ANGELA CARTER Second Edition

At the time of her death in 1992, Angela Carter had already become an important and widely read British author. In this fully revised and updated second edition of his popular study, Linden Peach provides a wealth of new material including:

- contemporary critical approaches to Carter's work
- one of the first discussions of the Italian film director Frederico Fellini's influence on her fiction
- an engaging study of Carter's interest in the aesthetics of the circus and music hall
- extended analysis of her most widely-studied novels, including *The Passion of New Eve* and *Nights at the Circus,* and her long essay *The Sadeian Woman.*

Arguing that Carter's fiction anticipates current debates around concepts such as 'postfeminism' and 'postfeminist Gothic', this lucid account of Carter's contribution to the modern novel features exciting re-readings of her key works and examines the impact she has had on other women writers for whom she paved the way. It is an ideal introduction for anyone who is looking for an approachable but sophisticated, twenty-first-century assessment of Carter as a novelist.

Linden Peach is Professor of English at Edge Hill University and an Honorary Research Fellow at Swansea University. His previous publications include books on Toni Morrison, Virginia Woolf, Crime Fiction, and contemporary Irish and Welsh fiction.

Angela Carter

Second Edition

Linden Peach

palgrave
macmillan

First edition published 1998
Second edition published 2009 by
PALGRAVE MACMILLAN

Palgrave Macmillan in the UK is an imprint of Macmillan Publishers Limited, registered in England, company number 785998, of Houndmills, Basingstoke, Hampshire RG21 6XS.

Palgrave Macmillan in the US is a division of St Martin's Press LLC, 175 Fifth Avenue, New York, NY 10010.

Palgrave Macmillan is the global academic imprint of the above companies and has companies and representatives throughout the world.

Palgrave® and Macmillan® are registered trademarks in the United States, the United Kingdom, Europe and other countries.

ISBN: 978-0-230-20282-5 hardback
ISBN: 978-0-230-20283-2 paperback

This book is printed on paper suitable for recycling and made from fully managed and sustained forest sources. Logging, pulping and manufacturing processes are expected to conform to the environmental regulations of the country of origin.

A catalogue record for this book is available from the British Library.

A catalog record for this book is available from the Library of Congress.

10 9 8 7 6 5 4 3 2 1
18 17 16 15 14 13 12 11 10 09

Printed and bound in Great Britain by
CPI Antony Rowe, Chippenham and Eastbourne

For Angela

Contents

Acknowledgements

The author and publishers wish to thank the Estate of Angela Carter, c/o Rogers, Coleridge and White Ltd, 20 Powis Mews, London W11 1JN, for permission to use copyright material from *Shadow Dance*, © Angela Carter 1966; *The Magic Toyshop*, © Angela Carter 1967; *Several Perceptions*, © Angela Carter 1968; *Heroes and Villains*, © Angela Carter 1969; *Love*, © Angela Carter 1971; *The Infernal Desire Machines of Doctor Hoffman*, © Angela Carter 1972; *The Passion of New Eve*, © Angela Carter 1977; *Nights at the Circus*, © Angela Carter 1984; and *Wise Children*, © Angela Carter 1991.

1

Introduction

THE LIFE AND THE ACHIEVEMENTS

Angela Carter (1940–1992) was born Angela Olive Stalker in Eastbourne, where her mother, her maternal grandmother and her eleven-year-old brother had moved to escape the bombings in London. The prospect of a German invasion through the south coast meant that the Stalker family moved again and the first five years or so of Carter's life were spent with her maternal grandmother in Wath-upon-Dearne, a village in the South Yorkshire coalfield. Her father, a journalist, remained in London during the war. After the war, Carter and her mother returned to their London suburban home in Balham. But they did not find what Carter described in her essay 'The Mother Lode' (1976) as 'a solid, middle-class suburb, lace curtains, privet hedges and so on'. The area had been much changed by the war and 'had had the residue of respectability bombed out of it' (*Shaking A Leg*, p. 11).

On leaving school, Carter followed in her father's footsteps and began work in 1959 as a junior reporter on the Croydon Advertiser. However, she did not pursue a career in journalism, but in 1962 accepted a place to read English at Bristol University, specialising in the medieval period. Her maternal grandmother died, aged ninety, the following year. Carter was married twice: in 1960 to Paul Carter, whom she left to go to Japan, where she took a Japanese lover for a while, and in 1977 to Mark Pearce, with whom she settled once again in South London; their son, Alexander, was born in 1983. When her mother died, her father decided to return to his home town, Macduff, in Aberdeenshire. Although Carter spent some time in Australia and the USA, it was probably the years when she lived in Japan, 1969–1972, that proved the most significant for her intellectual development. Her time there stimulated her to think about 'cultural foreignness', a concept that clearly informs her essay, 'My Father's House' (1976): 'The Japanese have a phrase, "the landscapes of the heart", to describe the Romantic correlation between inside and

1

outside that converts physical geography into part of the apparatus of the sensibility. Home is where the heart is and hence a moveable feast' (*Shaking a Leg*, p. 18). Since the seeds of the defamiliarisation and deconstruction which are so pronounced in her post-1970s work are evident in her early fiction, I am reluctant to see the period which she spent in Japan after she and her first husband separated in terms of a watershed. Sage (1994a) has suggested that it was 'the impetus she had built up through her own early work that had sent her on her travels' (p. 29). But clearly, the period in Japan, according to Salman Rushdie (1995) 'a country whose tea-ceremony formality and dark eroticism bruised and challenged Carter's imagination' (p. x), was important. As Gerrard (1995) points out, Carter herself believed: 'In Japan, I learned what it was to be a woman, and became radicalised' (p. 23).

Carter completed nine novels: *Shadow Dance* (1966; reprinted in America as *Honeybuzzard*, 1966), *The Magic Toyshop* (1967), *Several Perceptions* (1968), *Heroes and Villains* (1969), *Love* (1971), *The Infernal Desire Machines of Doctor Hoffman* (1972; reprinted in America as *The War of Dreams*, 1977), *The Passion of New Eve* (1977), *Nights at the Circus* (1984) and *Wise Children* (1991). Although the works written before *Nights at the Circus* (1984) are relatively short, even they are crammed with an extraordinary range of ideas, themes and images. She also published several collections of short stories: *Fireworks: Nine Profane Pieces* (1974), *The Bloody Chamber and Other Stories* (1979), *Black Venus's Tale* (1980) and *Black Venus* (1985; reprinted in America as *Saints and Strangers*, 1987) in addition to *American Ghosts & Old World Wonders* (1993), which was published posthumously. Of her non-fiction works, the most relevant to an appreciation of her novels are *The Sadeian Woman: An Exercise in Cultural History* (1979; reprinted in America as *The Sadeian Woman and the Ideology of Pornography*, 1979), *Nothing Sacred: Selected Writings* (1982) and *Expletives Deleted: Selected Writings* (1992). There are also four collections of children's stories, a work in verse entitled *Unicorn* (1966) and four radio plays. Because of her interest in editing fairy stories, that genre had a profound influence on her fiction and, especially, her short stories. She edited and translated *The Fairy Tales of Charles Perrault* (1977) and *Sleeping Beauty and Other Favourite Fairy Tales* (1982) and also edited two collections for Virago: *The Virago Book of Fairy Tales* (1990) and *The Second Virago Book of Fairy Tales* (1992).

Her work won prestigious literary prizes as well as favourable reviews during her lifetime. *The Magic Toyshop* won the John Llewellyn Rhys Prize and *Several Perceptions* won the Somerset Maugham Award. *Nights at the Circus* was the joint winner of the James Tait Black Memorial Prize in 1985. In the same year, the film *Company of Wolves*, based on *The Bloody Chamber* and a rewriting of 'Red Riding Hood', was released. During the period 1976–1978, Angela Carter was Arts Council of Great Britain Fellow in Sheffield. Further recognition of her work and her skill as a teacher of writing came with prestigious appointments which included Visiting Professor at Brown University, Rhode Island, USA; tutor on the MA in Writing at East Anglia University, UK; and writer-in-residence at the University of Adelaide, South Australia. She achieved international recognition as a teacher as well as a writer, holding writing residencies at Austin, Texas, Iowa City, and Albany, New York State.

SOCIAL ORIGINS

Carter began writing in the 1960s, and had completed her first five novels by the end of the decade. She recalled the 1960s in 'Notes From the Front Line':

towards the end of that decade there was a brief period of public philosophical awareness that occurs only very occasionally in human history; when truly, it felt like Year One, that all that was holy was in the process of being profaned ... I can date to that time and to some of the debates and to that sense of heightened awareness of the society around me in the summer of 1968, my own questioning of the nature of my reality as a *woman*. (Wandor, 1983, p. 70)

However, the radical nature of her work is rooted not just in the 1960s but in the contrast between the 1960s and the 1950s. Admittedly, the 1940s/1950s saw the introduction of the National Health Service, increased educational opportunities and social mobility. And the 1950s was a radical decade for the arts, which saw the 'Angry Young Men' in Britain, the Beat Generation in America and the existentialists in France. But Carter's family also experienced the austerity of the 1950s, and advertising campaigns which encouraged women to believe their place was in the home. Lorna Sage (1994a) pointed out that 'the prevailing style of British writing and of film-making (and of grey-and-white television) was neo-realistic – of a piece with the general atmosphere of austerity' (p. 2). The protest voices of the 1950s were male, and men benefited more than women from the increased educational and social opportunities. Indeed, the importance of Carter's origins in the dialectic between the 1950s and the 1960s has been noted by Carter herself who, in 'Notes from the Front Line', declared: 'I am the pure product of an advanced, industrialised, post-imperialist country in decline' (Wandor, 1983, p. 73).

Steven Connor (1996) reminds us that in the post-war period 'Britain came progressively to lose its confident belief that it was the subject of its own history' (p. 3). It appeared increasingly subject to outside pressures and influences, including the unpredictable forces of international capitalism which lay beyond the control of any one state. For Carter, there were positive aspects to Britain's changing position: 'The sense of limitless freedom that I, as a woman, sometimes feel *is* that of a new kind of being. Because I simply could not have existed, as I am, in any other preceding time or place' (Wandor, 1983, p. 73). But, whatever one's perspective on the matter, there could be no denying that the psychology of Britain was changing.

In her early novels, Carter depicts Britain in what one school of psychoanalysis might call a 'depressive condition'. In psychoanalysis, the depressive condition is the one in which infants begin to separate themselves from their mothers and experience a sense of loss. Carter herself did not regret the passing of imperialist Britain as such. Convinced that 'Western European civilisation as we know it has just about run its course', she believed that 'for the first time for a thousand years or so, its inhabitants may at last be free of their terrible history' (Wandor, 1983, pp. 72–73). But not everyone saw things this way, of course, and the experience of decline for the country after the war was also for many the cultural experience of loss.

In *Several Perceptions* (1968) and *Wise Children* (1991), Britain's waning power is linked with the decline in the prestige and influence of the English theatre. Whatever the subsequent benefits for women, Carter acknowledges that Britain as 'post' – post-imperialist, post-industrial – is cast, albeit temporarily, into a condition of loss; as a nation, Britain after 1945 began to separate from its mythical 'mother', industrialised, imperialist Britain. This view of Britain is incorporated in her first novel, *Shadow Dance* (1966). An auction sale is held in the gutted corpse of what had once been an Edwardian department store, 'where tall, thin pillars topped with fading garlands of gilded leaves insinuated hints of departed elegancies' (p. 23). The two junk shop owners know that there is a market for objects which evoke a period of lost elegance and glory. They are interested in a cake tin because it was produced as a souvenir of the coronation of Edward VII and a bidet because it depicts a pastoral scene of nymphs and shepherds. In *Several Perceptions* (1968), the decline of imperialist Britain is reflected in the run-down bohemian district of Bristol where the main street 'had once been the shopping promenade of a famous spa and still swooped in a sinuous neo-classic arc from the Down' (p. 9). Joseph Harker also alludes to this sense of cultural loss later in the novel when he regrets the passing of 'Victorian shooting jackets, Eskimo anoraks lined with wolf fur and military greatcoats of the elegant past' (p. 123). In Carter's final novel, which is discussed in Chapter 6, a sense of cultural loss is pursued through the disappearance of some of the icons associated with London, such as the Lyons teashops, and through the figure of a stand-up comedian who has the Empire tattooed on his body. Performing on stage, flexing his muscles to patriotic tunes, his ageing body positions parts of the Empire in less than complimentary places.

CRITICAL REPUTATION

When Angela Carter died of cancer in 1992, she was one of the best known British authors of the twentieth century, whose novels, short stories, reviews and journalism won her both critical acclaim and controversy. But, nearly twenty years after her untimely death, what do we see now as her contribution to the British novel?

At one level, it is misleading to think of Carter's writing in terms of the separate genres in which she worked. It is always hard to separate out the various strands in a prolific author's *oeuvre*, and it is especially difficult in Carter's case. The many connections between Carter's novels, short stories, children's fiction and even non-fiction are testimony to her interest in blurring the boundaries between them, challenging our perceptions of what we mean, for example, by a 'novel' or a 'short story'. However, the novel is the genre which still dominates British literary publishing and is read and studied more than any other. It is also the genre which in English culture in the middle of the twentieth century appeared to be in crisis, with some critics even talking of the end of the novel.

Nearly twenty years after her death, it is clear why Carter's work generated so much controversy, and it is still difficult to quarrel with Margaret Atwood (1992), who observed in her obituary of Carter, with only a hint of exaggeration, that she 'was born subversive, in the sense of the original root: *to overturn*' (p. 61). But, nearly twenty years on, Elaine Jordan's (1992) claim that 'I'll please no one least of all her, by trying to say she's not offensive' (p. 120) seems to have lost its edge due to the way in which in the academic nature of her work now stands more revealed.

While Carter was still alive, there was no greater bone of contention among critics than her representation of women. Paulina Palmer (1989) criticised the female characters in *The Passion of New Eve* who seek to liberate themselves from qualities associated with femininity in the early 1970s, such as dependency, passivity and masochism, but are 'composed of attributes which are predominantly "masculine"' (p. 16). Robert Clark (1987) criticised Carter for unwittingly repeating the 'self-alienation' to which patriarchal power relationships give rise. Even Jordan (1992) admitted that she had had her 'moment of horror and cold feet at what I was letting myself in for ... [Carter] started out writing as a male impersonator, with a strong streak of misogyny' (p. 16). In reading *The Infernal Desire Machines of Doctor Hoffman* (1972), Sally Robinson (1991), too, had reservations. Although she found that 'there is, quite simply, *no place* for a woman reader in this text', she was prepared to argue that the novel challenges 'the reader to occupy a position on the outside of that narrative' (p. 105). At times, Carter revelled in her provocative reputation, once sending a note to Elaine Jordan, referring to two leading feminist writers: 'If I can get up Suzanne Kappeller's nose, to say nothing of the Dworkin proboscis, then my living has not been in vain' (Sage, 1994a, p. 332). In some respects, Carter's fiction anticipates what has come to be called 'post-feminism', which some feminists argue 'participates in the discourse of postmodernism, in that both seek to destabilise fixed definitions of gender, and to deconstruct authoritative paradigms and practices' (Gamble, 1998/2001, p. 298). It is a term which is also used to identify feminists, such as Naomi Wolf, Katie Roiphe and Natasha Walter, who attack 'feminism in its present form as inadequate to address the concerns and experiences of women today' (ibid.).

Five years after Carter's death, Bristow and Broughton (1997) claimed that her most popular collection of short stories was *The Bloody Chamber and Other Stories* (1979) and her most widely read novel was *Nights at the Circus* (1984) (p. 1). This is probably still the case, and in some ways it has skewed her reputation. The emphasis in Carter scholarship has been upon a writer who, Bristow and Broughton (1997) maintain, 'delved into the most unsettling depths of Western culture, only to transmogrify its myths and unleash its monsters' (p. 1). Their view of her is typical of how Carter was seen in the decade immediately following her death. Nikki Gerrard (1995) argued that she was 'the one-off'. And what made her 'the one-off' at the time was the subversive nature of her 'strange, ribald novels': 'undecorous, overripe and mocking tales in which nothing is sacred and nothing natural' (p. 20).

Certainly Carter's novels are not in the English mainstream. Indeed, it might be argued that they are not 'novels' in the conventional sense at all, given the way in which their characters, often parodic and overly symbolic, are schematically drawn and how their plots are marked not by an interaction between characters and places but the unfolding of a speculative narrative. But now the initial shock waves created by her preoccupation with desire, sexuality and excess have subsided, there is a better understanding in Carter scholarship of the intellectual projects in which she was engaged.

The tide has turned against the emphasis in 1980s Carter scholarship on the mocking, monstrous feminine in Carter's novels, consistently with a wider change in contemporary Gothic writing. Stéphanie Genz (2007), in a discussion of post-feminist Gothic, a concept to which I will return later, argues:

> What comes to the fore in postfeminist Gothic is not the monstrous feminine that has been the figure of subversion and excess in H. Rider Haggard's *She* (1887) and Angela Carter's *Nights at the Circus* (1984). Quite the contrary, the postfeminist Gothic monster is neither abject nor excessive, but strangely conventional and, dare I say, trivial. (p. 69)

Possibly arising from the tenor of what Genz calls 'postfeminist Gothic', there is a discernible scepticism in feminist criticism toward Carter's monstrous, female 'figures of subversion and excess' that can be traced to the end of the 1990s. Sara Martin argues that although Carter's *Night at the Circus* (1984), Fay Weldon's *The Life and Loves of a She-Devil* (1983) and Jeanette Winterson's *Sexing the Cherry* (1989) are concerned with women who enjoy power over men, there are questions to be asked about their effectiveness in adding 'a new direction to the portrait of women in British Fiction' (p. 193). However, Martin's approach is typical of attempts in the second decade after Carter's death to contextualise her work through comparison with other female novelists. The studies by Rubinson (2005) and López (2007) compare Carter with Jeanette Winterson. Nicola Pitchford (2002) takes a different approach, comparing Carter with Kathy Acker, for whose novels she coins the term 'unreasonable texts'.

Helen Stoddart (2007), following critics such as Isobel Armstrong and Christina Britzolakis, believes that Fevvers in *Nights at the Circus* is reflected in the energy, excess and vulgarity of the prose, which 'is aligned with the popular'. However, as is typical of twenty-first century Carter criticism, she adds a note of clarification: 'Yet what is distinctive about Carter's writing is the way that these same popular attributes are also applied to the explication of intellectual and sometimes abstract concepts' (p. 114). Now the dust has settled around the controversy which Carter caused, the exuberant enthusiasm which she generated and her perceived preoccupation with excess and the monstrous Gothic, there is a greater emphasis in Carter scholarship on the intellectual depth of her work. Sarah Sceats (2001), focusing on the Gothic trope of the vampire, suggests that Carter's representation of sexual desire and predatory sexual behaviour is a vehicle for exploring political oppression. In much of the new criticism, Carter's intellectualism is linked, as here, to intertextuality. All texts inevitably contain traces of other texts which signal different ways of reading them. Julia Kristeva (1969) has pointed out: 'Tout texte se construit comme mosaique de citations, tout texte est absorption et transformation d'un autre texte' [Every text builds itself as a mosaic of quotations, every text is absorption and transformation of another text] (p. 146). At Bristol University, Carter became familiar with European art, and the French Symbolists and Dadaists are obvious influences on her writing. Later, she became more conversant with European critical theorists, especially the post-structuralists and the feminist psychoanalysts. The literary influences on her work include Chaucer, Boccaccio, Shakespeare, early modern dramatists, Jonathan Swift, William Blake, Mary Shelley, the Marquis de Sade, Edgar Allan Poe, Herman Melville, Dostoevsky, Lewis Carroll and Bram Stoker. Her close friends included postmodernist fiction writers such as Robert Coover and Salman Rushdie. She was an avid devotee and scholar of European and world cinema. Indeed, perhaps one of the reasons why Carter's work has aroused such controversy is that it is not typically English. Her novels are closer to the speculative fiction of writers such as Swift, the fiction of European Romantic writers, European film, folk tales, fairy stories and American Gothic than they are to the traditional English novel.

The influence of twentieth-century cinema on Carter's work should not be underestimated and the self-conscious eclecticism of New Wave French cinema, through the work of Jean-Luc Godard especially, was undoubtedly responsible for inspiring the highly allusive nature of Carter's fiction. Her novels often exploit the creative possibilities in shifting between different frames of reference and in subverting the cultural forms and traditions which structure our thoughts, perceptions and actions. Whereas the early works are, to employ Kristeva's viewpoint, a 'mosaique de citations', the intertext in subsequent novels is often more clearly the totality of a particular cultural or literary tradition. Eventually, intertextuality became not so much a characteristic of her writing as a boldly thematised part of it. At times, it seems that the novels' chief area of interest is the way in which meanings, boundaries and identities are rendered 'real' through cultural and linguistic metaphors. In this regard, Carter's fiction portrays Western culture as 'foreign'. The texts are driven by the twin processes of 'defamiliarisation' – making the literary and the familiar strange – and 'deconstruction'. The latter provides a means of looking critically at what we take for granted; the original meaning of the word 'deconstruction' is 'to take things apart'.

Contemporary Carter scholarship distinguishes between 'postmodern ludism', in which textual allusion is part of a wider 'play' with cultural referencing undertaken largely for its own sake, and intertextuality as a deliberate, intellectual and even academic strategy in which traditions, mythologies and conventions are subjected to sophisticated scrutiny. Though Carter was once seen as the *doyenne* of the former, her work is increasingly aligned with the latter. Munford (2006), with reference to select cultural and literary influences on Carter, including Jean-Luc Godard, Marcel Proust, Charles Dickens and Surrealism, argues that intertextuality is one of the most important drivers in Carter's fiction. Anna Watz Fruchart (Munford, 2006), examining surrealism in *Shadow Dance*, borrows Susan Rubin's term 'double allegiance' for the way in which allegiance to the source material in Carter's work coexists with a critique of it. This is certainly true of Carter's interest in Sade, discussed in Chapter 6, and, in some respects, of the influence of the Italian film director Federico Fellini on *Nights at the Circus*, discussed in Chapter 6. However, Carter's use of her source material is always complex.

There is considerable 'critique' combined with 'allegiance' in Carter's intertextuality, as Fruchart says, and Carter's ideological critique is as important in twenty-first-century as in twentieth-century Carter scholarship. Anna Katsavos's posthumously published interview with Carter on her interest in deconstruction continues to determine the majority of critical approaches to Carter's novels. There Carter explains that she is interested in 'what certain configurations of imagery in our society, in our culture, really stand for, what they mean, underneath the kind of semireligious coating that makes people not particularly want to interfere with them' (p. 12). Carter appears determined to challenge the comfortable and familiar way in which many of these ideologies are accepted as part of everyday reality. This is something which Carter's work shares with Bertolt Brecht's. He explained: 'The new alienations are only designed to free socially conditioned phenomenon from the stamp of familiarity which protects them against our grasp today' (Willett, 1964, p. 192). Carter's fiction encourages us to perceive for ourselves the processes that produce social structures, sociohistorical concepts and cultural artefacts.

Katsavos's interview with Carter is the springboard for Maria Perez-Gil's (2007) argument that 'Carl Jung's assumptions concerning the archetypal feminine and the androgynous self fall within the range of "semireligious" discourses that Carter satirically demythologizes in *The Passion of New Eve*' (p. 216). Perez-Gil argues that Carter not only dismantles these traditional stereotypes but turns Jung's concept of 'individuation' into a feminist narrative that subverts it. Patricia Smith (2006) argues that, while *The Magic Toyshop* is a feminist, 'modern day fairy-tale fantasy celebrating the awakening of adolescent female sexuality', it is also a 'complex web of signification that Carter weaves in an elaborate allegory of 1960s Britain that engages and retropes the works and philosophies of T. S. Eliot, D. H. Lawrence and W. B. Yeats' (p. 333). Smith maintains that Carter employs an 'allusory system' that, like modernism, combines high and low culture. But in Carter's work she sees the 'endgames' of modernism brought down 'in a tumultuous decade of social, cultural, and individual change' (p. 333).

Thus, 'deconstruction' remains the most consistent thread running throughout Carter scholarship. Sarah Gamble (2006), arguing that deconstruction of binaries lies at the heart of Angela Carter's artistic agenda, has defined Carter as being concerned with 'domestic deconstruction'. Other critics have focused on Carter's allusive metaphorical style and have veered toward a postmodernist, deconstructive intertextuality in Carter's fiction, emphasising the confidence trick and lucid game. The latter are at the heart of Jennifer Gustar's (2008) exploration of the structural and thematic elements that circulate in Carter's *oeuvre*. The recurring academic interest in deconstruction in Carter's fiction is not surprising, as her feminism focuses on the oppression of the 'signified' and how in the conventional heterosexual male gaze women are 'fixed' by what they are perceived as 'signifying'. Carter's work probes the subtleties of this process, of the different ways in which women are oppressed by cultural meanings, and through the process of deconstruction it seeks to reclaim women as 'signifiers' within their own narratives rather than as 'signified' objects in someone else's narrative.

WHAT KIND OF NOVELIST?

Carter's work has eclectic origins, in, for example, prenovelistic narratives, fairy stories, romance, pornography, Sade and European cinema, especially the films of Jean-Luc Godard and, as I mentioned above, the films of Federico Fellini. Attempts to 'label' Carter's fiction inevitably fail because they come up against the extraordinary eclecticism and the formidable intertextuality that give Carter's fiction its intellectual depth.

   Positioned at the boundaries between 'realism' and 'fantasy', Carter's novels seem to have more in common with a range of subgenres and popular narratives, such as Gothic, horror, fantasy narrative, speculative fiction and even sexploitation, than with the mainstream English novel. In the 1980s, and even the 1990s, scholarship seemed preoccupied with debates over what kind of writing Carter produced. Helen Carr (1989), believing that this posed a particular problem for Carter's readers, even suggested that 'Carter's novels became much more acceptable in Britain after the discovery of South American magic realism: her readers discovered that she was writing in a genre that could be named' (p. 7). It was a description of her work which Carter herself found problematic, explaining that the kinds of social forces that produced Gabriel Garcia Marquez, who is most often associated with this mode of writing, were very different from those that produced her (Haffenden, 1985, p. 81). Isabel Allende's definition of magic realism suggests some of the characteristics of Carter's later work: 'Magic realism really means allowing a place in literature to the invisible forces that have such a powerful place in life...dreams, myth, legend, passion, obsession, superstition, religion, the overwhelming power of nature and the supernatural' (Lewis, 1993, p. 26).

But 'dreams, myth, legend, passion, obsession, superstition, religion' cohere around the wider concerns that Carter's novels share with literary subgenres such as horror and the supernatural: victimisation arising from oppressive discourse. Carter's interest in legend, religion and myth is more astutely linked than in magic realist fiction to the way in which cultural discourses inform oppressive social practices and preconceptions, and her concern with passion, obsession and power informs her wider deconstruction of gender categories, depolarising of archetypes and demythologising of sexual pleasure.

Twenty years after her death, the debate as to whether Carter's fiction is 'magic realist' appears to have dwindling relevance. Of more interest to contemporary Carter scholarship is her mapping of new significance, otherness and subversion in premodern narratives that had a complexly ambivalent relationship with the bourgeois and the domestic, such as fairy stories and Gothic fiction. This led Carter to a way of 'knowing' the world which was sceptical of 'realism' as a vehicle of sociocultural critique. It is a commonplace that, although realism is based on a particular, historically located mode of awareness as partial as any other, over the last few hundred years it has been the preferred mode for writers with a commitment to social change. Carter's novels, on the other hand, are parodic, allusive and, often, elusive. Such artistic innovation has been regarded by social realist Marxist critics and writers, such as George Lukacs, as too decadent, introverted and 'bourgeois'. However, as Angela Burton and I have argued elsewhere (Peach and Burton, 1995), writers such as Dennis Potter have recognised that, as society changes, different strategies and techniques are needed to write effective social critiques (p. 31). Social realist fiction 'naturalises' what it portrays so that we trust what we are reading. Non-realistic fiction distances, or even alienates, us so that we are disturbed, puzzled, confused and possibly very critical of what we are reading. As a student of English at Bristol University, Carter would have been familiar with 'alienating techniques' through the work of writers such as Bertolt Brecht. Certainly in Carter's fiction, as in Brecht's work, everyday things are 'raised above the level of the obvious and automatic' (Willett, 1964, p. 92).

Non-realistic fiction usually presents the reader with new insights into how society is structured, into the forces behind it and into how it is organised according to the interests of particular powerful groups. In *Heroes and Villains* to some extent, but especially, as I shall discuss later, in the post-1970 novels, Carter acknowledged that the mode of awareness which in the previous three hundred years or so had been associated with realism had broken down. Although Carter's novels do not offer any clear, coherent alternatives, they are written from the realisation that many of the traditional principles which have governed our perception and organisation of 'reality' have been brought into question by modern and postmodern European and Euro-American thinking.

Beginning with Carter's attraction to Gothic and to premodern narratives and the way in which she may be seen as anticipating what post-feminist Gothic has identified as 'a new critical space beyond the Female Gothic' has enabled me to suggest that, if anything, her novels are 'postgenre'. In saying this, it is not my intention to exchange one problematic 'post' for another. What I mean to suggest by this term is that one of the principal lines of development in Carter's novels is the extent to which it brings forth unpredictable and transgressive forms. Thus, at the centre of Carter's novels is a speculative and creative space that is, may I dare say, 'post-feminist', 'post-Gothic' and 'post-genre'.

THE NOVELS

Carter's works are best read not as independent texts, but as part of an ongoing process of writing. Whilst to some degree this may be true of any author, it is especially true of Carter. In the chapters that follow, each of the novels is related to each other. Although many valuable insights are to be gained from a chronological consideration of her work, there is also a strong cyclical dimension to her *oeuvre*. Carter herself seems at pains to draw attention to it. Apart from the recurring preoccupation with key themes and ideas, details such as the names of characters are repeated across a range of the texts. Honeybuzzard in *Shadow Dance* (1966), for example, recurs as two characters in *Love* (1971); Toussaint in *Several Perceptions* (1968) is resurrected in *Nights at the Circus* (1984); and the names of two of the characters in *The Passion of New Eve* (1977) are borrowed from a passage in *Heroes and Villains* (1969). There are pointed similarities between characters in different novels, as, for example, between Mrs Boulder in *Several Perceptions* and Fevvers in *Nights at the Circus* or between Desiderio in *The Infernal Desire Machines of Doctor Hoffman* (1972) and Walser in *Nights at the Circus*. Carter employs similar scenarios in different contexts, such as the psychiatrist–client interview between Joseph and Ransome in *Several Perceptions* which occurs again between Lee and Annabel's doctor in *Love*. Moreover, where Carter engages with the characteristics of a literary tradition, for example, the fairy story or the apocalyptic novel, rather than with particular texts, the engagement is frequently carried over a number of her novels.

In the chapters that follow, discussions of individual works are structured to help readers who may not be familiar with all of Carter's novels and are designed to illuminate important interpretative issues in her work as a whole while providing extended treatment of topics and features particular to each book. Several works are juxtaposed, such as *Several Perceptions* and *Love* or *The Passion of New Eve* and *The Sadeian Woman*, where there is a clear *raison d'être* for reading them together, while key texts, such as *The Magic Toyshop*, *Nights at the Circus* and *Wise Children*, are the subject of single chapters. Although *Shadow Dance*, *Several Perceptions* and *Love* constitute a trilogy, concerned with the bohemian district of Bristol with which Carter was familiar in the 1960s, *Shadow Dance* is singled out. It plays a key role in discussing whether Carter is a 'Gothic' writer or whether her work anticipates, to employ a term which has become current in twenty-first-century scholarship, the 'post-Gothic'. However, the emphasis of the chapter is on how far the Gothic genre becomes a means of engaging with other perspectives, including realism, Jungian philosophy and twentieth-century psychoanalytic theory. *Shadow Dance* is seen as a novel particularly indebted to the work of Melville and Dostoevsky and to Carter's own critique of the Marquis de Sade in its pursuit of key Euro-American literary tropes such as the 'man of sorrows', body horror associated with 'necrophagy', and the 'double'. However, it is also suggested that the novel can be approached through a particular psychoanalytic framework provided by what has become known as object relations theory.

Several Perceptions (1968) is seen as continuing the interest of the previous novel in the particular type of melancholy to be found in German Romantic and early nineteenth-century American literature. The emphasis of the critical discussion, however, falls on the significance for the novel of David Hume's concept of the mind as a kind of theatre and upon the importance of the influence of Shakespeare's last plays in which the distinction between reality and illusion is blurred in potentially stunning pieces of experimental theatre. While *Love* (1971) shares many of the preoccupations of the other two parts of the trilogy, the novel is seen as primarily, but not exclusively, concerned with a preoccupation that Carter no doubt discovered in the work of the nineteenth-century American writer, Edgar Allan Poe: the price paid by those who take too subjective a view of the world.

Chapter 4 is concerned with the first of a group of novels which have certain features and subjects in common with the texts discussed in Chapters 2 and 3 but in other respects are closer to the later non-realistic fiction. Unlike the novels of the trilogy, *The Magic Toyshop* (1967), discussed in Chapter 4, and *Heroes and Villains* (1969), examined in Chapter 5, are each narrated from the perspective of a female consciousness, specifically an adolescent girl. They also confirm that Carter's work is different from the conventional English novel in the extent to which she is indebted to European literature and to prenovelistic modes of writing such as fairy stories, 'warning tales', the European picaresque narrative and German Romantic tales. Although they are different novels in many respects, *The Magic Toyshop* and *Heroes and Villains* have much in common. Literary allusions are more sharply focused and coherent than in the trilogy, and as such are used to call into question some of the grand narratives of Western culture – particularly those pertaining to the way in which female subjectivity and sexuality are normally constructed.

The salient narratives and assumptions of Western culture are also subjected to scrutiny in *The Infernal Desire Machines of Doctor Hoffman* (1972), the text discussed in Chapter 5 alongside *Heroes and Villains*, written during or after Carter's period in Japan. It develops ideas to be found in the earlier work, especially the unusual sense of 'foreignness' with which Carter, although born and brought up in England, tended to associate English and Western culture. However, it stands apart from the other novels in the boldness of its treatment of this theme, the less realist and more philosophical mode of writing, and the way in which it pursues themes and tropes of *The Magic Toyshop* and *Heroes and Villains* through a number of differently imagined societies.

Chapter 6 develops Carter's engagement with key debates of the 1970s, such as biological essentialism, the masculinist bias in Freudian psychoanalysis, separatist feminist movements and American survivalist movements as well as wider philosophical and social issues. But *The Passion of New Eve* is seen in relation to Carter's interest in pornography in *The Sadeian Woman*, particularly in what she perceives there as the limitations of 'traditional' pornography. There is a particular emphasis upon Carter's interest in sadomasochism and upon the plurality of desire in relation to the multiplicity of 'selves' based in any one body.

Carter's final novels, *Nights at the Circus* (1984) and *Wise Children* (1991), are discussed in Chapters 7 and 8 respectively, in relation to Carter's interest in the circus, music hall and theatre. As Salman Rushdie (1993) has observed, although Carter made the fable-world her own, her 'other country is the fairground, the world of the gimcrack showman, the hypnotist, the trickster, the puppeteer' (p. xi). In particular, these chapters examine the ways in which Carter explores the traditional connection between the theatre, the circus and what has come to be called the carnivalesque. Chapter 7 argues that *Nights at the Circus* is not an exploration of carnivalesque as such, important as this trope is to the novel, but of the overlap between the circus and the carnival. It breaks new ground in the extent to which the novel is seen as being influenced by the films of Federico Fellini, Carter's interest in the ways in which the Victorian circus, especially the female acrobat and trapezist, was perceived 'pornographically', and her wider interest in the circus aesthetic. Chapter 8 argues that Carter's concern with the music hall and variety theatre in *Wise Children* is similarly based upon an interest in the overlap between what is conceived as 'illegitimate' theatre and carnival. The chapter breaks new ground in arguing that Carter's primary concern is in the relationship between the aesthetic of popular and 'serious' theatre. The final chapter, recognising that *Wise Children* is the only novel narrated by an elderly woman, examines Carter's interest in the body, paying particular attention to the themes of illness and ageing. Chapter 1 examines Carter's changing critical reputation since her death, but the Afterword to this book examines Carter's contribution to the modern novel through some of the writers who were influenced by her.

2
Post-feminist and Euro-American Gothic: *Shadow Dance* (1966)

POST-FEMINIST GOTHIC

Carter's early work, particularly, betrays the influence of a wide variety of Gothic sources. These include nineteenth-century American writers such as Herman Melville and Edgar Allan Poe and, through their work, German Romance; European authors such as Dostoevsky; nineteenth-century Gothic texts such as Bram Stoker's *Dracula* and Mary Shelley's *Frankenstein*; the explorations of sadomasochism in the work of the Marquis de Sade; and the cinema, especially, but not exclusively, European cinema, particularly New Wave French cinema of the 1950s and 1960s, the vampire films of the 1960s, and the work of Alfred Hitchcock, particularly *Psycho*.

As mentioned in Chapter 1, a recurring concern in Carter scholarship during her lifetime was her perceived ambivalence toward 'feminism' or, at least, certain feminist positions. This is a subject to which I will return in Chapter 6 in a discussion of the *The Sadeian Woman*, a cultural essay which attracted more controversy from a feminist point of view than many of her novels. Rebecca Munford (2007), in a short essay on Angela Carter's (post-)feminist Gothic heroines, points out that hostile feminist criticism of this text saw it as 'more concerned with celebrating Sade than with tackling the implications of the gendered, sado-masochistic relations underpinning the pornograph' (p. 62). As I argue in Chapter 6, *The Sadeian Woman* has a complex relationship to pornography. Carter's depictions of sadomasochism ask questions, as in *The Passion of New Eve*, about who is in control in sadomasochistic relationships and about heterosexual play.

Carter's work might now be seen as sitting more comfortably with what has come to be called 'post-feminism' than within feminism.

17

At one level, the origins of post-feminism lie in critiques of 'second wave' feminism, associated with the women's liberation movement of the 1960s, as being, for example, too white and middle class and obscuring race and disenfranchisement (Springer, 2002). Post-feminism might be seen as continuing a strand of power feminism, associated with feminists such as Naomi Wolf, but even in the 1990s it was a moot point as to whether 'post-feminism' evolved from or in conflict with 'feminism' (Whelehan, 1995; Steinem, 1995). Benjamin Brabon and Stéphanie Genz (2007a) in their introduction to a special issue of the journal *Gothic Studies* argue:

> On the one hand, post-feminism is perceived as a pro-patriarchal, anti-feminist stance, a backlash against feminism and its values, whereas, on the other hand, it is seen to denote a postmodern and post-structuralist feminism that discredits discursive homogeneity and a unified subjectivity. (pp. 1–2)

Some 'post-feminists' use the term 'third wave' feminism to avoid the nuances of the prefix 'post', which could be taken to imply 'anti-feminism', but also to suggest that post-feminism embraces a greater multiplicity of identities and sexualities than feminism. This dimension of 'third wave' or 'post-feminism' is alignable with Carter's interest in heterogeneity. Carter's fiction also anticipates the re-visioning of popular cultural images in 'third wave' feminism. The re-visioning of popular images, from the vampire slayer to the female nude, is part of the cultural activism of 'third wave' feminism, and, again, is alignable with Carter's interest in the oppressive nature of cultural discourse. Indeed, some 'post-feminist' writing straddles, like some of Carter's work, a thin line between using cultural activism as a way of confronting the oppressor and using it as a site of postmodern 'play'. Carter's fiction challenges the inclusion/acceptable and exclusion/unacceptable binary which feminism applied to types of feminism and which at times prevented it from being sufficiently daring. Her work anticipates what Brabon and Genz describe as that 'postmodern and post-structuralist feminism that discredits discursive homogeneity and a unified subjectivity'.

Carter's novels are also ahead of their time in anticipating what has come to be called 'post-feminist Gothic'. Like 'post-feminism', it is a term fraught with difficulty. But it is generally seen as being based on moving beyond the oppressor and oppressed framework within which much feminist Gothic has worked. 'Post-feminist

Gothic' represents for many critics what Brabon and Genz (2007a) have called 'a new critical space beyond the Female Gothic (and its ghosts of essentialism and universalism)' (p. 7). Carter reads the Gothic in a way which, even in her novels written in the 1960s, anticipates post-feminist Gothic. Helen Meyers points out that post-feminist Gothic has come to be seen as a site of negotiation between the scripts of 'male vice and female virtue' and perceived as a site of 'gender scepticism' (cit. Brabon and Genz, 2007a, pp. 7–8), a description which also immediately brings Carter's novels to mind.

In her essay on Carter's Gothic heroines, Munford (2007) approaches the concept of post-feminist Gothic somewhat sceptically. She invokes a familiar argument in relation to Carter's female Gothic: that 'her early works most frequently draw on representations of the Gothic heroine as orphaned, passive and masochistic adolescent' (p. 64) and that her later work introduces 'power feminism', represented, for example, by Fevvers in *Nights at the Circus* (p. 66). Although Munford is wary of the concept of 'power feminism', which, 'like "victim feminism", is similarly defined by the structures within which it is enacted' (p. 67), she offers a reading of Carter which appears to locate her as a 'post-feminist' rather than a 'female Gothic' writer. The latter, as Brabon and Genz argue in their introductory essay in *Gothic Studies*, follows an oppressor/oppressed model, which post-feminist Gothic 'depolarises', and has a limited engagement with patriarchy. As a post-feminist Gothic writer, Carter, Munford says, 'moves beyond the narrativisation of the Gothic character of woman's experience under patriarchy, and refuses an unproblematic understanding of gendered power relations' (p. 67). Avoiding the term 'post-feminist Gothic' in her conclusion, she maintains that the 'interrelationship between feminist Gothic and Gothic discourse [in Carter's work] offers up the possibilities of reading beyond narratives of victimhood and victimisation' (p. 67). Munford appears to follow those critics mentioned earlier who expressed doubts about the feminist potential in Carter's representations of monstrous women, alerting readers to the dangers in post-feminist Gothic heroism. However, she insists it has to be admitted that Carter's novels often move 'beyond narratives of victimhood and victimisation'.

Given Carter's recurring ludic play with the Gothic hero–villain and heroine–victim, her parodic experimentation with a plethora of Gothic motifs, and deeply rooted gender scepticism, Brabon and Genz (2007a) might have given Carter's work more attention. In their concerns with paradoxical female embodiment, psychopathic misogyny, pleasuring masochism, sadistic mothers, transformative narratives and 'desubjectifying' spectacle, her novels anticipate the twenty-first-century interest in the complications that emerge from reconfiguring the intrinsic maleness and essential femaleness of Gothic fiction, reconceptualising feminism and approaching what might be called 'post-pornography'. It is Carter's post-pornography to which a number of subsequent women writers, such as Sarah Waters, are indebted.

SHADOW DANCE AND THE BRISTOL TRILOGY

Shadow Dance, *Several Perceptions* and *Love* are Angela Carter's first, third and fifth novels respectively. In between writing them, she published two novels, *The Magic Toyshop* and *Heroes and Villains*, which anticipate the less realistic style of the later fiction. Although Sue Roe (1994) has argued that formally *Love* stands alone in Carter's *oeuvre*, these three novels, despite the differences between them, have much in common. Indeed, acknowledging that they all share a recognisable contemporary setting, O'Day (1994) has called them Carter's Bristol trilogy, a view supported by Lorna Sage (1994a, p. 22). Sage, however, is troubled by O'Day's description of them as 'realist' texts. Whilst, as O'Day argues, they do not possess the 'magic realist' qualities of Carter's later fiction, she believes that they have 'the extra density of fiction squared' (p. 22).

O'Day's main argument for seeing these three novels as a trilogy is that each is a fictional mediation of aspects of the area of Bristol in which Carter lived: the auction room, junk shop and derelict houses in *Shadow Dance*; a bedsit, a large mansion and the Downs in *Several Perceptions*; and a two-room flat, the park and (Mecca) ballroom in *Love*. More significantly, the trilogy presents us with an imaginative response to provincial bohemian life as it happened at the time in bedsits, flats, cafes and coffee bars where somehow the boundaries between art and life became blurred. However, O'Day also suggests that the novels deploy a similar array of characters, variants of a similar plot structure, comparable forms of narration, and themes and motifs concerning 1960s counterculture.

There are further reasons why these novels may be regarded as a trilogy. Each novel, at various levels, including parody, is indebted to Euro-American Gothic. In particular, through a combination of

Gothic and psychological fantasy, Carter pursues themes and motifs from nineteenth-century American writers, especially Herman Melville and Edgar Allan Poe. Carter's view of American Gothic writing was undoubtedly mediated through Leslie Fiedler's critical study *Love and Death in the American Novel* (1960), which quickly became required reading for students of literature in the 1960s when Carter was a student at Bristol University. One of the epigraphs to the novel *Heroes and Villains* (1969) is from Fiedler's book and suggests that Carter was particularly interested in his perception of Gothic American literature: 'The Gothic mode is essentially a form of parody, a way of assailing clichés by exaggerating them to the limit of grotesqueness.' Certainly many of the characteristics of Carter's early writing recall Fiedler's summary of the principal features of Gothic writing: the substitution of terror for love as a central theme; the vicarious flirtation with death; an aesthetic that replaces the classic concept of 'nothing-in-excess' with 'the revolutionary doctrine that nothing succeeds like excess'; and a dedication 'to producing nausea, to transcending the limits of taste and endurance' (p. 126).

Each of the novels constituting the Bristol trilogy explores the negative aspects of the psyche – a project which leads inevitably to the Gothic tale, traditionally a vehicle for ideas about 'psychological' evil rather than evil as an external socio-political force. In the Afterword to the first edition of *Fireworks* (1974), Carter makes clear that even in the mid-1970s this was how she thought of the European Gothic tale:

> cruel tales, tales of wonder, tales of terror, fabulous narratives that deal directly with the imagery of the unconscious – mirrors; the externalised self, forsaken castles, haunted forests; forbidden sexual objects. ... Characters and events are exaggerated beyond reality, to become symbols, ideas, passions. Its style will tend to be ornate, unnatural – and thus operate against the perennial human desire to believe the word as fact. Its only humour is black humour. It retains a singular moral function – that of provoking unease. (pp. 244–245)

Carter's early novels, however, are not 'Gothic' in the traditional sense of the term. The Gothic genre is itself subversive, giving expression to what is culturally occluded, such as sexual fantasy and female desire. However, Carter's novels are subversions of the

Gothic genre which might be described as 'post-Gothic'. Themes and ideas first explored in Gothic writing are re-examined, challenged and expanded. The Gothic becomes a mode of awareness within the novels which challenges, contradicts or confirms other perspectives, as diverse as social realism, Jungian psychoanalysis and 'projection' theory, and is in turn subverted and/or expanded by them. This hybridity creates different possible ways of reading the texts, giving them the 'extra density of fiction' to which Sage refers. However, the dominance of the Gothic mode of writing within these early novels subverts the close relationship between word and referent which characterises realism. As Elizabeth MacAndrew (1979) points out, the all-pervading symbolism of the Gothic tale is 'almost, though not quite allegorical' – the 'referents are deliberately hazy' (p. 8). In the early novels, as in the later non-realistic, philosophical fiction, Carter exploits the hybridity of Gothic writing and its capacity for ambivalence and ambiguity.

In this trilogy, Carter appears to be re-visioning the sequence novel which, according to Connor (1996), underwent a remarkable revival after the Second World War. He points out:

> The world of the sequence has the self-sufficient density it supposes of the 'real' world. It is closed and complete in itself, a parallel universe or working simulacrum of the real not only in the encyclopaedic abundance of its narrative detail but also in its plethora of different possible perspectives; typically the novel-sequence will combine and juxtapose not only different experiences of different characters but also the same experiences revisited from different points of view. (p. 136)

Unlike the conventional novel-sequence which Connor describes, and more like the playwright Beckett in his *Trilogy*, Carter's sequence resists offering the reader a complete, coherent and self-sufficient world. Each of the novels in the Bristol trilogy enacts a complex, repetitious and paradoxical narrative.

SHADOW DANCE AND (POST-)GOTHIC BODY HORROR

Shadow Dance (published in the USA as *Honeybuzzard*) was completed in 1964 whilst Carter was a student of English literature at Bristol University. It is the novel which has received least attention, partly because it was out of print from 1966 until 1994, and maybe because it has a number of obvious weaknesses, to which Claire Harman (1994) has drawn attention; for example, the surreal characters, the constant threat of melodrama and its loose ends.

Although the novel is narrated in the third person, the story is told from the point of view of one of the male characters, Morris, and, as Lorna Sage (1994a) says, 'the female characters are scattered at large in a man's world' (p. 10). The specifically male focus is evident, for example, in Morris's attempt to justify what his friend Honeybuzzard has done to Ghislaine, the attractive woman with whom Morris has a disastrous one-night stand: 'She was asking for trouble ... Running around like she used to do, daft bitch, late at night, and nothing on under her mackintosh' (p. 33). It is also apparent in the way in which he describes his junk shop as a worthwhile place to work because it attracts lots of Americans in the summer, 'Especially females. In Bermuda shorts' (p. 35). Nevertheless, *Shadow Dance* is a complex, feminist and psychoanalytical exploration of post-1950s England. Morris's perspective, as one of many in the novel, is challenged and undermined by the wider interaction of voices within the text, which also encourages the reader to regard it sceptically.

Although *Shadow Dance* invokes a provincial 1960s urban landscape, the representational codes of realism in the text are locked in a continuous dialectic with fantasy. The distinction between the two is blurred in the focalisation of Morris himself, in much of its imagery and in the exchange between an owl and a child who mimics the bird's call so that the two sounds, the real and the fictitious, become indistinguishable. For the most part, the dialectic between the two modes is present in the novel as ironic comedy or, with more *gravitas*, in the spirit of the nineteenth-century American novelist Herman Melville, the nineteenth-century German Romantic writers who influenced Melville and his 'Gothic' American contemporaries such as Nathaniel Hawthorne and Edgar Allan Poe, mentioned earlier.

Honeybuzzard, at one level, is a comic stereotype of the Gothic villain: he wears false noses, false ears and plastic vampire teeth, retaining only his habitual dark glasses. Here Carter seems to be anticipating the late twentieth and twenty-first-century concept of the post-Gothic, but with a typical Carteresque slant. She seems to be thinking of post-Gothic as written from a place beyond Gothic, in which it is then possible to engage with Gothic in a kind of ludic play. Morris is a less parodic adaptation than Honeybuzzard of the Gothic protagonist. He is a recreation of the German Romantic protagonist who, in early nineteenth-century German literature, is pursued by the guilty secret of some terrible past deed. In pursuing these two approaches to Gothic material, Carter appears to be reflecting on the difficulty of transposing nineteenth-century Romantic tropes to the late twentieth century, especially for readers whose taste for the Gothic has been influenced by Hammer horror films and their subsequent parodies. Nevertheless, it is at the level of horror–fantasy that *Shadow Dance* is a shocking book.

In regard to the cinema, vampire films can be traced back to *The Vampire* (1913) and the first supernatural vampire horror, *Nosferatu* (1922). The first cinematic connection between sexuality, seduction and vampirism was made in *Dracula* (1931) and *Dracula's Daughter* (1936). However, the 1960s was the decade in which vampirism, sexuality and victimised females were closely linked; ushered in by *Horror of Dracula* (1958) and developed through films such as *Kiss of the Vampire* (1963), *Dracula Prince of Darkness* (1966) and *Dracula Has Risen from His Grave* (1968). David Hogan (1986) points out that *Brides of Dracula* (1960), like *The Kiss of the Vampire*, 'flirts with vampiric incest' (p. 146). Moreover, as Hogan maintains, vampirism and sexuality are increasingly linked in the 1960s with 'physical cruelty': 'When he bites a young lady's throat he is not merely feeding but experiencing (and inducing) a moment of orgasmic ecstasy' (ibid.). It goes without saying that the 'vampire kiss' invokes the tropes of oral sex and, even, the child feeding at its mother's breast. But a further, more contentious, trope is the subject of complicity and desire in male rape/violent sex, discussed further in Chapter 6.

After the disastrous one-night stand with Ghislaine, Morris tells his flamboyantly violent friend Honeybuzzard, with whom he runs the junk shop, to 'teach her a lesson'. He is unprepared for what Honeybuzzard does. In a graveyard, she is raped and slashed with a knife, after which her face is left monstrously scarred. However, she returns from hospital to haunt Morris in ways which are reminiscent of *Brides of Dracula*, where, as Hogan (1986) says, 'the victimized beauty...in turn levels her sexuality at others' (p. 147). Eventually, she takes Honeybuzzard away from his new woman-friend, Emily. Sarah Gamble (2006b) contrasts Ghislaine's 'moral vacuity' and 'malleability' with Emily, who for all the issues that her presence raises in the novel, 'does not lose herself in Honeybuzzard's world' (p. 54). Bizarrely, it might appear, but in keeping with the vampire films of the 1960s, Ghislaine is willing to accept Honeybuzzard as her master. Taking her to an old house, he eventually murders her near a plaster crucifix in an ironic reversal of the way in which the crucifix traditionally offers protection against the vampire. The exploration of female victimisation is a key theme which Carter's *Shadow Dance* shares with the vampire movies of the 1960s. But there are further influences on this novel, including, as mentioned earlier, French New Wave cinema, in which women are linked with victimisation, especially Jean-Luc Godard's *A Bout de Souffle* ['Breathless'] (1960), *Vivre sa vie* (1962) and *Bande a Part* (1964), influenced by American gangster films, in which two men fall in love with the same woman. Sarah Gamble (2006b) argues: 'Novels such as *Shadow Dance* and *Love* echo Godard's tactic in films like Vivre sa vie – that of showing female victimization in the process of construction and, in so doing, laying the mechanisms of oppression open to subversion and revision' (p. 51). Gamble draws attention to parallels between Carter's Ghislaine and Godard's Nana, a mother and aspiring actress who is forced into becoming a prostitute to support herself, in *Vivre sa vie*: 'Nana is similarly bound to the imperatives of masculine desire, seeming to have very little sense of herself that exists independently of men's regard' (p. 51).

Gamble (2006b) also points out that, for both Ghislaine in *Shadow Dance* and Nana in *Vivre sa vie*, 'obliteration lies at the end of their idealistic search for love, for they are trapped in a landscape in which, like one of Escher's optical illusions, every avenue of escape only brings them right back to where they started' (p. 53). A profound similarity between New Wave French cinema and Carter's post-feminist, Euro-American Gothic is the way in which her villains, like Godard's Michael in *Breathless*, are a parody of an American movie figure, Humphrey Bogart and the gangster in the case of Godard's film and Dracula in *Shadow Dance*. The savage ways and moods in each text reflect the rootless anxiety of Euro-American male youth in the mid-twentieth century, but in each text it is the women to whom the men become attached who seem to really understand the meaninglessness of life. In *Shadow Dance*, that meaninglessness is taken to extremes, representative of an immoral world of savagery, perhaps inspired by the more literal translation of *Breathless* as 'At the End of Breath'.

FLESH AND ABJECTION

As mentioned earlier, the fact that Ghislaine is mutilated in a grave-yard and murdered close to a crucifix, on which Honeybuzzard had envisaged taking turns with Morris to lay her, is significant. These details compound the horror arising from the way in which women are seen as 'flesh' and 'meat', especially as Honeybuzzard also thinks of selling pornographic photographs of Ghislaine on the crucifix. The interrelated but contrasting tropes of flesh signifying pleasure and of meat as signifying economic objectification occur throughout Carter's fiction, which seeks to explore the boundaries between them. In *The Sadeian Woman* (1979), discussed in more detail in Chapter 6, Carter explains:

> The word 'fleisch', in German, provokes me to an involuntary shudder. In the English language, we make a fine distinction between flesh, which is usually alive, and, typically, human; and meat, which is dead, inert, animal and intended for consumption... the pleasures of the flesh are vulgar and unrefined, even with an element of beastliness about them, although flesh tints have the sumptuous succulence of peaches because flesh plus skin equals sensuality. (pp. 137–138)

The Sadeian Woman is based on the Marquis de Sade's *120 days of Sodom*, in which four libertines – a duke, a bishop, a judge and a school friend of the Duke's – shut themselves away with four brothel madames, a crowd of young men and women and their own wives for 120 days. During that time, they recount the details of every sexual perversion they have encountered and the libertines try to perform them. However, investigating and challenging the distinction between 'flesh' and 'meat' was not peculiar to Carter's work in the 1960s and not confined to fiction. Carolee Schneeman's performance art piece, *Meat Joy*, first performed in 1964, was based on what was then a scandalous amount of nudity and 'forbidden' contact with the raw flesh of fish and chickens. Carter's critique of the work of the Marquis de Sade in *The Sadeian Woman* provides a retrospective commentary on how the flesh/meat trope is developed through what happens to Ghislaine in *Shadow Dance* and upon the particular dimensions of 'body horror' which the novel explores. Carter explains in her reading of de Sade: 'The strong, abuse, exploit and meatify the weak' (p. 140).

The image of 'meatifying' the weak also occurs in Carter's parody of de Sade in the later novel, *The Infernal Desire Machines of Doctor Hoffman* (1972), influenced by Japanese cinema and popular culture. There the women who are kept in the Count's cages have 'hides...streaked, blotched and marbled' (p. 132). The 'meaty' connotations of the word 'hides' are developed in the description of the girl who appears to have been recently whipped: 'torn and bleeding she was the most dramatic revelation of the nature of meat that I have ever seen' (p. 133). Moreover, in that novel, the Reality Testing Laboratory, in which the Determination Police, a latter-day equivalent of the German SS of the 1930s and 1940s, torture their suspects, smells of roast pork (p. 22).

In *The Sadeian Woman*, Carter observes that it is 'the shocking tragedy of mortality itself, that all flesh may be transformed, at any moment, to meat' (p. 140). The reference to 'any moment' here is applicable to the vampire genre, in which the victim is taken suddenly by the vampire, as by death, and what was once human becomes non-human. The transformation of the human into simply flesh, a body without soul, and the boundary between the body and the corpse are key tropes in vampire films of the 1960s. This sense of horror at the transformation of 'flesh' into 'meat' in death is very strong in *Shadow Dance*. Morris, for example, is reminded of it every time he opens the door of his junk shop and is 'punched in the stomach' by the smell of rotting meat from the butcher's shop next door. Indeed, this may be what encourages him to think of his sick wife, Edna, as 'a poor flat fillet on the marble slab of her bed' (p. 13). This image is disturbing for what is absent: there is nothing alive or sensual about it. It anticipates Edna's condition as a corpse, bereft of any compensatory symbolism. Jean Baudrillard (1993) has pointed out that every society has

> always staved off the abjection of natural death, the *social* abjection of decomposition which voids the corpse of its signs and its social force of signification, leaving it as nothing more than a substance, and by the same token, precipitating the group into the terror of its own symbolic decomposition. (p. 180)

Julia Kristeva (1982) is also relevant in this regard. She argues that 'refuse and corpses *show me* what I permanently thrust aside in order to live' (p. 3). The fillet metaphor is particularly disturbing because not only does it turn Edna's body into meat but also, in turning the bed into a butcher's slab, associates it with necrophagy.

Necrophagy, 'the exposition of the meatiness of human flesh', as Carter points out in *The Sadeian Woman*, 'parodies the sacramental meal' (p. 140), thereby associating Edna with Ghislaine's death at the crucifix. In *The Sadeian Woman*, Carter explains: 'Substitute the word "flesh" in the Anglican service of Holy Communion; "Take, eat, this is my meat which was given for you..." and the sacred comestible becomes the offering of something less than, rather more than, human' (p. 137). The image of the vampire drinking blood, of course, similarly subverts, and mocks, the symbolic drinking of Christ's blood as wine in the Sacrament. 'Fillet' suggests not only the pleasure of carving meat, associating Morris's fantasy of his wife with Honeybuzzard's mutilation of Ghislaine's face, but the anticipatory pleasure of eating meat. It is the suggestion of necrophagy in Honeybuzzard's face that exacerbates the horror of what he has done to Ghislaine: 'It was impossible to look at the full rich lines of his dark red mouth without thinking: "This man eats meat"' (p. 56). His association with a bird of prey through his name is reinforced by the nature of his mouth, which is said to suggest 'snapping, tearing, biting'.

Meat eating is a recurring trope in Carter's work, evident in *The Bloody Chamber and Other Stories* (1979), which, as Margaret Atwood (1992) has pointed out, is 'arranged according to categories of meateater' (p. 122). Although these stories are based on fairy tales, such as Perrault's 'Little Red Riding Hood', they are not 'versions' or, as the American edition of the book said, 'adult' fairy stories. Carter herself explained that she sought 'to extract the latent content from the traditional stories and to use it as the beginnings of new stories' (Haffenden, 1985, p. 84). In them, Carter develops the connection, first mooted in *Shadow Dance*, between the perception of women as property and the objectification of women as 'flesh' in ways which elide the connotations of 'flesh' and 'meat'. The association is taken further in the emphasis placed upon an active, unruly female sexuality which women have been taught might devour them. The first three stories, 'The Bloody Chamber', 'The Courtship of Mr Lyon' and 'The Tiger's Bride', are cat family narratives where, Merja Makinen (1992) argues, the wild felines signify 'the sensual desires that women need to acknowledge within themselves' (p. 11). The last three stories in the book are wolf family stories, concerned with a more unruly, animalistic sexuality. Critics have argued over how to read these stories. Makinen suggests that the beasts be seen as the 'projections of a feminine libido' and challenges critics, such as Patricia Duncker, who see the beasts as men. Here, again, there is a parallel with the vampire genre in which, as discussed earlier, the victimised female 'levels her sexuality at others'. The stories invite a number of different, and even competing, readings, as does most of Carter's fiction. They are a development from *Shadow Dance* in that they are not only an exploration of women's sexuality but of the ways in which men have sought to control that sexuality, of how both men and women need to reconfigure their sexualities, and of the commodification of women as 'flesh'.

The trope of cannibalism is close to the trope of vampirism, in which the vampire devours its victims through drinking their blood. In Carter's work cannibalism is closely connected to its interest in oppression. She explains in *The Sadeian Woman* that she saw cannibalism 'as the most elementary act of exploitation, that of turning the other directly into a comestible; of seeing the other in the most primitive terms of use' (p. 140). In vampire films, these are precisely the terms in which the victimised female, like Ghislaine, is seen. In the opening tale of *The Bloody Chamber and Other Stories*, Carter provides a male protagonist drawn particularly closely on the Marquis de Sade's cannibal, Minski. Although not the organising principle, cannibalism is an important trope, too, in the earlier *The Infernal Desire Machines of Doctor Hoffman* (1972). Not only is Desiderio adopted by river people who intend to eat him because they believe in that way they will acquire his knowledge, but, in a parodic scene, the Count is boiled alive by an African tribe whose chief's cannibalistic methods of discipline maintain his authority. There is, however, a difference between cannibalism as it is practised by the river people and that employed by the chief or suggested by the bird of prey in Honeybuzzard's name. Baudrillard (1993) maintains: cannibals 'don't just eat anybody ... whoever is eaten is always somebody worthy, it is always a mark of respect to devour somebody since, through this, the devoured even becomes sacred' (p. 138). This is very different from the meat eating which takes place in Western European society: 'We think of anthropophagia as despicable in view of the fact that we despise what we eat' (ibid.).

Contentiously, *Shadow Dance* associates the mutilation of Ghislaine with a latent necrophagy in society as a whole, which is also suggested in the body/flesh transformation and the link between them. It is surely significant that, when Emily first sees the mutilated Ghislaine, she is standing in the street outside the junk shop when the butcher next door receives a delivery of meat. The description of the meat underlines its transformation from flesh: 'great joints of meat, red sides of beef and amber-rinded pork and white legs of lamb and rosy shoulders of mutton' (p. 152). The nouns which remind us of animals – joints, sides, shoulders, legs – also remind us of what is human. But they are combined with words that deny the origins of meat as flesh: 'beef', 'rinded', 'mutton' and 'pork'. Yet what is denied is reintroduced by the description of the butcher in his 'filthy blue apron and bloodstained straw boater, around which the flies already buzzed'. The butcher, like the vampire, is a figure whose life is lived in close proximity to blood, flesh and death, to abjection in fact, and the kind of transformations and boundaries mentioned earlier.

The last verb in the above quotation reminds us of Honeybuzzard himself and significantly occurs before the account of Ghislaine standing in the street, waiting to confront Emily with what he has done to her face. It also recalls the fly that buzzed as Morris confronted Honeybuzzard over what he did to Ghislaine, while the Janus nature of Honeybuzzard's face, in his case 'cherub' and 'buzzard', is reflected in the description of the butcher. In developing the comparison between the butcher and Honeybuzzard, Carter once again focuses on the process of denial. The boater signifies a traditionally English view of what is elegant and civilised, but the bloodstains suggest what civilisation tends to deny or render as 'other'. This denial is suggested also by the fact that before Emily sees Ghislaine she is on her way to the lavatory, signifying the disposal of unpleasant matter, and, when Ghislaine and the meat appear, the laundry starts up and begins to 'hum'. Indeed, the presence of the laundry not only reinforces the notion of removing what is unpleasant from public view, but places the process in an institutionalised context.

Thus, in the description of the butcher receiving his order of meat, Carter inscribes the tension between society's recognition of its scatological elements, albeit in order to remove them, and its denial of them. Honeybuzzard's mutilation of Ghislaine is contextualised within this Janus aspect of society. Society turns flesh into meat on a daily basis, but simultaneously denies this by locating abattoirs out of public view and in reconfiguring flesh as cooked food, masking its origins. The word 'hum', of course, can suggest a musical sound, something attractive and transcendental, or the smell of rotting matter.

Emily's obsessive cleanliness enables her to cope with the contradictory nature of society and of the roles which she is required to perform. This is evident after her one-night stand with Morris, in which she serves as his surrogate mother as much as, if not more than, his lover; she is able to expel him like so much dirt. Significantly, when Ghislaine arrives shortly afterwards at her door, she cries 'Let me in!' (p. 154). Ghislaine is asking to be admitted not just to the shop but to Emily's consciousness. In making Emily kiss her scar, Ghislaine forces her to acknowledge Honeybuzzard's violence: 'he would cut me up like that if I did anything he didn't like. Like going to bed with anyone else. Or getting pregnant' (p. 166).

A key to the association of flesh with meat, necrophagy and the crucifix in Carter's early work is provided by the psychoanalytical criticism of Julia Kristeva (1987), albeit in another context. In an analysis of the painting *The Corpse of Christ in the Tomb*, by Hans Holbein the Younger (1521), Kristeva responds to the minimalism of the work: that Christ is entirely alone in the tomb; that the body is not idealised in any way; and that there is no suggestion of tran-scendence or of passion. In other words, Kristeva is concerned with the way in which the painting brings the viewer into close proxim-ity with death, bereft of any compensatory symbolism. This may also bring the vampire genre to mind, for there the space which the vampire inhabits is nothing but death. At one level of signification, the crucifix is a transcendental symbol. Normally, representations of Christ provide us with a way of enlarging our imaginary and symbolic means of coping with death. However, at another level, the crucifix reminds us that at one time the cross was a cruel and commonplace instrument of torture and execution. Bereft of any compensatory symbolism, death, as in Holbein's painting and Carter's *Shadow Dance*, disrupts the compensatory Symbolic Order. Both texts challenge our imaginary capacities. Carter's novel, like Holbein's painting, forces us to imagine what is in the gap between death and its 'denegation' through symbolic language and between flesh and meat.

Kristeva attributes the kind of detachment and coldness in Holbein's presentation of death to the Reformation and the emer-gence of a 'melancholic moment'. Here she makes a connection, essential to our understanding of Carter's work, between Holbein's view of death and the state of mind of the melancholic. As John Lechte (1990) argues 'Holbein's dead Christ...goes very close to illustrating the denial of *denegation* and the evacuation of drive affect characteristic of the melancholic's constructions' (p. 188). Similarly, in her depiction of melancholia, Carter focuses on the failure of the imaginative and the symbolic, as I shall discuss in the next section.

MELANCHOLY, DOUBLES AND SHADOWS

The shadow and the body without a soul are often haunting presences in the vampire genre. However, Carter's use of the concept of the 'shadow' may have been triggered by Fiedler's *Love and Death in the American Novel* (1960), in which he points out that the Shadow is 'the most variously developed of all the Gothic symbols' (p. 125). The word 'shadow' in the title of the novel has a number of connotations. At one level, it invokes Jungian psychology. But, at another level, *Shadow Dance* refers the reader to Psalm 23, in which we are said to 'walk through the valley of the shadow of death'. This is certainly appropriate to both Morris and his friend Honeybuzzard, who specialise in stealing Victoriana from derelict houses and subsequently selling it in their junk shop. This line of work only serves to feed Morris's dark, brooding personality:

> Beds with the shallow depressions in them that men and women, like rivers, mould out for themselves over the years. And piles of photographs of other people's darlings, smiling from outmoded clothes in forgotten summers at Torquay and elsewhere. And books signed inside, with love; up for sale, now, dead love for sale. (p. 25)

An important influence here is a story, 'Bartleby', by Herman Melville, whom Carter regarded, according to 'Notes From The Front Line', as one of her 'male literary heroes' (p. 75). The story concerns a man who, it is suggested, was affected by his work as a clerk in the Dead Letter Office. The Dead Letter Office, as the name signifies, was concerned with documents, and personal effects enclosed with them, relating to people who had died. Like Morris, Bartleby spends much of his life meditating upon mortality, the brevity of life and upon objects that were once part of someone's life but are now 'junk' or of value only as antiques.

As I have pointed out elsewhere, in creating Bartleby, Melville drew upon a figure well established in European romance, which he read in translation: the 'man of sorrows' (Peach, 1982, pp. 155–156). The stranger in Tieck's 'The Runnenberg', for example, typically admits to Christian: 'tonight I grew so sad as I never was in my life before: I seemed so lost, so utterly unhappy; and even yet I cannot shake aside that melancholy humour'. Melville and his European predecessors approached this type of melancholy within a particular metaphysical framework of the time. The optimistic disposition of a confident protagonist, such as the narrator of 'Bartleby', is undermined by the presence of the 'man of sorrows', a figure whom we might describe today as suffering from melancholia, just as Bartleby is affected by his work in the Dead Letter Office. The presence of the 'man of sorrows' disturbs the binarism between a positive subject position, or optimistic mode of thought and being, which the nineteenth-century British writer Carlyle summarised in *Sartor Resartus* as the 'Everlasting Yea', and a negative subject position, arising from a sceptical turn of mind, which Carlyle summarised as the 'Everlasting No'. Melville, like Dostoevsky, another of Carter's literary heroes, found the latter subject position so horrific as to be almost beyond contemplation. The narrator of Melville's 'Bartleby' concludes: 'What miserable friendlessness and loneliness are here revealed! His poverty is great; but his solitude, how horrible!' Nevertheless, Melville suspected that the 'Everlasting No' may have offered a more accurate reflection of life and the human condition than the 'Everlasting Yea'. Throughout Melville's work, under the influence of Carlyle, 'the articulate lovely' appears to the enquiring mind but a veil for 'the inarticulate chaotic' (Peach, 1982, p. 144). This aspect of Melville and also of Dostoevsky's work certainly interested Carter. In 'Notes From The Front Line', she observes: 'both of them lived so close to the edge of the existential abyss that they must often, and with good reason, have envied those who did not have enquiring minds' (p. 75). In the emphasis upon the meaninglessness of life, Melville and German Gothic Romance chimes with the depiction of mid-twentieth-century Europe in the New Wave cinema of the 1950s and 1960s, discussed earlier. But there is a further similarity between early nineteenth-century Euro-American Gothic and European New Wave cinema in the dialectic between the figure who is searching for meaning and those who embrace the 'Everlasting No'.

In *Shadow Dance*, Carter approaches Morris from different yet overlapping perspectives. Whilst one can be appropriately discussed in terms of the nineteenth-century metaphysical framework which she undoubtedly found in Melville's work, the other is influenced by twentieth-century psychoanalysis and anticipates the work of French psychoanalysts such as Julia Kristeva. According to Kristeva, the melancholic is someone for whom despair and pain, as in Bartleby's case, provide the only meaning. Thus, the melancholic's identification with suffering and death, evidenced by

Morris and Bartleby, is part of their failure to transform suffering in imaginative language. Kristeva (1987) argues that the melancholic's sadness is:

> the most archaic expression of a non-symbolisable, unnameable narcissistic wound that is so premature that no external agent (subject or object) can be referred to it. For this type of narcissistic depressive sadness is in reality the only object. More exactly, it is an ersatz of an object to which he attaches himself, and which he tames and cherishes, for want of something else. (p. 22)

From this perspective, the fact that Morris is a failed painter is an index of his melancholia, providing evidence of his failure to develop his imaginary and symbolic capacities. In fact, Morris tends to translate life into death. He imagines the old woman who works as a skivvy at the cafe, for example, creeping nearer and nearer the grave and envisages the loneliness of her death. He thinks of her as the 'Struldbrug', the name given to the immortals in Swift's *Gulliver's Travels* who only get older and uglier. Confessing to his friend Oscar that the cafe makes him sad, he sees his meringue as 'whited sepulchres with dead men's bones inside them' (p. 32).

Although Morris is a failed painter, the fact that he struggles to paint distinguishes him in a crucial respect from Emily and Honeybuzzard. He is at least able to appreciate the loss of life in the destruction of a bluebottle's eggs, unlike Emily, who manifests her failure to develop the imaginary. Her only response to one of Morris's paintings, which she tries to 'read' as a visually impaired person feels Braille, is that it is 'quite big reely' (p. 104). Indeed, Melville's argument that an important aspect of the enquiring, symbolic imagination was the capacity to appreciate 'the inarticulate chaotic' makes Emily's initial reaction to Morris's junk shop significant. When Morris pointedly tells her that 'the unseemly chaos around her was the norm', a sentence which has metaphysical ramifications beyond the shop to which it refers, she seems unperturbed, even spitting out a raisin pip as if in defiance. In its stress upon the inarticulate chaotic, *Shadow Dance*, once again, can be aligned not only with Euro-American Gothic but also with New Wave cinema, which emerged from the chaos of post-war Europe. Indeed, the way in which investment in the symbolic imagination is pitched against the 'realism' and chaos of post-Holocaust Europe in New Wave cinema is echoed in Carter's early fiction.

Suffering in *Shadow Dance* comes with love and a capacity to believe in some ideal. In his regret over what happens to Ghislaine and over the mistaken killing of, in his terms, the Struldbrug, Morris demonstrates a capacity, albeit undeveloped, for love. His troubled conscience is symbolised by his constantly aching teeth which, when he tells Edna that Honey mutilated Ghislaine, begin 'to ache, all together, in concert; all the canines and molars sang in chorus' (p. 50).

Morris's troubled state of mind stands in contradistinction to Honeybuzzard's indifference, a concept for which Carter is again indebted to Melville who, unlike Carlyle, saw the state of indifference as more than a transitory condition. The influence of Melville's preoccupation with what he called 'bitter blanks' is evident in the way Carter, too, associates 'indifference' with an inner void. When Morris tells Honeybuzzard that Ghislaine has been discharged from hospital, he notes how Honeybuzzard's face is 'a mask of nothing' (p. 59). In one respect, his face is redolent of the death mask of the vampire who is indifferent to his female victim, other than as a source of nourishment, and, in the 1960s vampire films, an (implied) source of sexual gratification. However, Dostoevsky is an additional influence on Honeybuzzard who is also described as having 'Raskolnikov eyes, like dead coals' (p. 42). Like Dostoevsky's Raskolnikov prior to his redemption, who cannot believe that his murder of an old woman was a crime, Honeybuzzard does not feel any remorse over what he has done to Ghislaine or over his apparent killing of the old woman from the cafe. Indeed, the emphasis shifts from his cruelty, evidenced in the extent of Ghislaine's injuries, to his indifference: ' "I don't care. Let her go, let her go!" He flung Ghislaine to the winds, with the gesture of the sower in the parable' (p. 61).

As I indicated earlier, in Western European culture the figure of the crucified Christ became one of the most potent symbols for the transformation of suffering and death, providing a way of enlarging the symbolic means of coping with death. Hence, Honeybuzzard's indifference to the crucifix which he and Morris find in a derelict house is an important indicator of his psychic disposition: '[Christ's] plaster nose was chipped, there were cobwebs in his beard and Honey's booted foot crunched a hand to dust in the darkness' (p. 131). However, indifference in Carter's work becomes 'in difference', the portmanteau term coined by the French philosopher Jacques Derrida to conflate the senses of 'difference' and 'deferment'. Derrida's thesis that meaning is never finite but always 'deferred' because of its dependency upon an endless interplay of shifting signifiers within language is appropriate to Carter's representation of Honeybuzzard.

As mentioned earlier, the allusive nature of Carter's work reflects New Wave French cinema, especially Godard's films. In addition to the films already mentioned that *Shadow Dance* recalls, it is worth drawing attention to a further famous film of the 1960s, Hitchcock's *Psycho*. Based on a novel by Robert Bloch, it concerns a psychopathic hotel owner with a fixation for his dead mother, whose skeleton he keeps in her bedroom. In the dream in which Morris mutilates his wife, he screams that there is too much blood. In *Psycho*, the film's psychopath, Norman Bates, reacts in a similar way to the amount of blood after the infamous 'shower scene' in which, dressed as his dead mother, he commits the first murder we witness on the screen. In fact, Hitchcock's film is a particularly appropriate intertext because Robert Bloch's novel, on which the film is based, is itself a reworking of the case of Ed Gein, a murderer who ate his victims. However, it is the allusion to the scene at the end of Hitchcock's film which perhaps has the most relevance for Carter's book, serving to highlight the elusive as well as the allusive nature of the novel. The details of the episode in which Honeybuzzard learns of Ghislaine's release – his face slipping for a moment into 'a mask of nothing' and the reference to the buzzing fly in the silence – are redolent of a scene at the end of *Psycho*. Bates sits alone in a police cell while a psychiatrist provides a long and unconvincing explanation for the murders which Bates has committed as his mother. The camera focuses on a fly, which Bates, believing himself to be watched, refuses to swot so as to give the impression that he would not harm a fly. For a split second, his face changes to that of a skeleton. At one level, this shot suggests a blank void, an amoral nothingness, which cannot be easily rationalised or summarised, the kind of indifference exhibited by Honeybuzzard. It is one of a number of camera shots that, throughout the film, appear to look into and behind Bates's eyes to discover only an unfathomable darkness. This image of a void stands in contradistinction to the psychiatrist's narrative which suggests that the human psyche is knowable. But, of course, Melville and Godard, in their different ways, peered into nothingness. The different intertextual references which Carter employs in describing Honeybuzzard suggest that, like Norman Bates, he, too, cannot be easily pinned down. The reader learns that his 'high-held androgynous face was hard and fine and inhuman', but also, as 'the beautiful, terrible Angel of the Annunciation', he appears to be 'a spectre, a madman, a vampire' (p. 136).

Honeybuzzard, as 'Honey' and 'Buzzard', is typical of the particular way in which the Janus nature of reality is configured in Euro-American Gothic. This configuration is evident, for example, in Melville's *Moby Dick* in the image of the sphinx. As originally described by Carlyle – 'There is in her celestial beauty – which means celestial order, pliancy to wisdom; but there is also a darkness, a ferocity, a totality which are infernal' – this particular image takes pride of place in the novel. In *Shadow Dance*, this configuration is evident not only in the face worn by Honeybuzzard, half Cherub and half devil, but the disfigured Ghislaine: 'When she laughed, half her face was that of a happy baby and the other half, crinkled up, did not look like a face at all' (p. 153).

Shadow Dance also appears to follow American Gothic in suggesting that to deny one side of the mask is to risk destroying the whole. We learn from the later novel, *Love* (1971), in which Honeybuzzard is split to reappear as Honey and Buzz, that, in describing the cherubic aspect of Honey, Carter had in mind Melville's story *Billy Budd*, in which a man is doomed because he is too perfect. Like Melville, Carter incorporates into her novel the Other against which American Gothic is defined – transcendentalism, belief in an idealised 'reality' immanent in or beyond the ordinary appearances of the world. Developed under the influence of German idealism and English romanticism, transcendentalism became the cornerstone of a New England movement from approximately 1830 to 1860. One of its basic tenets is evident in Morris's description of the fishmonger's window, which presents 'a transcendental vision of mystical ecstasy': 'all held some numinous significance, ideal forms from a universe where dead women walked and the past could run back on itself and there was palpable, tangible joy in the air' (p. 161). As in Melville's writing, however, such transcendental idealism, fails at the level of the individual. Morris tries to shut Ghislaine, and what Ghislaine represents, out of his mind:

And she walked into his empty mind again and sat down. Ignore her, don't think of her – Ghislaine. Think of pretty things, instead; think of white cats and black waistcoats and cheerful Hallowe'en feet. (p. 79)

Like Dostoevsky's Golyadkin in *The Double*, Morris appears to project deeds which he dare not commit onto his 'double', in his case Honeybuzzard. The 'double' haunts nineteenth-century European literature from the tales of the German writer Theodore Hoffmann to Robert Louis Stevenson's *Dr Jekyll and Mr Hyde*. Initially, it was a device for expressing the reflected self and the split personality. But the 'double' functions as a more complicated and ambivalent trope in Carter's writing than in the work of either Melville or Dostoevsky, even though she was influenced by them. At one level, the 'double' in Carter's fiction is employed to suggest the immutability of patriarchal society. At another level, it suggests the plural and shifting nature of identities. At even a third level, it provides a means of challenging the kind of binary thinking which too readily distinguishes, Carter suggests, reality and imagination, masculine and feminine, legitimate and illegitimate, good and evil, and custom and taboo.

PHANTASIES AND OBJECTS

The 'double' trope in *Shadow Dance* is developed within a framework drawn partly from American Gothic fiction and partly from twentieth-century psychoanalytical theory. The word 'shadow' in the title brings the analytical psychologist Jung to mind. In *Two Essays on Analytical Psychology*, Jung used the word 'shadow' to refer to negative aspects of the psyche. Whilst Jung believed, like Freud, that the personal unconscious is developed during the individual's lifetime, he also argued for the existence of a collective unconscious which presents itself in the conscious mind. According to Jung, the personal unconscious incorporates two sets of attributes from the collective unconscious, one positive and the other negative. But the novel itself develops the concept of 'shadow' in ways which in broad terms bring to mind not only Jungian psychoanalysis but a branch of twentieth-century analytical psychoanalysis known as 'object relations theory'. According to this school of psychoanalytical theory, we project negative attributes onto 'others'. Object relations theory provides an appropriate framework in which to read Carter's novels written in the 1960s, even if her own engagement with it was limited in terms of detail because of the extent to which her fiction employs 'projection' as twentieth-century Gothic texts. MacAndrew (1979) stresses the importance of 'projection' in Euro-American Gothic, maintaining that the monsters in Gothic tales 'are the shapes into which our fears are projected' (p. 8).

According to leading twentieth-century psychoanalysts such as Melanie Klein, projection and the internalising of our projections are crucial in the formation of our identities. The infant learns to keep 'good' and 'bad' apart in a process which involves dividing one from the other and which continues into adulthood. This process also involves absorbing those aspects of an Other which are perceived as positive, but dispensing of negative aspects of the self by projecting them onto others. However, one of the dangers in this process is that, in what Klein calls 'the paranoid-schizoid state', one-dimensional, single-characteristic part-objects are created as a solution to internal conflict. From her study of fairy tales, Carter would have been familiar with such part-objects in, for example, wicked stepmothers and fairy godmothers. They also occur in nineteenth-century novels such as *Dr Jekyll and Mr Hyde*, with which Carter was, of course, also familiar.

In *Shadow Dance*, the character most obviously regarded as a part-object by another character is Ghislaine. Before she is disfigured by Honeybuzzard, Morris sees Ghislaine as an idealised fantasy: 'She used to look like the sort of young girl one cannot imagine sitting on the lavatory or shaving her armpits or picking her nose' (p. 2). Morris's wife, Edna, also, sees Morris as a part-object. We learn that, according to whom she is talking to, she describes Morris as either an antique dealer or a painter. These little pretensions are projections of her anxieties onto him as he projected his own, far more serious, anxieties onto her. The appropriateness of a Kleinian framework is evident also in the way in which Morris's idealisation of Ghislaine is a defence, as Kleinian theory suggests, against persecutory fantasies. Indeed, one of the reasons why Morris wanted Honeybuzzard to teach Ghislaine a lesson was the way in which she seemed to challenge men, and himself in particular:

> She would say: 'I lost my virginity when I was thirteen', conversationally, as she lit a cigarette, or she would complain of the performance of her last partner, or she would ask you if your wife satisfied you sexually. ... Or she would describe her menstrual pains; and he [Morris] remembered the graphic recital of a course of treatment for a vaginal discharge. (pp. 9–10)

Moreover, in trying to theorise violence within the psyche, Klein focused on the fantasies that a child sometimes has of mutilating its parents. Morris's guilt over what has happened to Ghislaine, even though he did not specifically tell Honeybuzzard to disfigure her, is similar to that which bedevils the child in Kleinian theory who believes that thinking something can make it happen. When a bottle is thrown at Morris in the street from a passing car, he concludes: 'there was a dimension, surely, in the outer nebulae, maybe, where intentions were always executed' (p. 11).

As a traumatised individual, Morris is pursued by Ghislaine both literally and in his fantasies. Here Carter may be inverting Fiedler's (1960) description of the Gothic Shadow, to which I referred earlier, as 'the villain who pursues the Maiden' (p. 125). However, in developing this aspect of Euro-American Gothic, Carter blurs the distinction between the pursued and the pursuer. The text asks: Who is the Shadow? In the dream in which Morris cuts Ghislaine's face with jagged glass their bloods significantly flow together. Tormented by guilt and traumatised by what Honeybuzzard has done to Ghislaine, Morris ceases to exist as an autonomous psychic identity: 'he ran out of himself at every pore and the black sleep ran into him' (p. 18). This psychic and physical disintegration demonstrates Kristeva's point that meaning, identity, system and order collapse when confronted with 'what does not respect borders, positions, rules' (1982, p. 4). It raises questions about Morris's autonomy. Where, the novel asks, are the boundaries to be drawn between Morris and Honeybuzzard? To what extent are individuals, male and female, complicit in acts of intimidation, degradation and violence in which they are not directly involved?

Dostoevsky's *The Double*, to which I referred earlier, suggests the doubleness and sickness of all personality. Carter develops this thesis in *Shadow Dance*, suggesting that Morris's 'doubleness' is the result of the social construction of masculinity. She may, once again, also be taking her lead from Fiedler, who, in his account of the Gothic shadow, points out that 'there is a sense in which the evil principle is mythically male' and that 'it is the Shadow projected as male which most impresses itself upon the imagination' (p. 125). Thus, Morris's instruction to Honeybuzzard to teach Ghislaine a lesson is the product of particular social discourses which sanction male dominance over women and legitimate men's right to abuse women. Although Honeybuzzard mutilated Ghislaine by himself, in 'the outer nebulae', Morris is present as well. It is a significant detail that Ghislaine was naked beneath a shiny black raincoat. But this piece of information is learned at one of the points of the novel where fact and Morris's fantasies become indistinguishable. Ghislaine is described as if she were an object of male, and in particular Morris's, fetishistic fantasies. Morris's sense of complicity with Honeybuzzard specifically and with society's way of seeing women generally is reinforced by the black cat which emerges from the bushes and spits at him. As a witch's familiar, the black cat reminds us of how the persecution of women as witches provided a means of controlling and punishing women's sexuality. Morris, like Desiderio in the later novel *The Infernal Desire Machines of Doctor Hoffman*, is forced to confront his complicity in the dehumanisation of the objects of his desire.

The influence of social discourses in constructing Morris's perceptions is evident in his reading of one of the cards on the tobacconist's notice board: '15-year-old girl seeks riding lessons, *own* jodhpurs' (p. 22). Morris reads the card as if it were a cryptic advertisement for 'personal services' in a telephone box or pornographic magazine. Here Carter includes in the novel pornography which at its point of entry into the text ceases to be pornography as such and becomes one of the novel's tropes. Whilst two years ago a real fifteen-year-old put the card on the notice board, in Morris's fantasy she becomes an icon for a young woman, not necessarily fifteen, but on the cusp of childhood and adulthood. She becomes a part-object, 'a panting, wet-lipped nymphet with jutting nubile breasts'. Unlike the real fifteen-year-old who has got older – the card has begun to brown – the part-object conjured up in Morris's imagination is outside time. The 'real' and the 'fantasy' card occupy different spaces in which the words 'riding lessons' and 'own jodhpurs' acquire different connotations. In *Shadow Dance*, Carter is interested in the space in which these two sets of meanings collide.

The way in which Morris sees Ghislaine as a part-object is the product of both his individual psyche and the way in which society perceives women as part-objects. Baudrillard (1976) argues that every kind of body is articulated in terms of, and is a version of, the 'negative' of the ideal upon which it is based (p. 114). Although the notion of a 'negative ideal' may seem contradictory at first, the concept itself is interesting and relevant to Carter's work. Baudrillard argues that in medicine, in which the healthy body is the positive ideal, the 'negative ideal' represents the failure of medicine, the corpse. In religion, concerned with human spirituality and the transcendence of the body, the 'negative ideal' is the animalistic body, all instinct and appetite. In *Shadow Dance*, Morris's imagining of his sick wife as dead flesh reduces her to the phantasm of the corpse on which medical discourse about the body is based. At one level, Emily is the ideal housewife. Virtually her first act on arriving at

Morris's shop is to wash all the sheets, linen and clothing she can find in strong soap. As such, however, she is reduced to the phantasm of the robot, the 'negative ideal' type on which the housewife in cultural discourse is based. She is actually said to behave like 'a well-trained house-robot' and to perform her services with 'the competent impersonality of a cafeteria attendant' (p. 101).

The familiar virgin and whore phantasms to which male representations reduce women are literally realised in Ghislaine's disfigured face. Initially in Morris's focalisation, she has a personality which is a kaleidoscope of different emotions and motivations. However, he thinks of her increasingly in terms of binary opposites: a young picture-book girl or a shocking, rude woman. The one image, like the one side of her face, is soft and compliant, while the other is disturbing and embarrassing. Her Janus face forces Morris to confront a contradiction which is within both himself and the masculinised, sociocultural realisation of women as whole or part-objects.

3

'Realities', Illusions and Delusions: *Several Perceptions* (1968) and *Love* (1970)

Like *Shadow Dance*, *Several Perceptions* (1968), written between March and December 1967, is a third-person retrospective narrative. Again the focalisation is through the consciousness of a single, male character, Joseph Harker, who, like Morris, is prey to dreams and fantasies. Like Morris, he is haunted, but by death rather than by a woman. While Morris contemplates suicide in the first chapter of *Shadow Dance*, Joseph attempts it. The narrative charts his recovery, culminating in a miraculous party at the end of the novel.

Joseph, like Morris, is an adaptation of the Euro-American Gothic trope the 'man of sorrows', discussed in Chapter 2. At times, Joseph appears like 'a big, fat, soft, stupid, paper Valentine heart squeezing out a soggy tear at the sorrows of the world' (p. 5). His occupation as a hospital orderly brings him even more than Morris's antique business into proximity with death and abjection, 'cleaning up shit and amputations' (p. 98). Yet, as for Morris and Melville's Bartleby, it is the personal effects of the deceased which arouse melancholy:

> On the other hand, false teeth, spectacles and watches were scrupulously returned to the bereaved of the deceased; when Joseph asked what happened to glass eyes, they were peremptory with him, as though he had committed a breach of taste. (p. 12)

Like Morris, Joseph has a melancholic's identification with suffering and death. As is characteristic of Euro-American Gothic, the effect that they have on him is contrasted with the response of a friend who is less affected, in this case Viv. Unlike Joseph, Viv is resigned to mortality, to the sufferings of the old, and to the horrors of the Vietnam War. Like Morris, too, such is Joseph's melancholy that he is unable to develop his imaginary and symbolic capacities. Indeed, after Charlotte has left him, he sets fire to books in the public library. The intertextual references to T. S. Eliot's poem, *The Wasteland* – the novel contains references to the burial of the dead, the London pub and the hanging man of the tarot cards – are obviously significant in this regard since the failure of the imagination to rejuvenate the wasteland is one of the main themes of Eliot's poem. Indeed, Carter's description of Joseph's parents' living room appears at one level as a piece of realist writing, a window on a living room furnished in a style characteristic of the 1960s. But, at another level, it appears informed by the kind of disillusionment which characterises the depictions of tacky, twentieth-century materialism in Eliot's poem, albeit with stronger suggestions of violence:

> At home he sat in an uneasy chair urging the plaster ducks to try and fly across the wall. There was a tooled leather *TV Times* cover and a brass Dutch girl concealing fire-irons in the hollow of her back. These things seemed wholly threatening; the leather cover was a ravenous mouth smacking brown lips and the Dutch girl must use her little brushes and shovels as cruel weapons since there was no other use for them. (p. 7)

Of particular significance is Mrs Boulder's identification of Joseph with the hanged man of the Tarot cards (pp. 108–109). The hanged man is the card in Eliot's poem which Madame Sostris, in 'The Burial of the Dead', is unable to find, reinforcing the aridity of the wasteland since it signifies Christ or the hanged god from Fraser's *The Golden Bough*. In this context, it is ironic that Joseph is unable to satisfy Mrs Boulder sexually, and she then reminds him of the Tarot card.

Like Morris, Joseph also tends, as in his descriptions of the elderly, to translate life into death:

> Everywhere Joseph looked, he saw old people with sticks and bulging veins in their legs and skulls from which the flesh of their faces hung in tattered webs; they advanced slowly as if this might be their very last walk. A man with a metal hook instead of a hand passed by and then a hunchbacked woman. (p. 9)

While this passage describes physical features usually associated with ageing, in Joseph's mind they seem to be exaggerated. It is as if, being over-aware of these physical characteristics, he then projects them onto the people he is observing so as to turn them into part-objects, strongly suggesting Baudrillard's 'negative ideal' of the corpse to which I referred in Chapter 2.

Like the other two novels in the 'Bristol trilogy', *Several Perceptions* invites reading from a realist perspective, but also conflates the factual and the fantastic. In fact, it is less reliant than the other two novels on realist techniques. O'Day (1994) argues, developing Lorna Sage's point that the novel is constructed like a strip cartoon, that actions and interactions in *Several Perceptions* are not linked by cause and effect. Time in the novel seems like that which we find in fairy tale, myth and dream and, more so than in *Shadow Dance*, the nature of the narrative mimics the condition of the central male consciousness. The desultory, shiftless social world of the novel reflects the depressive, disillusioned and slippery nature of Joseph's mind. In many respects, Joseph exemplifies what Julia Kristeva (1987) describes as the typical melancholic's condition. Kristeva explains that there is no object for the melancholic, only 'an ersatz of an object to which he attaches himself', a vague 'light without representation' (p. 22).

The dreams in the novel are a displacement of the 'shadow' of Joseph's psyche. As in *Shadow Dance*, they are related to how the central protagonist has sought to deal with the negative aspects of his subconscious. At one point, in a narrative redolent of 'Red Riding Hood', Joseph dreams that he is a child walking home from the 'Wolf Cubs'. Here Carter wittily gives a Gothic twist to a social institution of the time, for the werewolf was one of the means by which Gothic writing sought to explore the repressed collective unconscious. The maniac who follows Joseph with a knife, recalling Honeybuzzard from *Shadow Dance*, would seem to represent the suppressed parts of his own psyche. The street through which he walks is exaggeratedly neat and clean; 'privet hedges and clean milk bottles' (p. 5). It may be that it signifies the conscious mind's denial of polluting objects, represented by the maniac and the wolf. In the dream, 'mad for sanctuary, Joseph the child burst through a front gate and beat his fists on the nearest door' (ibid.). Here, the child would seem to represent an innocence that Joseph would like to reclaim.

The way in which the suppressed, such as Joseph's childhood fears, can re-emerge and destabilise the conscious mind is mirrored in the novel in the way in which dreams, usually incorporated as metanarratives within the main narrative, and fantasy disrupt and destabilise the realist mode of narration which relies on coherence and closure. Catherine Belsey (1980) maintains that the realist novel is predicated on a 'declarative text' which imparts ' "knowledge" to a reader whose position is thereby stabilised, through a privileged discourse which is to varying degrees invisible' (pp. 90ff). Her reference to 'invisible' here reminds us that the realist novel purports to hold a mirror up to the world and, as readers, we tend to accept this, overlooking the ways in which the novel has constructed what we are looking at. However, within the realist text, we can also encounter metanarratives, or embedded narratives, which have a different mode of address. While the dominant, declarative text suggests coherence, closure and stability, the latter are marked by conflict, indeterminacy and instability. We are presented with questions to which we are encouraged to find answers, while being made aware of the difficulties in doing so.

In *Several Perceptions*, the dreams invite the reader, who has been cast in the mode of a reader of a realist text, to consider them both in relation to the main narrative and to each other. They are part of a larger interplay within the narrative which undermines the stability and coherence which we normally look for in a realist text. They also invite the reader to occupy a psychoanalytic position. At one level, the interconnections between the dreams in the novel appear to offer the reader some degree of satisfaction, such as insight into Joseph's character. The garden dream, for example, like the Wolf Club dream, ends with Joseph looking into his own face. Both dreams bring Joseph's childhood to the fore; Joseph enters both dreams as a violent, murderous adult and both dreams suggest, through their sexual connotations, that this figure may be the repressed father and that the dreams articulate Joseph's identification with him but also his fear and hatred of him. Both dreams resist any neat interpretation. The man in both dreams is additionally associated with time. In the garden dream, he destroys both children and spring flowers, while in the second dream, his progress is as 'relentless as the clock'. While in the second dream, the maniac in pursuit, in Freudian terms, conjures up the child's fear of castration, in the garden dream he destroys the heads of the flowers and the children.

The difficulty of achieving a clear-cut interpretation of these dreams is an irony at the centre of the novel, for Joseph's biblical namesake is an interpreter of dreams. However, the irony is even more complex because the dreams, as a reflection of Joseph's psyche, betray the influence of twentieth-century psychoanalytic thought, in which Carter was interested but of which she was sceptical. As symbolic narratives, the dreams lend themselves too obviously to analysis. Moreover, Joseph's surname is Harker – the name of the narrator of Bram Stoker's *Dracula*. This complicates matters further, for dreams in this novel are part of a literary as well as a character's psychic history. The two become confused, as, for example, in the way in which Charlotte is recreated in Joseph's dreams as one of the vampires in Dracula's castle:

A picture of Charlotte was tacked over the gas fire. ... Her blonde hair blew over her face which did not in the least resemble the face he remembered, since that face reincarnated in fantasy after fantasy, recreated nightly in dreams for months after she left, had become transformed in his mind to a Gothic mask, huge eyeballs hooded with lids of stone, cheekbones sharp as steel, lips of treacherous vampire redness and a wet mouth which was a mantrap of ivory fangs. Witch woman. Incubus. (p. 15)

That *Several Perceptions* should invite the reader to occupy the position of analyst but offer no guarantee of satisfaction should not surprise us given the novel's epigraph: 'The mind is a kind of theatre, where several perceptions successively make their appearance, pass, re-pass, glide away and mingle in an infinite variety of postures and situations.' In the course of the novel, Joseph's own state of consciousness is directly associated with Hume's concept of the mind. When Kay and Joseph break into the zoo to free the badger, the reader is told: 'These thoughts flashed on to various screens in small sideshows of [Joseph's] mind but the main theatre was so busy with the escape itself' (p. 58). Charlotte becomes a symbol of the female victim of the vampire, discussed in Chapter 2, who then turns her sexual, vampiric gaze on others.

The impossibility of the analyst's position is parodied in the comic relationship between Joseph and his psychiatrist, Ransome, who pointedly admits that, as neither a Freudian nor a shaman, he does not interpret dreams (p. 84). The weariness in Ransome's physical appearance – 'his colourless eyes hung in nets of tired lines, like trawled fish' – is mirrored in his diagnosis of Joseph's problems: 'you use [the tragedy of war] as a symbol for your rejection of a world to which you cannot relate. Perhaps because of your immaturity' (p. 64). The diagnosis is based on a narrative that has a coherence and closure not available to Joseph. When threatening to jump, Joseph opens a window, disturbing the psychiatrist's papers. Significantly, Ransome's response is to reassemble them. His solution is to write Joseph a prescription for more tranquillisers and recommend that he get plenty of fresh air. Joseph's lateral response to being labelled 'immature' is to send excrement to President Lyndon Johnson as a protest against the war in Vietnam.

Joseph's destruction of the books in the library draws attention to what he does read as much as what he does not. His room is filled with books, newspaper cuttings and scrapbooks about the Vietnam War. As the first war which Americans witnessed in the media, it literally brought home the trauma of military conflict where there was no clearly defined front line. It was a war for which American combatants were psychologically unprepared and with which many tried to cope by taking hallucinatory drugs. In the confusion of fact and fantasy through the elision of propaganda and reportage, the Vietnam War became a 'theatre', which Coppola encapsulated in both the content and style of his film *Apocalypse Now*, mirroring the theatre of the mind described in the novel's epigraph.

At the heart of the novel, as mentioned in Chapter 1, there is a sense of loss which can be interpreted in both historical/cultural and psychoanalytic terms. At one level, it is the sense of cultural loss which resulted from the decline of Britain as an industrial and colonial power, which became increasingly obvious after the Second World War. It is alluded to when Joseph regrets the loss of 'military great coats of the elegant past' (p. 123) and also informs the description of the Down:

> It was a once-handsome, now decayed district with a few relics of former affluence (such as the coffee shop, a suave place) but now mostly given over to old people who had come down in the world, who lived in basements and ground floor backs, and students and beatniks who nested in attics. (p. 9)

However, this sense of historical/cultural loss is elided at the individual level with a psychoanalytical sense of lack. Kay's mansion is a mausoleum created by his dying mother: 'a footlights favourite of the 1930s, the world she knew was shot down in flames in 1940' (p. 11). Nearly all the characters in the novel have experienced a personal loss: Joseph has lost his partner six months prior to the date when his narrative begins; Anne Blossom has lost her child and may also have lost her father in the war; Old Sunny the music hall violinist has lost his violin; and Mrs Boulder has lost her lover. But Carter's fiction presents us with the experience of loss as also the experience of a frightening presence. As in the other two novels in the 'Bristol trilogy', the void in *Several Perceptions* is filled with what is sinister and violent, evident in the poster of the child murderer and the reaction it provokes; the violence in the pub; the references to the Boston Strangler; and even in the dog, 'built like a fur tank, about half the whole size of Sunny' (p. 8), which steals Sunny's cap.

In some respects, the conclusion of the novel appears to present the reader with innocence regained. Unlike *Shadow Dance* and *Love*, the novel has a carnivalesque ending that anticipates Carter's interest in the carnivalesque in the later novel, *Nights at the Circus*. Almost like a benevolent puppet master, the androgynous Kay presides over a miraculous carnival, in contrast to Uncle Philip in *The Magic Toyshop*. In *Several Perceptions*, Anne Blossom, who has been mysteriously crippled, is able to walk, Mrs. Boulder is reunited with her lover, and Old Sunny has a violin again. Even Joseph's cat has snow-white kittens. Carter appears to conclude with a metaphor for the collective, utopian future envisaged in 1960s hippie counterculture. Typically, however, all this is also ambiguous. The reader is left wondering how much of it is illusion rather than miracle. With hands trembling so much that he spills his drink and cannot roll a cigarette easily, Kay insists:

> [Anne] had hysterical paralysis... Anybody could have cured her, anybody who said to her in a firm enough voice, "Nonsense, you don't really limp at all". Not a miracle. No miracle. It wasn't a miracle. Was it? (p. 145)

Although the question mark here may introduce a countersense of doubt, even more devastating is Kay's admission that he doesn't really care about her and the way in which the decaying atmosphere of his mother's mansion is consuming him so that he appears desiccated.

The miraculous party which concludes the novel is in sharp contrast to the earlier carnival site in the novel, the pub, or more specifically, the public bar. The description of the bar places it outside conventional realist narrative: 'things were happening without a sequence, there was no flow or pattern to events' (p. 52). There is a theatrical element epitomised in the fandango dancer and Kay

Kyte's role as 'the demon king'. However, it is an ambiguous social space. The boy who plays the fruit machine wears jeans and a leather jacket with 'Drag City' on the back – the uniform of rebellious youth. There is an atmosphere of repressed violence created by the knife scars on the leather benches and the fandango danced by the black-eyed girl: 'It was a mating dance display and yet it had the freezing menace of a dance in an Elizabethan tragedy performed by disguised assassins concealing knives' (p. 51). But if the public bar provides a counterculture to the lounge bar, it is also defined, and even contained, by it. The youth may wear what he believes to be the uniform of nonconformity, yet, paradoxically, he is conforming to a definition of nonconformity, one of the paradoxes of 1950s and 1960s counterculture. In the enthusiasm for the 1960s, freedom of choice was not often distinguished from the illusion of choice. Two central images in this scene are the fruit machine and the juke box. Apart from the fact that both may be seen as icons of an increasingly widespread, bland Anglo-American uniformity, the juke box offers choice only from a predetermined and limited selection. Both machines pander to subversive activities: the fruit machine to gambling, and the juke box to rock-and-roll. Yet each is the product of a capitalist system which exploits those who appropriate them as sites of ostensibly subversive activities. Capitalism grows rich on the proceeds of both.

The public bar is not an alternative to the lounge bar but, to employ the French cultural critic Baudrillard's terms, discussed earlier, its 'negative ideal': 'The public bar was quite different to the lounge bar; it was far larger, far colder, no snug carpet underfoot but chilly, clinking tiles' (p. 50). The empty grate holds only squashed cigarette packets and 'a fresh gob of sputum' (ibid.). The word 'gob' is slang for a clot of spittle and for a worked-out seam in a mine. Significantly, the public bar is where two old people sit; under capitalism, the old are literally surplus to requirements. In capitalist society, the most precious commodity is time; time is literally money. The public bar with fruit machine and juke box is a site where time, in capitalist terms, is wasted.

The narrative voice in the scene directs the reader's response. There is regret that there is no fire in the pub's grate. The metaphorical meaning of lack of fire extends to the boy with the pink tie, who has 'taxidermy eyes like a dead, stuffed deer' (p. 51). But even more significant is the narrator's intrusion: 'if you looked long enough into his eyes, you would start screaming'. The narrator obviously wants a site of genuine carnival. There is hope here in the possibility of sudden transformation, of the kind of sudden change which Joseph witnesses when he emerges from the lavatory. But even this is ambiguous, for the source of the change, the fandango dancer, is acting a part.

In the 'play within the play' in Shakespeare's *A Midsummer Night's Dream*, Bottom is distressed at the idea of presenting death to the audience. He insists on the inclusion of a prologue making it clear that Pyramus is not actually dead and that it is not in fact Pyramus at all but Bottom the weaver. In other words, realism intrudes and all but destroys the illusion of the play they are planning. At the end of *Several Perceptions*, illusion intrudes to subvert the 'realism' of loss, pain and suffering. Shakespeare's play is recalled at Kay's departure:

> He wavered as he walked as if he were a piece of trick photography and might suddenly disappear altogether, so discreetly the air would not even be disturbed by his passage. As if his goodnight act were to cast sleep upon them, both Joseph and Anne lay down and closed their eyes as soon as he was out of the room, both, in their different ways, perfectly content; already this marvellous happening seemed quite natural, like the existence of Sunny's violin, incorporated into the actuality of the house. (p. 146)

However, in reading the final pages of *Several Perceptions*, we might also think of those plays by Shakespeare, such as *The Winter's Tale*, in which the world itself is turned into a theatre. Towards the end of the miraculous party in *Several Perceptions*, as towards the end of Shakespeare's last plays, the reader is made aware of the theatricality of the event, which, like Kay himself, appears to be like 'a piece of trick photography'. Realism as the dominant mode of the text dissolves and threatens to disappear altogether. Between them, Anne and Sunny identify two key elements of realist writing dispensed with at this stage in the novel. Sunny is to throw away his book of facts and Anne identifies 'time' as the enemy (p. 140). The party which closes the novel is more than just a carnivalesque conclusion. It returns us to the David Hume epigraph and the notion of the theatricality of the mind. The incorporation of Sunny's violin into the 'actuality of the house' destabilises the distinction between fact and imagination, as does Kay's hypothesis that Anne's lameness was in her mind. The ending of the novel is meant to appear theatrical and contrived, a fitting conclusion to a text which from its very epigraph deliberately confounds illusion and reality.

THE CULTURES OF *LOVE*

Although *Love* was published in 1971, it was written in 1969. Unusually, a revised edition was published in 1987 containing an Afterword written by Carter herself. Originally, she had intended to reveal her own opinions of the novel nearly twenty years after writing it, but she tells us that she chose instead to write some more of the original text. In fact, she tells us what has happened to the characters subsequent to the original narrative. At the outset, however, she pinpoints three criticisms which she would now have of the novel: 'its almost sinister feat of male impersonation, its icy treatment of the mad girl and its penetrating aroma of unhappiness' (p. 113). But, perhaps, her views should not be taken at face value. As in some of her later novels, it would require considerable insensitivity not to be critical of the male protagonists, whose views appear to be given priority. As a novelist, Carter invariably liked to work backwards, beginning by articulating positions and perspectives which are subsequently exposed, challenged and unravelled as the narrative itself unfurls.

The novel is concerned with a love–hate triangle of two half-brothers, Lee and Buzz, and Annabel, a middle-class drop-out, in 1960s bohemia. There are a number of additional cameo roles, to which Carter in the Afterword admits she now wishes she had given more depth. Lee and Buzz share the same mother, who went mad in spectacular fashion: running naked down the high street declaring that she was the whore of Babylon and, painted all over her body with cabalistic signs, bursting into her children's school playground. However, they have different fathers. Lee's father was a railwayman killed in the course of duty, while Buzz, born during a period when his mother worked as a prostitute after her husband's death, is the illegitimate son of an American serviceman whom he believes to be an American Indian.

Brought up in south London by an aunt with strong left-wing sympathies, Lee and Buzz move to Bristol during 1963–1964 when Lee gains a place, like Angela Carter herself, at Bristol University. Annabel, whom Buzz discovers has joined his half-brother in the flat when he returns from the 1960s North Africa hippie trail, is another cliché of the period: a middle-class girl from a sheltered, conventional background who drops into bohemia as an art student. Later, she emulates Buzz's lifestyle, adopting his drifter's working pattern and stealing.

Lorna Sage (1994b) points out that the prose of *Love* is characterised by 'a glowing patina of craft and indifference ... that exactly fits the artificial "nature" of the people' (p. 20). The novel is a disturbing fusion of the Gothic and the avant-garde which may have been suggested to Carter by Fiedler (1960), who, in describing how Beatniks 'mock the "squares" of San Francisco with the monstrous disorder of life', explains that 'the gothic is an avant-garde genre, perhaps the first avant-garde art in the modern sense of the term' (p. 127).

Buzz as the illegitimate son, as in Renaissance drama, is an important destabilising element in the text, where an important trope is the significance of what is repressed or denied. In many ways, *Love* looks back to Carter's first novel. Honeybuzzard is divided and reappears partly as Buzz and partly as the beautiful Lee ('Honey'), who took his name from a Western movie. Conventionally attractive with blond hair and blue eyes, he has entered the middle class via a university education and a teaching post in a grammar school but his working-class origins are revealed in moments of extreme emotion when, like Paul Morel in D. H. Lawrence's *Sons and Lovers*, he lapses into working-class speech. Buzz is Lee's 'shadow'; the Native American to Lee's Western cowboy. In many ways, the Native American can be seen as the repressed subconscious of white America. However, Buzz is also the 'shadow' of the kind of society which Lee has been able to enter. Unlike Lee, he went to a secondary modern school, so that between them the brothers reflect the kind of social schizophrenia that the eleven-plus system imposed on the country, dividing children into an able, *academic* élite and a less able, vocational underclass. Buzz is also the 'shadow' of middle-class, bohemian rebellion. His father left behind a finger ring with a skull and crossbones, a symbol of piracy adopted as a sign of rebellion in the 1960s by working-class subculture. Buzz also signifies a further 'shadow', the homoerotic element in the complex relationship between the two half-brothers: at a party they dance together, and when Annabel has sex with Lee she is dressed in Buzz's clothes. When Buzz is thrown out of the flat, he asks his brother whether he is 'Going straight?' (p. 65), to which he replies: 'I'm not divorcing you, for God's sake' (p. 66). This is an aspect of their relationship about which Carter is a little more explicit in her Afterword:

> The brothers are no longer in communication. ... Nevertheless, Lee is the only human being his brother ever felt one scrap for and he admits to himself, and occasionally to startled companions, that if there is one thing he would like to do before he dies, it is to fuck him. There is as much menace as desire in this wish. (p. 117)

The middle section of *Love* is given over to an analysis of the *ménage à trois* in interviews between Lee and Annabel's psychiatrist. Here Carter employs a more concentrated version of the scenes between Joseph and Ransome in *Several Perceptions* for a similar purpose. There is a comparable tension between the complexity and intensity with which Lee perceives things and the occasionally curt responses of the psychiatrist. At one point, not unsympathetically, she pronounces that his brother 'does not seem entirely normal' (p. 59); at another, she shrugs enigmatically; and at still another she laughs long and hard at what he says. As in *Several Perceptions*, the scenes with the psychiatrist are ones of black comedy and it is in these sessions that Lee falls in love with the psychiatrist. In a sequence which he might have imagined or one that might have happened and resulted in him being kicked, Lee finds himself on the floor at her feet, exploring her knees, her thighs and, eventually, between her legs.

In her Afterword to the novel, Carter calls the analyst '*the perox-ided psychiatrist*' (p. 115). The account of her life over the next twenty years provides a commentary upon both the 1980s and her behaviour with Lee. After Annabel's death, she seems to have no more concern for him as an individual than she displayed in the earlier interviews; he is prescribed tranquillisers which turn him into 'a virtual zombie'. She goes on to work in those areas which prove the most lucrative, becoming a director of a chain of extremely expensive detoxification centres for very rich junkies and the director of three pharmaceutical companies. With a Porsche, a successful radio programme and a best-seller under her belt, she epitomises the yuppie culture of the 1980s. However, she also serves to highlight the commodification of mental health and the confusion of professionalisation and commercialisation during this period, together with the way in which people have been seduced into becoming dependent upon prescribed drugs.

GOTHIC *LOVE*

In her Afterword, Carter maintains that she first obtained the idea of *Love* from a nineteenth-century novel, *Adolphe*: 'I was seized with the desire to write a kind of modern-day demotic version of *Adolphe*, although I doubt anybody could spot the resemblance after I'd macerated the whole thing in triple-distilled essence of English provincial life' (p. 113). Carter's admission that the idea 'first' came from *Adolphe* suggests, of course, that there were other sources for the idea of *Love*. One of the most important of these, I would suggest, was the work of Edgar Allan Poe. Buzz looks as if he is fresh from a visit to the tomb of Edgar Allan Poe (p. 36) and is later compared with Poe's Raven. Not only has Carter split the name 'Honeybuzzard' drawn from her first novel, but the name 'Annabel Lee' in Poe's poem is also divided to provide the names of two of the leading protagonists.

The intertextual references in *Love* to Poe's 'Annabel Lee' highlight the novel's concern with a subject on which Carter, according to Elaine Jordan (1992), is particularly convincing and insightful: 'narcissistic desire, self-preoccupied fantasies which interfere in the possibility of relation between people who are "other" in themselves, not just projections of each other's desires' (p. 121). In fact, in exploring what Jordan calls 'narcissistic desire', Carter has taken up two of the major themes of Poe's poetry: the dangers in withdrawing too far into an imaginary world and the negative aspects of the human psyche. Unlike in the case of Buzz, who appears to have inherited numerous fears about women from his mother, particularly that of the *vagina dentata* (p. 94), little explanation is offered as to why Annabel is as she is. There is a hint, however, that Annabel is severely repressed by her parents. As an only daughter, she is brought up, and caught up, in a classic Oedipal triangle. Within this particular family unit, she can be nothing but the (only) daughter. The visit of her parents, which subsequently results in Annabel being forced to marry Lee, provides us with a glimpse into the introverted nature of Annabel's childhood and adolescence, suggesting that she has not been able to achieve a fully developed adult identity.

If the use of the names 'Annabel' and 'Lee' suggests that Carter had Poe's poem in mind when writing *Love*, it is clear that *Adolphe* sowed the seeds of the narrative idea that took her to Poe's work. Written by Benjamin Constant [Henri Benjamin Constant de Rebecque] (1767–1830), *Adolphe* (1815) is the story of a man who falls in love with

Eleanor, the wife of Count E—. Unable to terminate the relationship through guilt, he is devastated when she dies. The poem, 'Annabel Lee', is concerned with the union of two souls, that of the narrative 'I' and Annabel Lee, which cannot be separated:

> But our love it was stronger by far than the love
> Of those who were older than we –
> Of many far wiser than we –
> And neither the angels in heaven above,
> Nor the demons down under the sea,
> Can ever dissever my soul from the soul
> Of the beautiful ANNABEL LEE:
>
> For the moon never beams, without bringing me dreams
> Of the beautiful ANNABEL LEE:
> And the stars never rise, but I feel the bright eyes
> Of the beautiful ANNABEL LEE:
> And so, all the night-tide, I lie down by the side
> Of my darling – my darling – my life and my bride,
> In the sepulchre there by the sea – In her tomb by the sounding sea.

However, the real subject of the poem is the perils of what in Poe's day, *pace* Coleridge, was known as the 'secondary imagination'. In particular, Poe explores how this creative faculty, in reshaping the world inwardly according to its subjective awareness of life, death, time and space, can lead to an unhealthy solipsism. In the poem, each stanza through repetition coils back on, and appears to, absorb its predecessor.

When the reader first meets Annabel at the beginning of *Love*, she occupies a world where the boundaries between fantasy and illusion have become blurred: 'All she apprehended through her senses she took only as objects for interpretation in the expressionist style and she saw, in everyday things, a world of mythic, fearful shapes' (pp. 3–4). Narcissistic desire is perhaps an ironic subject to choose for a novel. Normally, we think of a novel as 'a meeting point between the individual and the general, bridging the isolated subjectivity and peopled world' (Connor, 1996, p. 1). Carter's Annabel has 'a capacity for changing the appearance of the real world... which is the price paid by those who take too subjective a view of it' (p. 3). An interest in this kind of excessive subjectivity inspired Poe, as evidenced in his poem 'The Raven', to write about the progression toward an 'imaginative madness'. In 'The Raven', the protagonist moves from the known or 'real' world of time and dimension to a chaotic, fictive world. Here, only the imagination and its morbid fantasies exist. Similarly, it is the inward subjectivity of Annabel, which eventually gives way to an 'imaginative madness' *pace* Poe, that is stressed at the outset of *Love*. In her Afterword, even with hindsight, Carter is of the opinion that 'even the women's movement would have been no help to her and alternative psychiatry would have only made things, if possible, worse' (p. 113).

Annabel is a version of the Gothic 'doomed beloved', who, Fiedler (1960) says, 'bears the stigmata of a tabooed figure' and is marked as 'the carrier of madness and death' (p. 385). One of the first images that the reader encounters in *Love* is of a 'once harmonious artificial wilderness' having become dishevelled over time (p. 1). It is an image of the shift which occurs in Annabel's own mind from a perilously maintained balance of her faculties to their total disruption. In the park, Annabel is seeking the Gothic north, the 'shadow' of the Mediterranean south which bores her with its serenity. It is evidenced in a symbol, 'an ivy-covered tower with leaded ogive windows' (p. 2), which anticipates Annabel's subsequent withdrawal into herself. As in *Several Perceptions*, the mind is envisaged as a theatre; here the pillared portico and Gothic tower transform the park into 'a premeditated theatre where the romantic imagination could act out any performance it chose' (ibid.). The park itself seems like a metaphor for a more tumultuous version of the 'theatre of the mind' described in the epigraph to *Several Perceptions*. Almost a parody of a Gothic protagonist, 'a mad girl plastered in fear and trembling' (p. 3), Annabel is prone to visitations of 'anguish' and suffers from nightmares too terrible to be revealed.

In *Love*, Carter suggests that 'indifference', which she explored in her first novel, may be a symptom of too introverted a subjectivity. Indeed, Carter frequently uses the adverb 'indifferently' to describe Annabel's actions and responses: we are told that she 'indifferently stirred the paper with her toes' (p. 8); she answers Lee 'indifferently'; and, when they make love, she submits indifferently (p. 32). In the pornographic photographs given her by Buzz, Annabel is attracted to the bland, indifferent, motionless face of the model and the stark, cold juxtaposition of genitalia. She lies for hours on the cold boards 'as if she were on a slab in a morgue' (p. 19). Lee's relationship with her stands in contrast to the affairs he has with the philosopher's wife, with Carolyn and with Joanne, his fifteen-year-old school pupil. O'Day (1994) points out that most of the verbal dialogue in the novel takes place in these encounters rather than within the triangle of Annabel, Lee and Buzz (p. 51).

Annabel is possessed, like Melville's Bartleby and like Morris in *Shadow Dance*, with an infinite sense of sorrow: 'she had impressed her sorrow so deeply on the essential wood and brick of the place she knew for certain nobody could ever be happy there again' (p. 71). However, *Love*, more than *Shadow Dance*, develops the condition of extreme withdrawal into which Melville's Bartleby has fallen. Annabel, like Bartleby, becomes increasingly detached from the immediate world around her, spending more and more time gazing into space (p. 71). Bartleby turns his desk to a blank wall; Annabel boards up her window and is drawn to Buzz's room, where the window faces a blank wall (p. 31). However, once again, the influence of Edgar Allan Poe, as well as Melville, proves important. The apartment, like the enclosures in which many of Poe's protagonists in his tales find themselves, becomes a place of exclusion, where an individual is isolated from the world of time, reason and physical fact, creating what Carter calls in the Afterword to *Love* 'its penetrating aroma of unhappiness' (p. 113).

Even Lee associates Annabel's other-worldliness with death, accusing her of going out at night to trample on graves (p. 7). Unwittingly, and ironically, in cautioning her about wandering on the hillside at night in bare feet, Lee anticipates the ultimate consequence of her introversion: 'Oh, my duck, you'll catch your death' (ibid.). In *Shadow Dance*, Morris is unable to transform his awareness of suffering and death through art. Annabel's paintings also fail because they are life-denying. The tree of life she paints is like the Uppas tree of Java, which casts a poisoned shade (p. 32).

In exploring 'the price paid by those who take too subjective a view' of the world, Carter rewrites that aspect of the Gothic genre in which women are usually presented as preyed on by men. Annabel's decision to have Lee tattooed in, significantly, Gothic script and circled by a heart is a rewriting of Hester Prynne's punishment in Hawthorne's nineteenth-century American Gothic novel, *The Scarlet Letter*. In Hawthorne's text, the Puritan elders make her wear the letter 'A' embroidered on her gown as a punishment for adultery. There are a number of parallels between the two episodes. When Hester Prynne passes young women in the street, the scarlet letter which she wears is said to give a throb of recognition. Lee's tattoo similarly seems to 'throb and burn him' (p. 70). Once again, this trace of an earlier text opens up different possible readings of Carter's novel. Carter not only rewrites the patriarchal bias of Hawthorne's novel, but develops its interest in revenge and the way revenge can affect both its victim and its perpetrator. When the tattooist creates the heart on Lee's chest, Annabel looks on with a cold, almost sadistic, sense of satisfaction, reminiscent of the revengeful gaze of Roger Chillingworth in *The Scarlet Letter* as well as other cold-hearted observers who seem to recur in Hawthorne's work. Here, Carter is exploiting the potential of the horror story for the exegesis of guilt. The victim, in this case the wronged Annabel, becomes a cold-hearted monster who must be destroyed. However, the allusions to Hawthorne's *The Scarlet Letter* invite the reader to see Annabel through Hawthorne's moral framework. From this perspective, Annabel appears particularly disturbing because she unwittingly devises 'a revenge which required a knowledge of human feeling to perfect it' (p. 70). It is very likely that Carter had in mind the way in which this aspect of Annabel is represented when she referred to the novel's 'icy treatment of the mad girl' (p. 113).

In *Love*, Carter once again works creatively within and between different frames of reference. The concepts of excessive subjectivity and 'narcissistic desire' are developed not only with reference to paradigms from nineteenth-century American writers and her own earlier work, but also from twentieth-century psychoanalysis. Again, object relations theory provides an appropriate framework within which to discuss Carter's work. When he makes love to her, Lee has to undress Annabel as if she were once again a child and she regresses to the nursery. As the trope of regression suggests, Annabel, like Melanie in *The Magic Toyshop*, has not developed an autonomous sense of self. Like a child, she reconstructs the world according to her whims and populates it with imaginary elements. Even chess pieces, especially knights and castles, are fantasy objects which she introjects, falling into reverie, eyes fixed blankly on the chessboard. She also, of course, projects her fantasies onto Lee, imagining him paradoxically as a herbivorous lion or a unicorn devouring meat. The latter is a particularly important projection because it highlights that he is being destroyed by her. In Kleinian theory, projection destroys the object. Annabel comes to see Lee as an incubus and as dissolving in his own sperm (p. 35). Here there is a contrast between Annabel and Joanne. When Joanne eventually has sex with Lee, she is able to distinguish the reality of the married man from the teacher on whom she had a schoolgirl crush. In her Afterword, Carter stresses Joanne's intelligence and common sense because, more than the other characters, she seems capable of taking control of her own life.

Jacqueline Rose (1993) has pointed out that psychoanalytic theory has tended to concentrate upon the relationship between the over-controlling ego and the disruptive force of desire. It has paid less attention to 'the more difficult antagonism between the superego and the unconscious, where what is hidden is aggression as much as sexuality, and the agent of repression is as ferocious as what it is trying to control' (p. 143). *Love* is concerned with the 'difficult antagonism' of which Rose speaks, but particularly with what happens when negativity enters the psychic structure. Carter appears to have found in Poe's poem, 'Annabel Lee', a stimulus for thinking about the connection between the expression of love and 'destruction' or 'negativity' (*Nachfolge*) which Freud saw as linked to 'destruction' (*Destruktionstriels*). As such, *Love* embarks upon a difficult area of exploration for, as Rose maintains, thinking about negativity and its outer boundaries calls into question the very existence of boundaries (p. 164). Carter's novel suggests that when we allow for 'negativity' within our model of the psyche, we can no longer rely on the conventional boundaries between, for example, 'love' and 'destruction' or 'care' and 'the infliction of pain', nor assign to logic and sequence their traditional priority in an explication of human behaviour.

IN CONCLUSION, THE TRILOGY

Thus, it is plausible to read *Shadow Dance*, *Several Perceptions* and *Love* as a trilogy based on a fictional mediation of bohemian life at various points in 1960s Bristol, which invites reading from a realist perspective. However, it is no coincidence that, when Joanne takes Lee home to her bed in *Love*, they pass through the wrought iron gates of the park which 'neither permitted nor denied access' and seemed to negate a moral problem 'by declaring it improperly phrased' (pp. 110–111). Throughout each of the three novels, Carter is concerned with the significance of how things are 'phrased', that is, conceptualised. A range of different frameworks provides different ways of approaching and pursuing issues, just as the hybrid nature of the novels and the myriad of intertextual references provide different pointers as to how they should perhaps be read. Realism in these novels, as in all Carter's work, offers one way of looking at things, but it is disrupted by, and in turn destabilises, a combination of American Gothic and Freudian and object relations psychology. These novels demonstrate Carter's interest in the fictionality of 'realism' and of much that we regard as 'non-fiction'. In each novel, the boundaries between reality and illusion and between fact and fiction become blurred. Although each novel is a third-person narrative, they are identified, especially in the case of *Shadow Dance* and *Several Perceptions*, with a specific male consciousness. It is impossible to see these consciousnesses as that of the author and, as constructions, they are slippery, incoherent and difficult to map adequately. Carter appears to be interested, in these novels, in the different means which have been available at different times for mapping the mind. The reader soon becomes aware that ways of conceptualising the mind have a literary as well as a psychoanalytic history. In these early novels they are 'dehistoricised', perhaps because, as *Several Perceptions* illustrates, Carter is interested in the collage, a non-linear way of constructing fictions. Joseph's wall is covered with photographs of different periods:

There were some pictures tacked to the wall. Lee Harvey Oswald, handcuffed between policemen, about to be shot, wild as a badger. A colour photograph, from *Paris Match*, of a square of elegant houses and, within these pleasant boundaries, a living sunset, a Buddhist monk whose saffron robes turned red as he burned alive. Also a calendar of the previous year advertising a brand of soft drinks by means of a picture of a laughing girl in a white, sleeveless, polo-neck sweater sucking this soft drink through a straw. And a huge dewy pin-up of Marilyn Monroe. (p. 15)

In Joseph's room, these photographs exist in new spatial and temporal relationships with each other. The pictures of the monk and of the houses from the French magazine, for example, have been lifted out of the framework in which the reader would normally encounter them, creating a new context in which the viewer might now 'read' each differently. In other words, conventional ways of 'phrasing' these events have been challenged. The ahistorical arrangement of these photographs is echoed in the early novels in Carter's use of intertextuality. In *Love*, we are told that Lee 'looked like Billy Budd, or a worker hero of the Soviets, or a boy in a book by Jack London' (p. 12). Here Carter juxtaposes in a concentrated way three pieces of representation which readers may not have thought of connecting for themselves. Lifted out of their usual cultural, geographical and temporal frameworks, and placed in this new spatial and temporal sequence, these references pose a problem for the reader. Which of these references is to be privileged over the others? To give priority to one rather than another may take our reading of Lee in a different direction from that suggested by the others. The association of Lee with Billy Budd, mentioned in relation to *Shadow Dance* in Chapter 2, would more than likely emphasise the feminine nature of his beauty and lead the reader to consider the ambivalence in the representation of Lee's relationship with his brother. On the other hand, placing Lee in context with idealised portraits of Soviet workers would invariably lead the reader to consider the importance to the narrative of the left-wing aunt with whom he was brought up, his own working-class origins and how they are betrayed (probably in both senses of the word), and how he represents himself in class terms, including in his relationships with Carolyn and Joanne.

The intertextuality in the Bristol trilogy may involve us in studying specific allusions, in tracing particular references and in comparing sources. At another level, it may encourage us to think in more general terms: recalling characters, plots, images and conventions from literary traditions which in the novels are appropriated, challenged or transformed. Thus, through their intertextuality, the novels may transform the way in which we think about intellectual frameworks, encouraging us to be more aware of, and open in, how we read, think and conceptualise within frameworks, and in the way in which we consciously and unconsciously police boundaries between fiction and non-fiction.

The focus of the next chapter is on a text which alludes to another literary tradition, the fairy story. Many studies of narrative have been concerned with the way in which key narrative modes have been determined by 'real life', or rather the way in which real life has been perceived in terms of linearity, coherence and closure. Carter, however, is interested in the way in which human thought and behaviour have been structured by literary and non-literary cultural forms such as fairy stories, folklore, myth, superstition and proverbs. Judie Newman (1990) has pointed out: 'human experience may generate literature – but such experience has already been filtered through forms of artistic organisation' (p. 114).

4
Pain and Exclusion: *The Magic Toyshop* (1967)

The Magic Toyshop, like *Heroes and Villains*, discussed in Chapter 5, is a third-person narrative, whose focalisation is through the consciousness of an adolescent girl who has lost one or both of her parents after an act of transgression on her part. Melanie, like Marianne, responds to the trauma of her parents' deaths initially through an act of self-mutilation; she breaks up her bedroom, while in *Heroes and Villains* Marianne cuts off her hair. This act of transgression and the parents' deaths initiate for Melanie, as for Marianne, a period of 'exclusion' in which she is forced to go and live in London, where she is an outsider in the Flowers family. It is her experiences with the Flowers family that are employed to advance Carter's concern, pursued in different ways in *Heroes and Villains* and *The Infernal Desire Machines of Doctor Hoffman*, with the rite of passage as a series of personal, corporeal and sociocultural experiences in which the social and ideological apparatus of oppression is deconstructed.

At the heart of *The Magic Toyshop*, as in *Heroes and Villains* and, more complicatedly, in *The Infernal Desire Machines of Doctor Hoffman*, there is a problematic relationship based on a combination of attraction and repulsion and in both *The Magic Toyshop* and *Heroes and Villains* the young women are raped, Melanie symbolically, as I shall discuss later, and Marianne literally. In using the rite of passage as a vehicle for challenging the social, cultural and intellectual dissembling by which oppression is justified or evaded, *The Magic Toyshop*, like all of Carter's work, is a critique of patriarchy, in this case very obviously present in the person of Uncle Philip, and further pursued through the relationship between Melanie and Finn.

Paulina Palmer (1987) has pointed out that, typically of women in a patriarchal society, Melanie, like Marianne, is 'pressured to seek refuge from one man in the arms of another' (p. 187). She argues that in both novels 'the contradiction between the romantic images of femininity reproduced in culture and art, and the facts of sexual violence' are highlighted (p. 184). In particular, the violence of the myths which have sustained patriarchy is signified in the recurrent images of mutilation and castration, such as Melanie's fantasy of the severed hand. However, the severed hand may also suggest the psychic severance women experience in patriarchal society.

Although *The Magic Toyshop* is not a fairy tale as such, it reclaims a number of elements from the genre. The word 'reclaim' is used deliberately here, for the fairy tale has been marginalised as a literary form, relegated to the non-serious world of children's fiction. In *The Magic Toyshop*, Carter rediscovers its imaginative potential, especially for the feminist writer. The storyline of the novel itself is reminiscent of a fairy story. Its heroine, Melanie, her brother Jonathan and sister Victoria are orphaned; the death of their parents in a plane crash is linked in Melanie's mind to an act of transgression – Melanie secretly trying on her mother's wedding dress one night – and the children are forced to live with a relative they hardly know who turns out to be an ogre. The stock fairy-tale motifs adapted by Carter include: the arduous journey, the children travel from their comfortable home in the country to their uncle's toyshop in south London; the dumb mute, their aunt in London has been struck dumb on her wedding day; metamorphoses, Uncle Philip's evil is revealed gradually in the course of the narrative; and the winged creature, in the form of the swan puppet which Philip makes for the show in which Melanie takes part.

Traditional fairy tales, rewritten by male writers, became vehicles for the socialisation of young women, producing a subgenre of 'warning tales'. Jack Zipes (1988) points out:

> Almost all critics who have studied the emergence of the literary fairy tale in Europe agree that educated writers purposely appropriated the oral folk tale and converted it into a literary discourse about mores, values and manners so that children would become civilised according to the social code of that time. (p. 3)

The stories acquired a moral, which often arose out of a young girl being punished or brought to 'wisdom' through realising the foolishness of transgression. In a discussion of Perrault, whose tales Carter translated, Zipes points out that such stories do not warn 'against the dangers of predators in forests', but warn girls 'against their own natural desires which they must tame' (p. 29). In other words, Carter, like many feminist critics, recognises fairy tales as a reactionary form that inscribed a misogynistic ideology. However, Makinen (1992) has pointed out that critics have not always questioned whether women readers would necessarily identify with the female figures (p. 4). Carter's attempts to write new versions of fairy tales in *The Bloody Chamber and Other Stories* (1979) have been the subject of much debate among critics. Some critics, following Andrea Dworkin (1981), have suggested that Carter has not adequately re-visioned the fairy-tale form, working within the straitjacket of their original structures, so that her attempts to create an active female erotic are compromised. Makinen (1992) takes issue with this view, arguing that 'it is the critics who cannot see beyond the sexist binary opposition' (ibid.); they have tended to assume that the fairy tale is a universal, unchangeable and 'given'. Although all narrative genres clearly do inscribe ideologies, as Makinen argues, later rewritings of a genre do not necessarily encode the same ideological assumptions.

Although *The Magic Toyshop* is not a fairy story as such, it anticipates how in her later collection, *The Bloody Chamber and Other Stories*, Carter adapted the form to criticise the inscribed ideology and to incorporate new assumptions. The novel incorporates the reactionary element of the fairy story in the consequences which befall Melanie's borrowing of her mother's wedding dress. However, it also undermines this inscribed ideology by emphasising what the misogynistic fairy stories suppressed, an adolescent girl's excitement about her body and the discovery of her emerging sexuality:

> she would follow with her finger the elegant structure of her rib-cage, where the heart fluttered under the flesh like a bird under a blanket, and she would draw down the long line from breast-bone to navel (which was a mysterious cavern or grotto), and she would rasp her palms against her bud-wing shoulder-blades. (p. 1)

Carter appropriates a Renaissance convention whereby the continent of America (of discovery and enjoyment) serves as a metaphor for the body: 'The summer she was fifteen, Melanie discovered she was made of flesh and blood. O, my America, my new found land' (ibid.). Richard Brown (1994) points out that the implied male colonial explorer is now a young woman, an index in the text of female self-possession (p. 92). Fredric Jameson (1986) has argued that one of the most potentially disruptive elements in narrative, and especially 'magic realist' narrative, is the appearance of the body (p. 307).

While I would not describe *The Magic Toyshop* as a 'magic realist' narrative, it has more in common with 'magic realism' than with 'realism'. As Jameson suggests, the body, in this case Melanie's, in *The Magic Toyshop* diverts the narrative in a number of directions. According to Jameson, in the realist novel, the disruption is resolved through fetishising the body as image. In *The Magic Toyshop*, this is clearly not the case. Indeed, the disruption is not only sustained, but thematised in the narrative. Through her fantasies enacted before her mirror, Melanie begins to explore her different potential identities and the contradictory roles that make up the female subject in art and society, such as a Pre-Raphaelite, a Lautrec model with her hair 'dragged sluttishly across her face', and a Cranach Venus. She indulges in secret acts of transgression, gift-wrapping herself for a phantom bridegroom and, after reading *Lady Chatterley's Lover*, sticking forget-me-knots in her pubic hair.

The novel's concerns with the female body and sexuality are typical of Anglo-American feminist art and literature of the late 1960s and early 1970s. It is important to place the zeal of such work, which from a later feminist perspective may appear intellectually a little crude, in the context of the times. Feminist artists and writers of the day were mounting a challenge to the way in which women's bodies were rendered invisible in art and culture other than as idealised objects in works produced by men within the tradition of the classic female nude. The focus of their challenge was this Western tradition's denial of women's experiences of their own bodies. In other words, they attacked the mythical sense of the integrity of the body and its boundaries in the representation of the female nude and drew attention to the internal bodily changes or bodily fluids which regularly crossed those boundaries and subverted the body's sense of closure. Lynda Nead (1992) has pointed out that artists such as Judy Chicago were claiming 'that vaginal and vulvic forms were an innate and natural language for female artistic expression' (p. 65). The notoriety which works such as Chicago's *Red Flag* (1971), depicting the removal of a bloody tampon, achieved was a result of the sanitised way in which the female body had hitherto been perceived in art. Much of the feminist artistic space now taken for granted had not been won at that time. Nead (1992) argues:

> The feminist claim of the 1970s to 'our bodies, our selves' put the issues of control and identity at the centre of the movement's political agenda ... art that focuses on images and aspects of the

female body, was one attempt within the sphere of culture to create a different kind of visibility for women. (p. 64)

The episode in *The Magic Toyshop* in which Melanie enters the garden at night, wearing her mother's wedding dress, begins with a description of Melanie's anxieties about tree-climbing since she began menstruating. As if to reinforce what culture had so long denied, the novel mentions periods, pregnancy, embryo, gestation and miscarriage within one short paragraph (p. 20). Although this may seem like straining for effect to contemporary readers, Carter is following the feminist concerns of her day to challenge, and work against, traditions which reified the cosmetically finished surface of the female body and denied the perceived 'abject' matter of its interior. Ironically, in London, Uncle Philip tries to turn Melanie into a fetishised object as spectacle, a wooden marionette. Palmer (1987) points out that the image of the puppet suggests the coded mannequin metaphor employed by the French psychoanalytic literary critic, Julia Kristeva, to represent the robotic state to which human beings are reduced by a process of psychic repression (p. 180).

The way in which the wedding dress episode is structured appears to suggest a young girl's first experience of sex and the anxieties around it. In *The Interpretation of Dreams* (1965), Freud observes that climbing in a dream signifies vaginal intercourse (p. 401). The purring cat at the centre of the tree she is about to climb gives Melanie the confidence to step out of the wedding dress and become naked. In her nakedness, she feels vulnerable, pulling her hair around her for protection. The cat unexpectedly hurts her, the dress which she had parcelled up and placed in the tree is symbolically ripped and there is now blood on the hem. Melanie now feels 'a new and final kind of nakedness, as if she had taken even her own skin off' (p. 21). Moreover, the season is the end of the summer – the end of childhood and 'innocence' – and the moon, the female symbol to which menstruation is linked, is 'beginning to slide down the sky'.

At this point in the novel, Carter rewrites the myth of the Garden of Eden. The reader cannot but be reminded of Eden by the tree itself, clearly the Tree of Knowledge, by the reference to the shower of apples, and by the allusion to Eve's realisation of her nakedness after eating the forbidden fruit: Melanie is 'horribly conscious of her own exposed nakedness'. However, if the biblical imagery reminds us of Genesis, there are counter-elements drawn from witchcraft, paganism and superstition: the cat is a well-known witch's familiar,

Melanie crosses her fingers, and there are references to blackness, the night, blood and nakedness. They remind us of elements absent from the biblical version of the Adam and Eve story and the novel seems to be challenging a myth which endorses the inferiority of women to men.

An important aspect of the novel's re-vision of the Adam and Eve story is the female focalisation, or point of view, which stresses not only a developing sexuality, but the excitement, fears and fantasies to which sexuality gives rise and through which it not only finds expression but is explored and developed. The emphasis eventually falls upon anxiety, pain and disillusionment. The initial reference to the domestic in this episode promises reassurance – the cat purrs as if someone had lit a small fire for it – but it proves to be unstable and cruel. The purring cat turns out to have paws 'tipped with curved, cunning meat hooks' (p. 21). Melanie's experience of nude tree-climbing leads to injury and, quite literally, agony. Here the novel may be prefiguring more than what is in store for Melanie as a consequence of her parents' death and her enforced move to London. It may also be giving expression to a centuries-old fear of women: that their husbands may turn out to be monsters and wedded bliss prove a nightmare. Ironically, while much of the passage suggests the irretrievable loss of childhood – Melanie has started her periods, decided to grow her hair long and has stopped wearing shorts – Melanie emotionally regresses to childhood: 'Please, God, let me get safe back to my own bed again.' Particularly important to the novel's concern at this point with Melanie explicitly and all women implicitly is the tension between desire and restraint which causes a scream to swell up in Melanie's throat. The unexpressed scream, of course, becomes a symbol of the condition in which Melanie, and perhaps many women, will come to live:

> Once a branch broke with a groan under the trusting sole of her foot and she hung in agony by her hands, strung up between earth and heaven, kicking blindly for a safe, solid thing in a world all shifting leaves and shadows. (p. 21)

IDEAL HOMES, DESIRE AND PSYCHOANALYSIS

Zipes (1988), drawing on Freud's theory of the uncanny, suggests that fairy stories have remained popular because they are concerned with the quest for an idealised notion of home which has been suppressed in the adult consciousness. In discussing the liberating power of feminist fairy tales, he suggests that they present us with a means by which the idealised home may be reclaimed. These include the ways in which the opposed protagonists learn to free themselves from 'parasitical creatures'. For Zipes, the latter are allegorical representations of the socio-psychological conflicts which have prevented the opposed protagonists from having a psychic realisation of home. In Zipes's psychoanalytic approach to fairy stories, they are also the conflicts which the reader, in a similar position to the opposed protagonist, needs to revisit.

Zipes's argument is particularly relevant to Carter's fiction, in which a number of characters are motivated by a desire to realise the ideal of home. Desiderio in *The Infernal Desire Machines of Doctor Hoffman* temporarily realises the ideal of home among the River People and even more fleetingly with Albertina, the object of his desire, among the Centaurs. However, Zipes's work is especially applicable to *The Magic Toyshop* and *Heroes and Villains*, where for Melanie and Marianne, as for so many of Carter's characters, their early home life is severely disrupted by trauma. After being raped by Jewel, on whom she projected her erotic fantasies, Marianne wants to escape, 'as if somewhere there was still the idea of a home' (p. 52). The description of the flat in London in *The Magic Toyshop* is in the third person, but the focalisation is Melanie's. The contrast between the new home and the one she has left opens up a new space in which Melanie imagines, locates and develops an ideal:

> Porcelain gleamed pink and the soft, fluffy towels and the toilet paper were pink to match. Steaming water gushed plentifully from the dolphin shaped taps and jars of bath essence and toilet water and after-shave glowed like jewellery; and the low lavatory tactfully flushed with no noise at all. It was a temple to cleanness. Mother loved nice bathrooms. (pp. 56–57)

She is cast as an oppressed protagonist. Even though Aunt Margaret, Francie and Finn love each other, making Melanie feel 'bitterly lonely and unloved', the Flowers family become the parasitical creatures of fairy stories. Finn, for example, is described as 'a tawny lion poised for the kill'. Melanie does consciously what Zipes argues all readers of fairy stories do unwittingly. She translates the parasitical creatures of fairy stories into the socio-psychological conflicts which separate her, and will continue to separate her, from the psychic ideal of the home. Finn comes to represent an 'insolent, off-hand, terrifying maleness' and the threat that he poses is suggested when, in order to comb out her hair, he 'ground out his cigarette on the window-ledge and laughed' (p. 45). For all the differences between Finn and his uncle, the laugh and the grounding gesture at this point blur the boundary between them.

From the outset, *The Magic Toyshop* is concerned with the importance not only of fantasy but also of ego disturbances within the psyche. These are often brought about by what Lorna Sage (1994b) has described as 'the bad magic of mythologies' (p. 18). In the novel, the psyche is perceived as constructed within a wide system of relationships including familial, social, cultural and political forces. Some of these, such as nature and sex, we tend to 'mythologise' and regard as if they are 'outside' history and social milieux. Desire and fantasy, especially, we tend to regard as 'universal' or 'archetypal', ignoring the way in which these, too, are socially constructed. Many teenagers, for example, may identify with the lyrics of chart-topping pop songs because they appear to reflect their emotions, anxieties and frustrations, without realising that these songs as part of popular culture contribute to the social construction of emotional identity, of gendered behaviour within relationships, and of desire itself. In her exploration of the different social roles and subjectivities available to women, Melanie not only challenges the notion of a singular female identity, but demonstrates how women have to negotiate a myriad of received assumptions and social conventions.

Thus, one approach to *The Magic Toyshop* would be to consider Melanie's acquisition of an autonomous identity in the context of the circumstances which befall her. In this regard, the text poses a challenge to conventional psychoanalysis, which has tended to be based on relationships within the kind of comfortable bourgeois family that collapses for Melanie. Jennifer Fitzgerald (1993) has pointed out in a critical essay on the African–American writer, Toni Morrison, that psychoanalysis has traditionally pathologised non-normative families. However, it is not really the function of literary criticism to examine characters as if they were people. Fitzgerald goes on to argue that it is the purpose of literary criticism to analyse discourses, not psyches. This seems particularly appropriate to Carter's novel, which is sceptical of many of the discourses, such as the Adam and Eve story, which circulate through it. This does not mean that we should not bring a psychoanalytic discourse to bear on a discussion of Melanie within the novel. It means that we should recognise that psychoanalysis is only one of a number of discourses, such as female identity, patriarchy and the family, circulating in this text, and that one discourse is always articulated within or against the frameworks of other discourses. In the account of the relationship between Melanie and Finn, there is a wide variety of allusions: to Romeo and Juliet, Tristan and Isolde, loveknots, and lovers in New Wave films. Any one of these might trigger a different reading of what happens between them.

Since Melanie's normative family life is disrupted, classical analytical psychoanalysis based on the traditional bourgeois family norm, which tends to pathologise non-normative families, may not be the most appropriate framework within which to explore what happens to her in the toyshop. An alternative psychoanalytic framework is provided by object relations theory, referred to in Chapter 2. In contradistinction to classical psychoanalysis, it recognises the range of relationships, including those within the family, which can influence the psyche. As explained in Chapter 2, according to object relations theory as developed by Melanie Klein, an infant experiences complex and contradictory emotions which are projected onto objects, including people, with which it comes into contact. These objects, subsequently transformed into positive or negative phantasy objects, or 'imagos', are 'introjected' back into the child's psyche. Eventually, the child forges a sense of its own identity out of these experiences and fantasies and begins to recognise others as separate individuals rather than 'imagos'. Clearly, one of the most powerful, negative 'imagos' in Melanie's childhood is the jack-in-the-box with a grotesque caricature of her own face which Uncle Philip, whom she had never met, sent her one Christmas and which turned the uncle himself into an 'imago'. The face is mocking and cruel, mirroring the way in which the father, according to Freudian psychology, imposes on the girl-child a sense of lack. Uncle Philip epitomises the intrusion of patriarchy: how the male will come between a young girl and her relationship with her mother and will seek to silence and control the female.

The novel's brief account of Melanie's childhood emphasises her reclusive nature, her privileged upbringing and a range of likely and unlikely 'imagos'. Inscribed almost exclusively in terms of 'projection' and 'introjection', it is clear that Melanie's privileged and limited childhood has prevented the full development of her own sense of identity. This is exacerbated by the trauma of her parents' deaths. She is unable to recognise that other factors which had nothing to do with her were responsible, and this in turn results in a form of self-loathing. In her own mind, she becomes the kind of part-object which, as I suggested in the discussion of *Shadow Dance* in Chapter 2, is characteristic of fairy stories: 'The girl who killed her mother' (p. 24). Unable to expel this imago – initially by vomiting – she projects it onto her mirror image, which she tries, unsuccessfully, to destroy. Ironically, she kills her parents a second time by destroying their photograph. However, the imago onto which she has projected her guilt now consumes her so that she becomes inhuman: 'She neither saw nor heard anything but wrecked like an automaton. Feathers stuck in the tears and grease on her cheeks' (p. 25). This description of her anticipates the puppet which Uncle Philip tries to make of her. The distinction between her own intense subjectivity and external objects becomes blurred; she refrains from cutting her hair short because it grew while her parents were alive. Although Mrs Rundle moves onto another family, Melanie continues to cling to her in her memories. Significantly, Mrs Rundle has created for herself an independent sense of self; although not married, she has chosen to be called 'Mrs' since it makes it easier for her to be 'acceptable' in a society geared towards men and married women. In the course of the novel, Melanie has to seek her own autonomous identity.

In London, Melanie's reactions to the people she meets is regressive. She projects her emotions onto them as external objects, introjecting the resultant 'imagos' as part of herself. This is partly the consequence of the intensity with which Melanie sees things, as suggested in the image of Aunt Margaret's coal fire, which is 'rendered more fierce by the confines of the small, black-leaded grate' (p. 41). In Melanie's case, the confines are those of Uncle Philip's flat and the guilt she feels over her parents' deaths. In the flat above the toyshop, the people she meets and the objects she encounters are rendered fiercer by these confines. Although it is the third-person narrative which introduces the fallen puppet – 'Lying face-downwards in a tangle of strings was a puppet fully five feet high, a *sylphide* in a fountain of white tulle, fallen flat down as if someone got tired of her in the middle of playing with her' – the focalisation is Melanie's: ' "It is too much", said Melanie, agitated. "There is too much" ' (p. 67).

In terms of Kleinian theory, the processes of identification and projection are particularly intense in Melanie's case. Regressively, she clings to the imago of a lover which she has derived from children's books and poems. While it is difficult for the reader to separate the reality of Finn from Melanie's perceptions of him, he at least draws her away from her past. Eventually, her idealised lover crumples: 'like the paper he was made of before this insolent, off-hand, terrifying maleness, filling the room with its reek. She hated it. But she could not take her eyes off him' (p. 45).

As the jack-in-the-box demonstrates, Melanie also becomes an object onto which others, whom we may suspect of not having forged an adequate sense of their own identity, project their own fantasies and desires. Not only does Finn insist on combing her hair differently almost as soon as she arrives, but he paints her secretly through a hole in her bedroom wall. Uncle Philip sees her as a nymph covered with daisies. At one level, the toy shop is a parody of patriarchy, under which women are silenced. It is significant, albeit rather crudely, that Aunt Margaret is struck dumb on her wedding day and only regains her voice when Philip discovers her locked in an embrace with Francie.

Nicole Ward Jouve (1994) points out that father figures in Carter's work are 'attacked, deconstructed, shown to be hollow or vulnerable' (p. 155). Uncle Philip's need to control and manipulate others – on the poster advertising his puppet show he is depicted holding the ball of the world in his hand – is evident in one of his favourite creations, the 'Surprise Rose Bowl'. The shepherdess which appears from a simulacrum of a rose made out of stiffened card or wood shavings performs a perfectly poised pirouette. But Philip is so obsessive and violent, worryingly evident in the way he 'attacks' the Christmas goose with the carving knife, that he appears to have serious and deep-rooted psychological problems. He seems driven by a repressed and violently tinged sexuality; in manipulating Melanie in his version of *Leda and the Swan*, he appears to be per-forming a surrogate rape. The narrative makes him an even more disturbing personality by comparing him with the Nazis, especially bearing in mind the way he is shown on the poster. Having attacked Finn because he has ruined the 'Grand Performance', Philip, we are told, shoves the body aside 'with the casual brutality of Nazi sol-diers moving corpses in films of concentration camps' (p. 132). Here Carter is introducing a popular connection between private sadism and the public brutality of totalitarian regimes. She is not necessar-ily arguing for the link, and indeed in the course of the novel it is not really developed. However, in the novel's more general exploration of private and socially sanctioned domination of one group by another, it is introduced as one position that can be, and has been, struck. Particularly ominous is Finn's blood-streaked vomit, a harbinger of the violence to come. The extent of Philip's callousness is reinforced by the way in which he laments the damaged puppet as a dead friend or sibling might be mourned in a Renaissance tragedy: 'Poor old Bothwell! All his wires gone!' But even more disturbing are the changes which occur in him. In the wake of the disastrous show, his language becomes increasingly crude and violent: Finn is accused of 'buggering me Bothwell' and the family are told to 'piss off' (p. 133). An especially chilling development is the way in which he becomes a parody of the wicked, incestuous uncle in insisting that Melanie now acts with his puppets: 'He rubbed his hands with satisfaction. "What's your name, girly? Speak up." ' (Ibid.) It is particularly disturbing that he addresses her as if he does not know who she is. The word 'girly' robs Melanie of her identity as his niece, reinforces her vulnerability and confirms his power over her.

In contrast to Philip's favourite toy, the movements of Finn's own creation of a yellow bear with a bow tie around its neck riding a bicycle are erratic. They permit an unpredictability which has no place in Uncle Philip's universe, and the toy itself is witty. In fact, Melanie's reaction to the toy is different from her response to the objects which filled her bedroom as imagos at the beginning of the novel. As it makes her laugh, the toy and Melanie remain distant from each other, so that it is able to represent the wit and perspective which Melanie needs to acquire in order to achieve a confident, autonomous self-identity.

At the end of the novel, Melanie and Finn escape from the toyshop, like Adam and Eve from the Garden of Eden, returning the reader to the biblical myth which is employed in the earlier description of Melanie's sexual awakening. In fact, Carter herself has said that she saw the novel in terms of the 'Fortunate Fall': 'I took the Fortunate Fall as meaning that it was a good thing to get out of that place. The intention was that the toyshop itself should be a secularized Eden' (Haffenden, 1985, p. 80). The 'Fortunate Fall' is not only from the toyshop but the cultural myths which have contributed to women's intellectual, emotional and sexual oppression.

The theme of a new Eden and the human race reduced to an elemental pair was common in speculative fiction of the 1950s and 1960s. Carter's adaption of it is ambiguous and possibly influenced by the art of the time, especially collage work suggesting that desire, as Thomas Crow (1996) maintains, is 'held hostage' by the Adam and Eve myth (p. 47). In Richard Hamilton's collage, *Just what is it that makes today's homes so different, so appealing?* (1956), Charles Atlas, the model body-builder of comic-book back pages, is the naked Adam and the pulp pin-up is Eve. In Hamilton's collaborative contribution, the same year, to the installation art exhibition *This is Tomorrow*, the primal male is the robot from *Forbidden Planet*, who holds a Jane-like figure in his arms. Next to him is Marilyn Monroe in a still from the pavement grating scene in Billy Wilder's film, *The Seven Year Itch* (1955). The latter, in which a married man has a fling with the girl upstairs, suggests through a series of dream sequences that desire is structured by the dominant fictions in society. At the end of *The Magic Toyshop*, Carter appears to imply, as she said, that the Fall was fortunate, but also that Melanie and Finn are trapped by the Genesis myth. It is ironic that in the fire 'everything is gone' but that the myth remains: 'At night, in the garden, they faced each other in a wild surmise' (p. 200).

The agency which Melanie needs to acquire in her own life is evident in the early part of *The Magic Toyshop* in acts of transgression such as trying on her mother's wedding dress and stealing her brother's books in order to raise the money to buy false eyelashes. Ironically, while, at one level, her desire for false eyelashes is a sign of her independence, at another, it is a symbol of the way in which her identity as a young woman is defined by discourses outside herself. Inevitably, these discourses take control over her own body from her. Even at fifteen, Melanie is beginning to feel a failure because she has not yet married or had sex.

Thus, the focalisation of *The Magic Toyshop* gives priority to a female consciousness. However, readers will probably find themselves assuming a complex, if not ambivalent, attitude towards the key female protagonist. These are novels where nothing can be taken for granted. The allusions to key literary traditions, such as the fairy story and the post-apocalyptic novel, are designed to call into question some of the grand narratives, such as the Western romantic view of suffering, which we have tended to accept unquestioningly. But they also alert us to ways in which human action is shaped by literary and other cultural forms. Hence, the reclamation of the fairy story as an appropriate genre for serious writers in *The Magic Toyshop* is also a deconstruction of some of the ways in which the genre was used to regulate female sexuality.

There is a sharp focus in *The Magic Toyshop* on how identity is produced in the process of other people's perceptions and rendered 'real' through linguistic and other symbolic mechanisms. The novel explores, for example, some of the consequences of the Genesis account of creation, especially its role in the construction of female subjectivity and sexuality within twentieth-century psychoanalytical thought, a topic pursued in Chapter 6 in relation to *The Passion of New Eve*. In *The Magic Toyshop* some of the more important of the linguistic and symbolic mechanisms, such as in the scene where Melanie tries on a number of different female roles, are presented in ways which alienate the reader from them. In other words, the text 'defamiliarises' them. This is, in turn, evidence of the way in which Carter was beginning to see her culture as 'foreign', possibly without realising the full implications of this position, even before her visit to Japan. This is a trope explored in the novels written on her return from Japan, discussed in subsequent chapters.

5

Symbolic Order, Myths and Transgression: *Heroes and Villains* (1969) and *The Infernal Desire Machines of Doctor Hoffman* (1972)

Heroes and Villains (1969) and *The Infernal Desire Machines of Doctor Hoffman* (1972) share a concern with the way in which different societies are shaped around particular values, beliefs and ideologies. However, in developing the competing ideologies around which different societies in these texts are formed, Carter examines the way in which European and American 'civilizations' have been forged by particular worldviews. Through her critique of the different societies in these texts, Carter presents a critique of aspects of modern European and American history.

At one level, these novels reflect aspects of the Bristol trilogy. Lorna Sage (1994b) has pointed out that *Heroes and Villains* mocks the cultural landscape of the 1960s, such as the glamour of underground, countercultural movements and the siege of university campuses (p. 18). However, they are different from the Bristol trilogy in ways in which Carter's fiction was to develop from the early 1970s onwards. *Heroes and Villains* is a version of the post-apocalyptic novel which was popular in the Cold War 1950s. Roz Kaveney (1994) has pointed out that *Heroes and Villains* draws upon an older, decline-of-civilisation genre which can be traced back to Mary Shelley's *The Last Man* (1826) and also to Richard Jefferies's *After London* (1885). More specifically, *Heroes and Villains* is based on tropes, such as living among the ruins, familiar in British and American post-apocalyptic science fiction written by women in the

1970s. Nan Albinski (1988) reminds us that in the 1970s and 1980s 'women writers increasingly foresee the destruction of the cities, with groups of survivors (sometimes groups composed solely of women) living in the ruins, scavenging the left-overs' (p. 133).

In *Heroes and Villains*, a nuclear war has transformed a mundane environment into a Gothic fantasy. Although there are numerous post-cataclysmic science fiction fantasies, Carter's novel is one of the few to highlight the effects on people and the landscape from a female focalisation. Marianne, from whose perspective the novel is narrated, runs away from what remains of civilisation: orderly communities based on farming and craftwork and guarded by soldiers who rule over them with the Professors, between whom there is little respect. She enters the outside, Gothic world of ruins and forests inhabited by the Barbarians, by whom she is taken captive, and by mutants who are the products of radiation. However, despite similarities between Carter's novel and post-apocalyptic science fiction written by women, it is unlikely that Carter had read much of it in any detail, if at all. Kaveney (1994) maintains that it is likely 'that she was interested in those aspects of the culture where ideas from SF were liable to make their mark' (p. 182).

Although a sense of loss pervades the novel at a number of levels – civilisation has all but been destroyed and Melanie loses her parents – Carter's novel avoids focusing on the decline itself. On a cursory reading, Carter appears to establish a clear polarisation between the two societies. The community of the Professors and soldiers is rigidly hierarchical, totalitarian, militaristic and sexually repressive. The society of the Barbarians is more strongly linked to the natural world, has a quasi-tribal structure and regards the community as a family. However, Carter does not establish a rigid binarism between the Professors/soldiers and the Barbarians or pursue the tensions between the soldiers and the intellectuals. The post-apocalyptic fantasy becomes a narrative space in which Carter explores the blurring of conventional boundaries and binarisms and the ways in which such artificial boundaries are maintained.

In playing 'Soldiers and Barbarians' with the son of the Professor of Mathematics, Marianne refuses to accept that she should always have the part of the Barbarian, the villain, and that, as the hero, he should always shoot her. The Professor's son thinks within a rigid, binary structure which he never questions and which has its external equivalent in the stout wall around the village, manned with machine guns and topped with barbed wire. The word 'manned' is significant, for within the compound life is structured, as the game of 'Soldiers and Barbarians' indicates, according to male rules and male logic. Even Marianne's own mother prefers her brother to her. In tripping up the Professor's son, Marianne disrupts the male symbolic structure. Overturned by this sudden act of violence, the boy loses command of language and is reduced to 'yowling' in the dust. Marianne, like Melanie, learns that in order to achieve an autonomous sense of self she has to disrupt the symbolic structures which have deprived her of control of her own language and of her sense of self and identity.

Marianne, we are told, is a child who 'broke things to see what they were like inside' (p. 4). This is an insight not only into Marianne but into Carter herself. Certainly, *Heroes and Villains* is as sceptical of mythologies as *The Magic Toyshop*. Both societies in the novel employ mythology and folk tales to maintain their geographical, cultural and intellectual boundaries, including those which define the 'otherness' of outsiders. The 'warning tales' told by Marianne's nurse, that the Barbarians slit the bellies of women after they have raped them and sew cats up inside them (p. 10) and wrap little girls in clay and bake them (p. 2), are echoed by the stories of the Barbarians themselves, who believe the Professors kill and bake Barbarians in their ovens (p. 35). When Marianne first meets Donally, he alludes parodically to the Barbarians' belief that women in the society of the Professors have sharp teeth in their vaginas in order to bite off the Barbarians' genitalia (p. 49). Of course, like the European 'warning tales' of the seventeenth century discussed by Zipes (1988), the stories Marianne is told warn children, especially girls, 'against their own natural desires which must be tamed' rather than against the Barbarians in the forest. The way in which the two communities regard each other, though, is redolent of the way Western explorers brought back tales from various parts of the world about their indigenous peoples. These tales fuelled the colonial project which continued to perpetuate stories of 'barbarism' in order to rationalise, justify and win support at home for their economic and cultural ambitions. Moreover, as a child, Carter lived through not only the mass killings and destruction of the Second World War, but the propaganda war, in which the enemy on all sides was denigrated with myths, as the two societies in *Heroes and Villains* perpetuate stories about each other.

Marianne, like Melanie in *The Magic Toyshop*, comes to realise that identity is produced in the perception of others and rendered real through linguistic mechanisms. Jean Baudrillard (1993) points out:

> the progress of Humanity and Culture are simply the chain of discriminations with which to brand 'Others' with inhumanity, and therefore with nullity. For the savages who call themselves 'men', the others are something else. (p. 125)

This is evident not only in the way in which folk tales and games are used in the society of the Professors, but in the mythologising of death – her brother is said to have 'gone to the ruins' – which Marianne is able to contrast with her own witnessing of his killing. Marianne realises that not only is the self located in the word, but when the word changes so does the concept of self. Increasingly, the ostensibly stable wor(l)d in the community of the Professors is exposed through the soldiers' slack use of language. On returning home, having committed an act of transgression by going into the ruins, Marianne discovers that her nurse has killed her father with an axe and then poisoned herself. The Colonel, her uncle, offers only the explanation that she was 'seriously maladjusted' (p. 15), which Marianne cannot equate with the love which the woman had shown them. This loose connection between fact and interpretation characterises the soldiers' discourse. The complex relationship between cause and effect, event and consequence, is frequently elided, as in the Colonel's response to the (symbolic) killing of the Professor of Psychology, which he believes to be justified because he, like Marianne's nurse, was 'maladjusted' (p. 17). At this point in the novel, Carter may well be parodying the way in which military language in the late twentieth century, employing evasive terms such as 'conflict management', has become increasingly diffuse.

A key text which the two societies in *Heroes and Villains* share, and which is tattooed on Jewel's back, is the myth of Adam and Eve. Encapsulating the story of Adam bewitched by Eve's smile, the tattoo signifies the ideologies through which Jewel's view of Marianne is mediated. Like *Shadow Dance*, *Heroes and Villains* places misogyny within a larger ideological and cultural context. Jewel's fear of Marianne is given as his explanation for raping her. However, his fear of her is also a product and reflection of the way patriarchal societies more generally fear the loss of control to women. Significantly, Jewel is happiest with Marianne in those moments when she has been subdued.

One of the most innovative aspects of *Heroes and Villains* is the way in which the confusion created by nuclear war, explored at the level of plot and theme in the conventional post-apocalyptic, futuristic novel, is pursued at the level of semiotics. The relationship between language and meaning is learned and arbitrary, as in the relationship between a word and the object to which it refers, and is always subject to change. However, meaning is conveyed through language because words relate to each other as part of a linguistic system. The wedding ceremony in the novel draws elements from so many different cultures and linguistic systems that they are unable to relate in any coherent way. Whilst Marianne wears a second-hand, white dress, Jewel wears a stiff, scarlet coat interwoven with gold thread that may have once belonged to a Bishop. Donally, who performs the ceremony, is robed from head to foot in a garment woven from bird feathers and wears a painted mask carved from wood. Although Donally reads from the *Book of Common Prayer*, the centrepiece of the ceremony is taken from Native American culture, the cutting of the bride's and groom's wrists and the mixing of their bloods. The semiotic confusion here is also an index of a greater confusion over identity created when traditional boundaries are crossed or blurred. Stepping outside the world which has been named and defined is exciting, as Marianne realises near the end of the novel; on the seashore, she discovers how losing the names of things is 'a process of uncreation' (p. 136). However, the novel also suggests that, without naming, everything reverts to chaos, to things 'existing only to themselves in an unstructured world'.

TATTOOS, PAIN AND SUFFERING

Towards the end of *Heroes and Villains*, a sick and slightly drugged Marianne admits: 'When I was a little girl, we played at heroes and villains but now I don't know which is which any more, nor who is who, and what can I trust if not appearances?' (p. 125). As in *The Magic Toyshop*, shifting frames of reference are used in *Heroes and Villains* to disrupt and deconstruct mythologies which have gone unchallenged for many years. Two of the most obvious are connected with post-Enlightenment European thinking. The novel confounds the conventional binarism in post-apocalyptic novels between 'civilised' and 'barbarian'. Jewel, for example, turns out to be an educated thinker. When he first meets Marianne, he quotes from Tennyson: 'It's the same everywhere you look, it's red in tooth and claw' (p. 18) and, much to Marianne's surprise, knows the zoological name for the adder which bites her (p. 28). This combination of encyclopaedic knowledge and primitive lore – he treats her with a folk remedy for snake bite – is an index of the way in which Carter has created a 'third space' in her narrative about the Barbarians which defies analysis along the lines of conventional binarisms. Marianne's father makes the mistake of associating the Barbarians only with instinct, a view of which she is disabused shortly after meeting Jewel. Whilst her father and the other Professors believed that the painted faces of the Barbarians were an indication of how they had 'reverted to beasthood' (p. 24), she discovers that their masks are worn for another reason: it makes them look more frightening to their enemies in battle. The social structure of the Barbarians also challenges Rousseau's myth of the noble savage, which is provocatively invoked at the outset of the novel. Whilst Rousseau envisaged natural man as an isolate, Marianne, the product of 'civilisation', is the outsider while the 'natural' people are social with a valued family structure.

Heroes and Villains also challenges the European Romantic notion of suffering, which has its origins in the Christian contemplative tradition and which valorises suffering as a pivotal experience whereby an individual becomes human. Post-apocalyptic narrative inevitably provides a space in which suffering, as a means to full human subjectivity at the individual level, can be expanded into the public realm, where there is an obvious communal need to make sense of suffering as part of the human condition. However, the way in which the soldiers reductively attribute acts of violence and human breakdowns to 'maladjustment' suggests the difficulty of doing so. The death of the Professor of Psychology suggests that a means of explaining the bizarre instances of suffering which pervade the opening of the novel has been lost to the Professors of Mathematical Sciences. It may be difficult in terms of psychology to discuss fully, for example, the actions of the worker who 'went mad' and burned his wife and three children to death before killing himself. However, it is even more difficult to do so within a metaphysical framework which attempts to valorise human suffering.

In *Heroes and Villains*, suffering makes one less real rather than brings one to full subjectivity. This is evident in Jewel's whipping of his brother, in which Precious swings under the blows 'like a carpet being beaten' (p. 113) and Jewel himself becomes 'mechanical' and 'a man no longer'. Jewel's muscle movements animate the tattoo on his back, whereby Eve offers Adam the apple in 'an uncompleted series of actions with no conclusion', suggesting that violence holds one prisoner within actions which cannot move beyond themselves or to any sense of completion. Indeed, pain and suffering in the novel frequently take away the power of language in which a sense of self and identity are located: Precious grunts in 'a mechanical repetition of sounds' (ibid.). Through the suffering inflicted on him by Donally, the boy whom Marianne first sees chained is regressed to pre-language, 'to a babbling murmur' (pp. 12–13). Indeed, extreme violence of any sort frequently has the same effect. Jewel 'howls' in fury before he strikes Marianne (p. 20) while his brothers, tearing at their meal of meat, issue screeches and foul abuse (p. 46).

The tattoo on Jewel's back is a permanent reminder of oppression and of the infliction of cruelty upon others; Jewel admits that when Donally tattooed him he was delirious and that only Mrs Green's care saved him from blood poisoning. It is also a reminder that suffering does not valorise pain but repeats the circumstances in which the suffering originated. Whilst Jewel believes that the tattoo on his back is impressive, Marianne is only reminded of the pain which it must have caused. For her, there is no question of the tattoo's beauty transcending Jewel's suffering, even though pain is eroticised. Asking Jewel why he allowed Donally to 'attack him' with the needles (p. 86), she wants to know how much it hurt him (p. 96). Indeed, Marianne is preoccupied with the imposition of pain upon one person by another. Carter's own retrospective essay, 'People as Pictures', in *Nothing Sacred*, on the subject of Japanese tattooing, 'irezumi', provides a gloss on what Donally has done to Jewel. Irezumi, Carter maintains, 'transforms its victim into a genre masterpiece' (p. 33), but the technique employed is particularly painful. Indeed, Carter observes that the novelist, Junichiro Tanizaki, describes one particular tattoo artist as a sadist: 'His pleasure lay in the agony men felt...The louder they screamed, the keener was Seikichi's strange delight' (p. 35). Donally's art is similarly sadistic, an extension of the abuse he inflicts on his own child. Significantly, he tattooed Jewel when he was young and made most use of green which, according to Carter's own essay, is one of the most painful colours to use. He was also responsible for the death of the little girl who died as he tried to turn her into a 'tiger lady'. Eschewing romantic valorisation of suffering enables Carter to explore the extent to which men are trapped within codes of violence and aggression which sometimes eroticise suffering, and the extent to which violence and pain are used to dominate women.

FEMALE RELATIONSHIPS

In the lives of both Melanie and Marianne, an older woman – Mrs Rundle and Aunt Margaret in *The Magic Toyshop* and Mrs Green, Jewel's foster mother, in *Heroes and Villains* – proves to be important. The relationships which Melanie establishes with Mrs Rundle and Aunt Margaret are much closer and less ambiguous than the relationship between Marianne and Mrs Green. As is evident when she gives Margaret her dress and lends her mother's pearls to her, Melanie comes to see Margaret as a surrogate mother. At another level, however, their relationship suggests that women might establish among themselves an alternative community to the male-dominated social structure represented by Uncle Philip (a concept of which Carter is explicitly critical, though, in *The Passion of New Eve*). When Margaret tells Melanie that Philip does not allow her any money, Carter describes 'an ancient, female look' that passes between them:

> 'I understand', said Melanie. An ancient, female look passed between them; they were poor women pensioners, planets round a male sun. In the end, Francie gave Melanie a pound note from his fiddling money. He slipped it into the pocket of her skirt and she hardly knew how to thank him. (p. 140)

The look that passes between them is evidence of a deeper female bond. At the puppet show, Margaret pushes a toffee into Melanie's hands, a compensatory gesture between two females. However, the word 'bond' is double-edged; the women are also brought together by their shared economic dependency upon men. Even though Finn helps Melanie, the basic problem remains the same; she is still a planet circulating around a male sun. Although Mrs Rundle has cared for the children, she is powerless to stop them from going into London and she has had to change her own title to that of a married woman to survive in a patriarchal society. Margaret may offer Melanie a toffee to console her, but she is unable to rescue her and the other children from the oppression of their uncle. Moreover, at one level, both Mrs Rundle and Margaret are complicit in their own and Melanie's oppression. The message which Margaret has written on the toffee paper reads: 'Look as though you're enjoying it, for my sake and Finn's' (p. 128). The toffee suggests the kind of consolation that a mother would give to a child. This in turn suggests that one of the risks in valorising the mother/daughter relationship as an alternative to the father/son relationship which is privileged in patriarchy, as critics such as Kristeva have done, is that it can locate the daughter in a state of childlike dependency.

The theme of women being complicit in their own oppression is developed further in *Heroes and Villains* when Marianne is regarded with suspicion by the other women of the tribe, who believe that she is possessed of dangerous powers and separated from them by her social background. Like Margaret, Mrs Green is dependent on the goodwill of the men. However, unlike Margaret, she identifies with the men, encouraging Marianne to do likewise, although there are moments when she sympathises and tries to be supportive of Marianne. Palmer (1987) points out that 'in a patriarchal society, contact between women is frequently ambiguous. They help to arrange each other's hair and make each other beautiful not for their own pleasure and satisfaction, but in order to attract men' (p. 192). Maintaining that often the only gift women can bestow on each other is 'tears, images of suffering and pity', Palmer draws attention to the fleeting moment of closeness between Marianne and her cousin, Annie:

> Annie shrank away but she was as much afraid of Jewel's displeasure as she was of Marianne and he had perversely ceased to give her signals. Marianne saw the baby's bleared, red face pressed against a breast from which it was too ill to suck and helplessly she began to cry. Her tears splashed on Annie's cheek. Annie touched them with her finger and then licked her finger to see if they were salt enough. Marianne slid down to her knees, sobbing as if her heart was breaking. Annie pushed the girl away and turned her back on her with a sigh. (p. 104)

However, the passage is even more ambiguous than Palmer suggests. Marianne is ordered by her husband to kiss Annie and she does so unwillingly, afraid that she will pick up an infection from Annie's baby. Although Marianne is moved to tears by Annie's baby, Annie is suspicious of her tears; she has to test the level of humanity, the salt, in them. Marianne can fall on her knees sobbing, but Annie, who has responsibility for the child, pushes Marianne away and turns her back on her, as if tears were an indulgence that, in different social circumstances from Marianne, she can not afford herself.

As in Melanie's case in *The Magic Toyshop*, Marianne's lack of an adequately defined, autonomous sense of self is evident in the intensity of her processes of projection and introjection. Like Melanie at the outset of the novel, her close identification with her possessions are important to her sense of self and identity: 'She marked all her possessions with her name, even her toothbrush, and never lost anything' (p. 3). From the moment when Marianne sees Jewel killing her brother, she projects onto him the fantasy of the *homme fatale*. Although Jewel has killed her brother instead of his own, she perceives the tattoo on his back as the mark of Cain, a figure that she then eroticises. The idealised nature of the fantasy which she projects on Jewel is evident in the appeal that even the word 'barbarian', 'the wild, quatrosyllabic lilt of the word' (p. 4), has for her.

MASCULINITY, DESIRE AND THE DEMON-LOVER

The focalisation of *Heroes and Villains* in the consciousness of a female character presents us with an erotic objectification of men from a female perspective. Marianne's eroticising of Jewel is a product of the way in which her own feelings are strange and unknown to her. Carter herself maintained in a letter to Elaine Jordan (1994): 'she *is* very much a stranger to her own desire, which is why her desire finds its embodiment as a stranger' (p. 198). The occasion during which, without the light of the moon, Marianne explores Jewel's face with her hands is a discovery of her desire as much as his body. The strangeness of his face to her is expressed in geographical metaphors so that it becomes a 'landscape' which is also the terrain of her sexual feelings. Once again, we are reminded of Jameson's (1986) argument that this kind of manifestation of the body is what remains in a culture where larger perspectives have lost their validity and older narratives have been neutralised (p. 321). And also that in this type of non-realist narrative, as in *The Magic Toyshop*, such a manifestation of the body diverts the narrative logic of the unfolding story in new directions.

Forced to wear a second-hand wedding dress, Marianne becomes, in terms reminiscent of Melanie, 'a mute furious doll' (p. 69). Again this reminds us of Aunt Margaret and of the scream that swells in Melanie's throat during the tree-climbing episode. Like many women, Marianne has been rendered mute, but her enforced silence is accompanied by a swelling rage. At one level, the dress suggests that there is a universal element to women's experiences, occurring as it does in both novels and located in two societies which have similar expectations of women. At the same time, the wedding dress, occurring in different circumstances in each novel, reminds us of the difficulties of, and dangers in, attempting to essentialise women's experiences.

The wedding dress which Marianne is made to wear has sweat stains left by the previous bride, reminding her of her own sexuality and her own desire, to which she is a stranger. However, as the bride, she is also a sacrificial victim. In fact, the way in which she is handed over to the male is linked to cannibalism. When Mrs Green adjusts Marianne's wedding dress, she brings with her 'the sharp smell of burned fat and roasting meat' (p. 69). The bodice of the dress itself is said to have 'crackled and snapped', like roasting meat. In the chapel, the congregation is turned out like animals, in rags and fur, reminding us that their leader, Donally, has his teeth filed to points, a detail which links him, tellingly, to Dracula.

In the relationship between Marianne and Jewel, Carter also rewrites a further traditional story, that of the demon-lover, of whom Jewel has many of the characteristics: he is powerful, mysterious and supernatural, and he can also be cruel, vindictive and hostile. However, in her depiction of him, Carter challenges the male–female binarism which ascribes so-called 'masculine' qualities to men and 'feminine' characteristics to women. In discovering the nature of her own desire, Marianne finds that male–female attributes exist within each individual. The demon-lover is also reconfigured as part of her eroticisation of the male Other. So Marianne is surprised, in exploring Jewel's face when he is asleep, to discover tears. Marianne, too, is not entirely the traditional victim of the demon-lover. Normally the victim is persuaded to leave home and travel to unknown places, but in *Heroes and Villains* it is Marianne who makes the decision to do so of her own volition. In fact, in some respects, Marianne is far removed from the conventional demon-lover's victim. Normally, the demon-lover returns to remind his victim of a bond from the past, but in *Heroes and Villains* it is Marianne who reminds the demon-lover of the bond: in this case the bond that developed between herself and Jewel when he killed her brother.

The way in which the initiative in *Heroes and Villains* is shifted from the demon-lover to the so-called victim, and the way in which Marianne subverts the role of the female in traditional demon-lover stories, are indications of the power which is ascribed to the novel's female focalisation. Melanie responds to her symbolic rape and Marianne to her literal rape with anger and indignation. Palmer (1987) points out how Carter highlights a distinction between the young women's physical vulnerability and the strength of their independence of spirit (p. 188). After marrying Jewel, Marianne, anticipating in many ways Justine in *The Sadeian Woman* (1979), which is discussed in more detail in Chapter 6, gradually turns from victim to predator, surmounts rape and humiliation, and takes Jewel's place as leader. Nevertheless, even this is ambiguous. She says to Donally's son: 'I'll be the tiger lady and rule them with a rod of iron' (p. 150). She seems unaware of the irony of her situation in talking to Donally's son in these terms, given the amount of abuse he has suffered at his father's hands.

CONSCIOUSNESS AND DESIRE IN THE INFERNAL DESIRE MACHINES OF DOCTOR HOFFMAN

Although there are parallels between *The Infernal Desire Machines of Doctor Hoffman* and *Heroes and Villains*, as 'last days' narratives, there are important differences between them. Elaine Jordan (1990) has pointed out that *The Infernal Desire Machines of Doctor Hoffman* draws on an especially eclectic range of narratives: 'pornography, the Gothic, fairy tales, horror films, boy's imperial adventure stories, anthropological idylls according to Rousseau or Levi-Strauss, and the fantasies of philosophy, the world as Will and Idea' (p. 34). It also conflates the 'rite of passage' and the quest narrative much more consciously than the other novel. While *Heroes and Villains* focuses on the binarism between two types of community, *The Infernal Desire Machines of Doctor Hoffman*, like Carter's subsequent novel *The Passion of New Eve*, features a number of differently organised social and community structures.

While Melanie in *The Magic Toyshop* and Marianne in *Heroes and Villains* have to acquire power in order to achieve a fuller sense of their own subjectivity, the protagonists of *The Infernal Desire Machines of Doctor Hoffman*, like Evelyn in *The Passion of New Eve*, have to lose power in order to do so. Unlike Melanie and Marianne,

they have to assume in serial fashion a number of different identities: Desiderio is forced to take refuge among the River People as
Kiku, is driven to join a travelling circus as its peep show proprietor's nephew, becomes a companion to a sadistic Count who takes
him to a Sadeian Brothel peopled with androids and automata,
falls among a tribe of cannibals, becomes involved with the masochistic religion of the Centaurs and ends up in the Gothic castle of
the Doctor himself. Roz Kaveney (1994) observes that the changes
through which the protagonists are put 'are remorseless, one might
almost say sadistic in their intensity' (p. 172).

In *The Infernal Desire Machines of Doctor Hoffman*, Desiderio, a
former confidential secretary to the Minister of Determination,
has been instructed to write down his memories of the Great War
between the Reality Principle and the Pleasure Principle. While
working for the Minister of Determination, Desiderio respected him
for his stand against Dr Hoffman, who represents an opposing mode
of apprehending 'reality'. The Minister of Determination represents
the positivist laws of science while the poet–physicist Dr Hoffman
represents their subversion. While the one stands for reason, law,
structure, restraint and philosophy, the other represents imagination, freedom, desire and anarchy. Carter appears to be recalling
Plato's *Republic* – Hoffman is after all a poet – and the banishment of
the poets from the Athenian city-state. In Plato's *Republic*, the poets
compete with the philosopher–king as Hoffman competes with the
Minister of Determination, threatening the stability of the state by
appealing to the irrational desires and the unruly appetites.

Up to a point, what Desiderio experiences in the meaningless plurality produced by Hoffman's ghosts is the postmodern,
consumer-oriented world dominated by media images. However,
it is also more than that. People, objects, landscapes and even time
are subject to the whims of the desire machines. Generating eroto-
energy, a force in opposition to rational knowledge, the machines
disrupt reality, making epistemological certainty an impossibility.

Neither of these novels can be fully understood without reference
to their intertexts. *The Infernal Desire Machines of Doctor Hoffman* is a
rewriting of the Oedipus story. Desiderio sets out with instructions
from his stern father to destroy Hoffman, but, in keeping with the
quest narrative, he is seduced by a woman, in this case Hoffman's
daughter. Like Oedipus, Desiderio eventually rids the city of its
pollution but has to pay a price for his victory and his new-found
knowledge. However, the most important intertext in the novel

is the work of twentieth-century linguistic philosophers, such as Ferdinand de Saussure. Of particular relevance is Saussure's argument that all linguistic signs have two aspects: the 'signifier' (an actual word, printed or spoken) and the 'signified' (the thing the word describes or the meanings associated with a word), which were arbitrarily linked. In the Minister's world, in *The Infernal Desire Machines of Doctor Hoffman*, there is no 'shadow' or slippage between a word and the object to which it refers; boundaries, rules and hierarchies are clearly defined and observed without ambiguity or ambivalence. Hoffman's world is one of simulacra, where signifier and signified bear only the most arbitrary relationship to each other. Boundaries are blurred and 'everything that is possible to imagine can also exist' (p. 97). Yet this binary distinction between the two worlds proves to be an illusion itself. Like Donally in *Heroes and Villains*, who tries to construct a social mythology for the Barbarians, the Minister of Determination and Dr Hoffman try to impose a particular set of perspectives on their societies. While Hoffman offers a surreal, liberating opposition to what the Minister represents, he is also the embodiment of capitalist control of desire through media technology.

Truth in classic realist fiction, as Steven Connor (1996) argues, is 'a matter not of correspondence to facts but of perspective' (p. 53). As a result, what is important in the realist novel is the establishment of a vantage point from which disparate issues and widely separated experiences can be grasped. In *The Infernal Desire Machines of Doctor Hoffman*, Carter focuses not so much on the experiences of the protagonists as on the difficulty of establishing vantage points. The opening lines of Desiderio's account of the Great War give us reason to doubt at least some of the narrative that follows, for he claims to have remembered everything perfectly. Although Desiderio emerges as a war hero, he has failed to find his master/ father figure or the object of his desire, since he has had to kill both. His heroic status is further undermined by his complicity in domination and exploitation. Ostensibly, Desiderio's focalisation derives from his commitment to rationality. But we soon discover that he is sceptical of rationality, of his Minister and of the Determination Police. Moreover, not only does he appear critical of rationality, but his own behaviour is much less rational than he thinks. It is no coincidence that Carter writes of the Minister's denial of shadows, employing the term which the twentieth-century psychologist Jung, mentioned in Chapter 2, used to refer to the negative aspects of the collective unconscious that enter the personal consciousness. The emphasis upon rationality denies not only the importance of the irrational but also the fact that what we perceive as rational behaviour, even in ourselves, may not be as rational as we might believe.

Once again Carter appears to be challenging a basic assumption of the classic realist novel, which, as Connor (1996) says, is normally regarded as a meeting point between reality and desire (p. 1). The realist novel can be seen as a concentrated fusion of how the world is, or appears to be, and the shaping force of imagination and/or fantasy. Desiderio's name actually means 'desire' in Italian and, of course, he falls in love with his fantasy version of Dr Hoffman's daughter, Albertina, modelled on Proust's androgynous Albertine in 'The Captive' from *Remembrance of Things Past*. Albertina awakens passion and desire in Desiderio, who until then has been merely a passive observer of Hoffman's fantasies. Indeed, the history is dedicated to her with all his 'insatiable tears' (p. 14). So, whilst he denounces the mirages created by Dr Hoffman, Desiderio spends much of his life chasing one. Even after her death, Desiderio cannot rid himself of his obsession with her, and hers is the final image of his memoirs. Albertina, of course, does not appear as a character in her own right in this novel, only as a creation, or projection, of Desiderio's fantasies. Sally Robinson (1991) points out that women in this novel, as in the quest story, are objects, 'put into circulation according to the logic of male desire' (p. 101). They function as fetish, foil or exotic/erotic objects.

Desiderio, who did not have a proper relationship with his mother, a prostitute, and never knew his father, whose genetic imprint he carries in the colour of his skin, was brought up after his mother's death by nuns. The perpetual presence of a sense of loss in the psyche of individuals who do not experience a close, fulfilling relationship with their mothers is a recurring trope in the novel. Mamie Buckskin, the 'phallic paradox', always wears a picture of her dead, alcoholic mother between her breasts, which themselves remind Desiderio of the 'bosom of a nursing mother' (p. 108). The way in which Desiderio interprets his time with the River People, too, suggests that he is impelled in a Freudian sense, like Melanie in *The Magic Toyshop*, to discover a sense of home as an ideal in his own psyche: 'If I murdered Desiderio and became Kiku for ever, I need fear nothing in my life ever, any more. I need not fear loneliness or boredom or lack of love' (p. 80). Here Desiderio lists three of the forces which disrupt the psyche. He wishes to eradicate all desire except for that associated with the pre-Oedipal. Indeed, there is a significant difference between the sound of the name 'Desiderio' and the sound of 'Kiku', which is much closer to the kind of sound that an infant would make at its mother's breast. However, Desiderio is not only returning to his absent mother, but also to his unknown father. For, although the River people's society is theoretically matrilineal, in practice all decisions are devolved to the males.

Similarly, Desiderio's idealised account of his and Albertina's life among the Centaurs reflects his own deep-rooted need to discover an ideal psychic home. His memoirs note how Albertina's skin responded well to the sun, how 'she would come home in the golden evenings, wreathed with corn like a pagan deity in a pastoral and naked as a stone' (p. 187). They also betray his masculinist bias; he is uncritical of the way in which the females have to work in the fields, while the men have a more leisurely lifestyle.

Another disturbing feature of Desiderio's account of life among the Centaurs is how the recreation of a pastoral innocence-cum-naïve primitivism is linked to his perception of his relationship with Albertina as a loving one between brother and sister. At one level, this is regressive on his part, an attempt to reclaim the ideal of the home. But the reader cannot forget that relationships between brothers and sisters often involve repressed desires, as, of course, does the pastoral itself. Indeed, incest is a recurring trope in Carter's work. Moreover, within its fantasies about sibling relationships, Desiderio's account sublimates the trauma which Albertina experiences, and that, even when her physical wounds following the rape are healed, she will not let him touch her.

MASCULINIST PERSPECTIVES AND DILEMMAS

Although the focalisation of *The Infernal Desire Machines of Doctor Hoffman* is male, the reader is not easily seduced into identification with this male point of view. Sally Robinson (1991) points out that the novel presents 'an epistemological revolution...in which culture's master narratives are losing the power and authority to order experience' (p. 78). The exception is the 'Oedipal narrative that places man in the position of questing, speaking subject, and woman in the non-position of object who is *subject* to male regulation, exploitation and violence' (ibid.). Initially, Desiderio is no more able than Evelyn/Eve in *The Passion of New Eve* to see the inequality and oppression in which they are both complicit. When the reader first encounters Desiderio, he lives and works in a city which, according to him, is 'thickly, obtusely masculine' (p. 15). In discussing the general character of cities, he employs a clichéd binarism, apparently unaware of the gendered nature of the assumptions underpinning it: 'Some cities are women and must be loved; others are men and can only be admired and bargained with' (ibid.). Women here are associated with love and, by implication, with the private and the domestic. Men, who, it would appear, do not need love, are associated with the public realm of business and bargaining, a point reinforced when we remember that this male city 'throve on business' and is 'prosperous'. While Desiderio recognises that many of the landmarks of the South American city from which he starts out were anointed with his forefather's blood, he does not bring the same level of critical acumen to his description of his mother, only observing that 'her business, which was prostitution of the least exalted type, took her to the slums a great deal' (p. 16).

As if to remind us that sight does not always mean insight, the peep show displays are, as Susan Suleiman (1994) points out, 'unmistakably male voyeuristic fantasies' (p. 114). In most of the societies which Desiderio visits, women are in a subordinate social position, but this is something of which he is insufficiently critical. Even though Desiderio observes that the River Women all moved in 'the same, stereotyped way, like benign automata', the only conclusion he draws is that it was possible to 'understand what had produced the prejudices of the Jesuits' (p. 73). Meanwhile, his subconscious desire to 'masculinise' women is revealed when he cannot help but approve of the practice whereby mothers of young girls manipulate their daughters' clitorises so that they approximate penises. This fantasy of 'masculinised' women renders many of his representations of women, such as his portrait of Mamie Buckskin, who always has at her thigh 'a gun, death-dealing erectile tissue' (p. 108), unreliable. She treasures, 'lovingly fingering', the weapons of dead male outlaws, such as Billy the Kid, Doc Holliday and John Wesley Hardin, from the American West, which was itself a masculine imaginary. We are also told that, for shooting a man, she was 'imprisoned in the far West' (ibid.). Ironically, this may also be taken to refer to the way in which she is entrapped in an essentially masculine fantasy.

The initial privileged position which Desiderio, like Evelyn in *The Passion of New Eve*, enjoys is reversed in the course of the narrative.

Once at the centre of all systems of representation, man has become decentred, and with him traditional notions of patriarchal authority. Like Eve/Evelyn, Desiderio suffers pain and humiliation through which he discovers what women have to endure. The most obvious example is Desiderio's rape by the Moroccan acrobats, which makes him realise what Albertina endured when she was raped by the Centaurs: 'The pain was terrible. I was most intimately ravaged I do not know how many times. I wept, bled, slobbered and pleaded but nothing would appease a rapacity as remorseless and indifferent as the storm which raged outside' (p. 117). Jordan (1994) points out that, initially, Albertina cannot accept that she was raped, convinced that, though every male Centaur has carnal knowledge of her, the beasts were only emanations of her desires (p. 208). But the account that we have of the rape and how it has affected her, which seems to preclude any possibility of trauma, is Desiderio's. A compounding irony is that when the Centaurs realise that Albertina is Desiderio's 'mate', that is, his property, they apologise for raping her. And he accepts the apology!

Part of Desiderio's problem is that he does not understand the 'feminine' even within himself. Throughout his memoirs, there are women as castrating Amazons, mutilated bodies or erotic toys. His 'othering' of Albertina is as inhibiting to the development of a fully reciprocal relationship as Marianne's projection of her fantasies onto Jewel in *Heroes and Villains*. At that moment among the Centaurs when Desiderio cannot understand why Albertina does not want him to touch her, she is more the Other in his imagination than at any other time. She becomes most erotic to him when she becomes most exotic: 'brown as an Indian' and 'wreathed with corn like a pagan deity' (p. 187). Her Mongolian skin is tangible; it places her in a specific part of the globe and gives her an identity and history. But, in eroticising her, Desiderio makes her 'abstract'. She acquires a body 'naked as a stone', a face that 'fell into the carven lines of the statue of a philosopher' and eyes 'which sometimes held a dark, blasting lightening' (ibid.).

The explanation offered in the novel for Desiderio's attitude towards women is that, as in Buzz's case in *Love*, he has been adversely influenced by his childhood experiences. Like Buzz, he has grown up with a sense of fear which he projects onto women. His fears are most vividly revealed in a dream in which, like Melanie in *The Magic Toyshop*, he is threatened by a swan. At one level, the black swan signifies the horror of nothing, which, as discussed in

Chapter 2, was central to much of Herman Melville's work, which greatly influenced Carter's early writing: 'a black as intense as the negation of light, black the colour of the extinction of consciousness' (ibid.). At another level, it makes Desiderio's fear of women explicit, for it is both a swan and female, turning eventually into Albertina.

RATIONALITY, TECHNOLOGY AND VIOLENCE

Desiderio, however, is not wholly blinkered. He witnesses cracks appearing in a mode of awareness which has dominated Western thinking since the Enlightenment: 'But I think I must have been one of the first people in the city to notice how the shadows began to fall subtly awry and a curious sense of strangeness invaded everything' (p. 15). Although at the outset of his memoirs Desiderio describes physical changes that appear to be happening in the city, such as the sudden erection of cloud palaces, his real anxiety concerns the emergence of a new way of looking at 'reality'. It is not simply that 'reality' has changed but that the conventional assumptions about the relationship between language and external referent have proved false and been shown to be illusory: 'Hardly anything remained the same for more than one second and the city was no longer the conscious production of humanity; it had become the arbitrary realm of dream' (p. 18).

From the post-Enlightenment emphasis on rationalism, denying the acceptability of beliefs founded on anything but experience, reasoning and deduction, developed the mode of awareness in literature and art normally referred to as 'realism'. In the Middle Ages, literature concerned itself with a world of ideals rooted in cosmologies which suggested that the human world was divinely ordained, ordered and controlled. However, in post-Renaissance England, the emergent world view was rooted in scientific and rational notions of comprehending the world, with 'real' human experience at the centre of it. In *The Infernal Desire Machines of Doctor Hoffman*, the dominant world view is shifting again, away from the rigid hierarchies and classifications of the rationalism in which Desiderio has been educated. The fruits which begin to appear in the market stalls are 'remarkable' because they defy boundaries: they are pineapples but have the colour and texture of strawberries and taste of caramel. They literally and metaphorically occupy a space outside the conventional classification of fruit, as, for example, oranges and apples, in which the conventional ideas about fruit are overturned. The market stall fruit are hybrids whose boundary crossing suggests the interleaving of ideas, ethnicities, classes and sects.

The way in which Desiderio criticises the Minister of Determination suggests that he is sceptical of the familiar post-Enlightenment myth that, through reason, human beings become most positively human. Moreover, the way in which reason and social progress have been habitually linked in Western thought is debunked by the description of the Determination Police. Desiderio, the first person to recognise that shadows are beginning to fall 'awry', has enough imagination to link the Police with the German SS of the 1930s and 1940s who have come from 'a Jewish nightmare' (p. 22). The 'Jewish nightmare' was itself a denial of the kind of interracial and intercultural realities which the fruit on the market stall suggest. But the reference to the Holocaust here also reminds us, as the appearance of the police reminds Desiderio, that rationality played a key role in the design of the Holocaust, of the concentration camps and of the gas chambers. This post-Enlightenment myth of an inextricable connection between reason and the progress of civilisation is also undermined by the concept of Reality Testing and the irony that, even though the Minister had 'a battery of technological devices' at his disposal, he had to resort to 'the methods of the medieval witch-hunter' (ibid.).

Carter's novel also disabuses us of any inevitable correlation between technological development and the betterment of humanity. Apart from the fact that technology may unwittingly have dire consequences for humanity, it has been employed in the creation of ever more imaginative ways of inflicting pain and torture on human beings. In the course of the novel, it becomes clear that rationality and imagination, although they are perceived as binary opposites, have come together in history to further rather than abolish the means by which one individual is abused by another. In a world governed by rationality, efficiency – as in the speedy despatch of 'undesirables' by the Third Reich – becomes a kind of morality. This is something that Desiderio observes but does not fully appreciate. He is quick to point out that the Minister of Trade, who later becomes the Minister of Determination, was 'always the model of efficiency' and that when he helped the Minister with the crossword puzzle the Minister admired the speed with which Desiderio completed the squares.

The Infernal Desire Machines of Doctor Hoffman, like *The Magic Toyshop* and *Heroes and Villains*, reminds us how important the dream of eradicating violence has been to ideas of 'human progress'. It encourages us to ponder why attempts to do so have failed, and, in the twentieth century, failed so spectacularly. Although Desiderio experiences different types of human community, with different social structures and at different stages of technological development, pain is employed within all of them as a means of social control. The Chief whom Desiderio encounters on the African coast, surrounding himself with women rather than men, controls his army of women by circumcision; the clitoris of every girl child born to the tribe is removed as soon as she reaches puberty, as are those of his wives and concubines brought from other tribes.

Within this framework, the inclusion of a parody of the Marquis de Sade's *The 120 Days of Sodom* in *The Infernal Desire Machines of Doctor Hoffman* opens up further possible readings of the text around debates pertaining to the supposed 'progress' of human civilisations. *The 120 Days of Sodom* is a work of the imagination which, in subverting traditional moral codes, seeks to push sexual fantasy to the point of creating 'evil', where fantasy becomes divorced from sexual pleasure. Gąsiorek (1995) points out: 'While Albertina hints at the benign effects of Hoffman's worldview, the Count discloses its malignant consequences' (p. 130). The Count and his servant, Lafleur, are modelled on the Marquis de Sade and his valet, Latour. In fact, he is a fusion of Sade and Dracula. In the Count's case, the liberation of desire leads to an endless search for increasingly perverse manifestations to satisfy an insatiable and increasingly sadistic appetite. Initially, as Robinson (1991) says, the Doctor is attractive in 'his ability to think beyond binary oppositions, to read the world in ways not wholly dependent on a logic which would repress the unconscious in a hegemony of logocentrism' (p. 99). However, his desires lead to exploitation and domination.

Thus, the Sadeian brothel scene is particularly disturbing in the way in which it elides masculinity, sexuality and excessive violence. When they enter the brothel, the Count and Desiderio are dressed for the occasion in special costumes which hide their faces, but which leave their genitals exposed: 'the garb grossly emphasised our manhoods while utterly denying our humanity' (p. 30). The Bestial Room to which they are led takes up where *The 120 Days of Sodom* leaves off, eliding Doctor Hoffman's Marcusean principle that 'everything it is possible to imagine can also exist' with the perversity of Sade's imaginative liberty. Sade only completed thirty of his 120 days, leaving sketches for the rest, which included the criminal passions and others which combined the comic with sheer cruelty. When they enter the room, the Count and Desiderio are confronted by monkeys turned into living candelabra and animals turned by a taxidermist into furniture. Then they notice the prostitutes kept in cages redolent of Victorian drawing-room birdcages. They are not women but 'sinister, abominable, inverted mutations, part clockwork, part vegetable and part brute' (p. 132). If all this were not horrific enough, Desiderio is shocked by the way in which the Count is aroused by it all.

Here, as subsequently in *The Passion of New Eve*, Carter parodies the principal tradition of pornographic writing. As she explains in *The Sadeian Woman* (1979), since pornography is 'produced in the main by men for an all-male clientele' it has 'certain analogies with a male brothel' (p. 15). Desiderio is the author of a narrative which, as Robinson (1991) says, 'enlists an array of misogynist sentiment and fantasy' (p. 102). However, here Carter, as a female author, is appropriating a male consciousness to expose how women are trapped, like the woman reader of this novel, in a male imaginary. Moreover, the narrative technique of ventriloquism, a female author speaking in a male voice, is employed to create not just pornography but an especially sadistic version of it. Hence, as a parody of pornography, Desiderio's account positions the (male) reader as voyeur but does not necessarily guarantee a voyeuristic, pleasure position for him.

While *The Infernal Desire Machines of Doctor Hoffman* might take up where Sade left off in its depiction of how evil can be created in the human mind, it offers an alternative understanding of evil as something which is likely to be produced when the external circumstances are congenial to it. The problem is that evil, like the subordination of women, has occurred in so many different cultures, societies and histories that generalising about those circumstances is difficult. In *The Sadeian Woman*, Carter points out: 'pornography reinforces the false universals of sexual archetypes because it denies, or doesn't have time for... the social context in which sexual activity takes place, that modifies the very nature of that activity' (p. 16). Throughout the novel, the creation of evil is seen as embedded in particular sociohistorical circumstances. The Count's account of himself to Desiderio, even if allowances are made for the context in which the Count relates his tales and for Desiderio's inevitable filtering of them as narrator, would suggest that he is the kind of person Sade believed the imagination might create: 'From the cradle, I have been a blasphemous libertine, a blood-thirsty debauchee. I travel the world only to discover hitherto unknown methods of treating flesh' (p. 126). Many of the serial atrocities he recounts betray particular contexts. But they also have much in common. Victims are people designated inferiors and marginalised, such as geisha girls in Japan, eunuchs in the Royal Court of Siam, people accused of witchcraft in Salem, Negro slaves in Alabama and a 'mulatto' whore in New Orleans. In Salem and Alabama, retribution is the product of a group of people afraid of losing their control and authority.

The novel, as is typical of Carter's work, does not offer the reader a fully developed thesis. Kaveney (1994) reminds us that Carter 'is not one for telling us what to do or what to believe' (p. 183). One proposition is introduced in opposition to another. Even the realisation that evil behaviour arises from specific contexts stands in contradistinction to other suggestions that it is linked to the 'shadow' aspects of the psyche. The description of the Determination Police suggests that there is something fetishistic about their uniforms; the coats are of black leather and the boots 'too highly polished', a criticism which has been made about the uniforms and regalia of the German SS. The fetishistic overtones are, in turn, linked to hints of repression in the ankle-length of the coats and in the fact that they are worn 'truculently belted' (p. 22). The atrocities committed by the Klansmen in Alabama are one thing; the fact that they ululate while watching the Negroes burn is another. Throughout the novel, a thesis that evil can only be understood in relation to specific contexts in which it emerges is countered by the horror of an evil that cannot be rationalised, signified in Desiderio's dream of the black swan, whose eyes 'expressed a kind of mindless evil that was quite without glamour, though evil is usually attractive, because evil is defiant' (p. 30). This perspective on violence is discussed in more detail in the next chapter, within a wider framework about sadomasochism, in relation to *The Passion of New Eve* and *The Sadeian Woman*.

6
Sexual Fictions: *The Passion of New Eve* (1977) and *The Sadeian Woman* (1979)

The narrator of *The Passion of New Eve*, Evelyn, describes his/ her movement from London to New York and from there to the desert. That the journey ends up in the desert, traditionally associated in Euro-American literature with sterility and death, seems particularly ironic, a parodic reversal of the myth of America as the land of opportunity and possibility. In the desert, Evelyn is captured by a band of feminist guerrillas controlled by Mother, who transforms him biologically into a woman but who does not have time to complete the psychosurgery before he escapes. Fleeing from her, s/he is captured once more, this time by a male tyrant called Zero, who, like Evelyn, is obsessed with a film star called Tristessa de St Ange. But, unlike Evelyn, Zero believes that Tristessa telepathically emasculated him during a showing of one of her films.

In the novel, linear time is often associated with the male and the onward drive of modernity, evidenced in technology, wars, cities and 'the space race', while cyclical or recurrent time is associated with the female. However, such an essentialist binarism, even though it is not fully endorsed in the narrative, becomes irrelevant to the novel's delineation of a postmodern Euro-America. At the centre of the novel, Tristessa's house of glass, an illusion sustained by light and a vast rotating apparatus of reproduction, signifies the postmodernist cycle of self-construction and self-replication which America, once signifying the European dream of spiritual greatness, has become.

Although in some ways *The Passion of New Eve*, like *Heroes and Villains*, is a 'last days' narrative, it is a different type of post-apocalyptic text from that novel. While *Heroes and Villains* appears to have been written with British post-apocalyptic specu- lative fiction in mind, *The Passion of New Eve* is distinctly in the American vein. Nan Albinski (1988) points out that the novel, which is almost wholly set in the United States, is partly a satire on the work of 'American separatist writers whose women cele- brate female rituals, and joyfully claim the pastoral world' (p. 134). Carter parodies a matriarchal society in the American desert – possibly thinking of the kind of society which Marianne as the 'tiger lady' would introduce – and, through a black American woman, ridicules the projection of gender, whether male or female, onto gods. Kaveney (1994) maintains that, while Zero is 'an unholy cross between the macho litterateur and Charles Manson' (p. 181), he is also a satire on another subgenre of American futuristic literature, survivalist narrative. A key element in Zero's harem is the violence with which the regime is run, and the novel holds up a mirror to American society that celebrates the part guns have played in its history, associating them with freedom and individual liberty. A crucial issue is the causal nature of the relationship between Zero's enthusiasm for guns, his violence and his misanthropy. Zero spends each afternoon shooting empty beer cans placed on sticks in the ground. It is quite clear that they signify people, and there are two disturbing dimensions to this activity. First, the choice of object suggests the contempt in which he holds people in general. Second, there is a thin line between shooting at an imaginative projection of a human target and attempting to kill a real person.

The Passion of New Eve appears to have been written from the point of intersection of two genres: American 'last days' futuris- tic fantasy and the British 'innocent Englishman/woman abroad' narrative which has a long lineage that includes works by authors such as Charles Dickens, Evelyn Waugh, David Lodge and Malcolm Bradbury. In keeping with the expectations of the latter, the focal- isation is from Evelyn/Eve as an Englishman in America. But, since the 'Englishman abroad' narrative is essentially a *Bildungsroman*, the emphasis is upon his 'education'. This particular focalisation is employed to provide not only a satire on the novel's central pro- tagonist, Evelyn/Eve, who undergoes an enforced sex change oper- ation, and a vehicle for exploring the nature of gender identity, but a mounting satire on the communities with which he/she comes into contact.

AMERICA

Although, as in *Heroes and Villains*, Carter is not interested in tracing the decline of civilisation, *The Passion of New Eve* explores how cultural myths may have contributed to the disintegration of Western, or, more specifically in the novel, American civilisation. The irony of the novel, to which its epigraph from John Locke's *Second Treatise of Government* draws our attention, 'In the beginning all the world was America', is that the myth of America once offered Europe an opportunity to return to a point of origin outside European history. However, the epigraph is ambiguous, especially when read in conjunction with Eve's assertion at the end of the book that 'we start from our conclusions'. That is to say, America is the future from which late capitalist Western society will have to begin again.

When Tristessa, a Hollywood star whose name suggests Tiresias, the prophet of Greek mythology who illicitly obtained knowledge of male and female sexuality, is discovered to be a man dressed as a woman, Eve observes in her face 'all the desolation of America' (p. 121). This scene is redolent of an incident in Carter's short story 'John Ford's 'Tis Pity She's a Whore', published in *American Ghosts and Old World Wonders* (1993), in which the play, by the seventeenth-century dramatist John Ford, becomes a Western. In the story, Ford's Annabella has become Annie-Belle and Giovanni has become Johnny. After their mother's death, they are left alone with their father and an incestuous relationship develops between brother and sister. Although Carter is suggesting hidden aspects of Ford's play, her story is really about America: 'The light, the unexhausted light of North America that, filtered through celluloid, will become the light by which we see *North* America looking at itself' (p. 338). Just as America was a step beyond the Old World, Carter has moved beyond John Ford's Jacobean text. While for men the American prairie traditionally represented openness and possibility, for women it could be oppressive, as Carter makes clear. Annie-Belle's mother 'died of the pressure of that vast sky, that weighed down upon her and crushed her lungs' (p. 332). America, as read through Carter's story, is made problematic by the loss of the mother and the celebration of the kind of masculinity associated with the mythology of the American frontier. Loss creates a void, which is inevitably filled with the presence of something darker than was there initially. In the case of America, the symbolic loss of the 'mother', through the way in which America as a nation privileges its frontier mythologies, creates a void of overwhelming emptiness and intense loneliness, which a ruthless, masculinist ideology seems to have stepped in to fill, resulting in the destruction of the wilderness and the genocide of the Native American.

But Annie-Belle's situation is more than just an allegory for America and the dominance of a national, masculinist mythology. The void left by her mother's death is filled by her mother-in-law when, pregnant by Johnny, she marries the Minister's son. But, in the space vacated by her mother, Johnny is transformed into a further threatening presence. In trying to get away from him, Annie-Belle drives her buggy, in an allusion to another text, 'lickety-split' to town (p. 345). This is a story where Carter often makes the briefest of references to other texts. 'Lickety-split' might suggest that Annie-Belle is Brer Rabbit running 'lickety-split' away from the tar baby, Johnny. Or, possibly, the tar baby is the American prairies. In the description of Annie-Belle as a 'repentant harlot', for example, we are told that 'she wore a yellow ribbon', an allusion to one of John Ford's most famous films (p. 346).

America in 'John Ford's 'Tis Pity She's a Whore' is riddled, like America in *The Passion of New Eve*, with confusion, pretence and illusion. In *The Passion of New Eve*, as I have said, Tristessa is a woman in a man's body masquerading as Woman and Evelyn becomes a man in a woman's body. In 'John Ford's 'Tis Pity She's a Whore', Annie-Belle 'cross-dresses' as her brother's wife, the community believe her to be pregnant by the Minister's son and Johnny is mistakenly regarded as a shamed member of her family. But it is perhaps the American literary critic Leslie Fiedler's *Love and Death in the American Novel* (1960), which, as discussed in Chapter 2, was an important influence on Carter's interpretation of Gothic, that provides the key concept which links both works. Fiedler argues that, 'when the last great communal myth system begins to collapse', the individual is left 'unsure of his relationship to the ego-ideals left him by the past' (p. 109).

In *The Passion of New Eve*, America is disintegrating: California is seceding from the Union and the Siege of Harlem is raging. In the course of *The Passion of New Eve*, Evelyn/ Eve finds him/herself increasingly 'unsure' about what Fiedler calls the ego-ideals of the past. At the beginning of the novel, the representation of civil war in California symbolically depicts the masculinist ego-ideals coming under attack from the female 'id' they have long sought to suppress and control:

> As the summer grew yet more intolerable, the Women also furthered their depredations. Female sharp-shooters took to sniping from concealed windows at men who lingered too long in front of posters outside blue movie theatres. They were supposed to have infiltrated the hookers who paraded around Times Square in their uniforms of white boots and mini-skirts. (p. 17)

The irony lies in the way in which the old fetish, 'uniforms of white boots and mini-skirts', returns in revenge on the old fetishists.

THE SADEIAN WOMAN: PORNOGRAPHY AND SADOMASOCHISM

Like *The Infernal Desire Machines of Doctor Hoffman*, *The Passion of New Eve* is a retrospective, picaresque, serial narrative. Although each novel is narrated from a male point of view, the novels invite their readers to assume a perspective outside the narrative. The male focalisation of *The Passion of New Eve* is often parodic, as in the above quotation, and in Evelyn's admission that a man's 'manhood' is much more vulnerable than his head (p. 17). Jouve Ward points out that the novel sets up and then frustrates a whole series of male pornographic expectations. In other words, like the account of the 'House of Anonymity' in *The Infernal Desire Machines of Doctor Hoffman*, *The Passion of New Eve* refuses to guarantee a voyeuristic subject position for its readers. Like the peep show and the brothel in *The Infernal Desire Machines of Doctor Hoffman*, the novel makes voyeurs of its readers and then undermines their voyeurism.

The Sadeian Woman (1979) provides a retrospective commentary on some of the issues which *The Passion of New Eve* raises in relation to sexual violence and the oppression of women. It was described by Carter herself as 'neither a critical study nor a historical analysis of Sade' but 'a late-twentieth-century interpretation of some of the problems he raises about the culturally determined nature of women and of the relations between men and women that result from it' (p. 2). It sheds light on Carter's recurring concern with cultural discourses of gender and sexuality that oppress not only women but also men.

In the decade following its publication, *The Sadeian Woman* was perceived as a disturbing essay and some critics were confused by it. Late twentieth-century and twenty-first-century criticism has taken this work and the subject of sadomasochism more seriously. Gregory Rubinson (2000) typically highlights Carter's interest in 'moral pornography' that provides a critique of relations between the sexes, especially of mythological notions of femininity. He argues: 'What Carter values in Sade's writings is his unrestricted disclosure of sexual power dynamics' (p. 717). However, the paradox at the centre of *The Passion of New Eve* is that, while the novel mocks the assumptions informing the archetypes of sexual behaviour, the effect of androcentric norms on Eve, Leilah and Tristessa, even at their most 'liberated', is still evident. The focus of *The Sadeian Woman* shifts from pornography in general to Sade's work in particular. But Rubinson's argument that Carter values the 'unrestricted disclosure of sexual power dynamics' stands in contradistinction to Sarah Henstra's (1999) warning that 'many readers may have imposed a syllogism here that makes the Marquis himself the moral pornographer...' (p. 98). Henstra complicates the authorial position in *The Sadeian Woman*, pointing out: 'Rather than aligning herself with predator or prey, Carter adopts a stance as onlooker, from which she 'thinks through' both experiences and allows them to cast each other into relief' (p. 109).

At one level, Carter's interest in sadomasochism reflects the period which she spent in Japan and her developing familiarity throughout those and subsequent years with Japanese culture, especially film. The work of Oshima Nagiska had an important influence upon her fiction. *The Passion of New Eve* and *Heroes and Villains* betray the influence of his films in their depiction of the cruel world of youth and their concern with hopelessness, cruelty, torture and rape. It is not surprising that Carter should have developed an interest in Nagiska's work, as both are iconoclasts who, as Maureen Turim (1998) says of Nagiska, 'create icons to attack other icons' (p. 19).

At another level, Carter's interest in sadomasochism chimes with the 1960s and 1970s in Europe, which saw numerous films about, or involving, sadomasochism, such as *Belle de Jour* (1967), *The Libertine* (1969), *The Night Porter* (1974) and *Story of O* (1975). Many of these films adopt, or seek to adopt, a viewpoint that, like Carter's *The Sadeian Woman*, attempts to sympathise with the predator and the prey and assumes an ironic voice, located in the way each perspective, as Henstra says, casts the other into relief.

The *Story of O* is one of the texts from this period which most consistently weave the dominant and submissive viewpoints in an ironic dialectic with each other. It is based on an erotic novel published in 1954 by French author Anne Desclos under the pen name Pauline Réage. It approaches the subject, like *The Passion of New Eve*, through ambivalent imagery. 'O', as the central protagonist is known, can signify 'object' or 'orifice'. A beautiful Parisian fashion photographer, O, is brought by her lover to a château where she is blindfolded, chained, whipped and made to provide various kinds of intercourse on demand. From there, she is handed over to a specific 'master', Sir Stephen, and eventually to an all-female community where she agrees to receive a branding and labia piercing with rings. O agrees to everything beforehand and her consent is sought throughout. At one level, the text parodies the concept of marriage, in which the father in the traditional ceremony hands his daughter over to a stranger while the obedient, silent O embodies the 'ideal' of the dutiful wife. But, like *The Passion of New Eve*, in the dialectic between master and submissive, it asks questions about which of them, the 'master' or the 'submissive', is really in control. For example, O's valet desires her. But when she refuses to look at him as he would wish, even though in return he promises not to whip her, he realises that, as the submissive, she is ultimately in control of him.

Throughout the film *Story of O* there are suggestions of a female camaraderie which, as in Zero's harem in *The Passion of New Eve*, is resistant to male power. At the château, the women form a community which sustains them and eventually O takes a female lover, Jacqueline. However, like *The Sadeian Woman*, the text breaks down the conventional male predator and female victim binarism. The sadomasochism presented in *Story of O*, as in *The Passion of New Eve*, is not solely inflicted by men. At the mansion Samois, in an all-female community, O is whipped by a woman whom she upsets and later is allowed revenge by whipping her. O eventually sends her new female lover, Jacqueline, to the château for 'training'.

Considering *O* and *The Sadeian Woman* in juxtaposition, through the way in which each text casts the spectator or reader as an outsider or onlooker, reveals the depth of irony in each work. However, it also reveals how Anne Desclos and Angela Carter, despite the differences between them, share an approach to sadomasochism, based on gender and identity roles as a kind of performance, which enables them to explore sadomasochism's different dimensions sympathetically. Both Declos and Carter appear to be interested in as full a representation of 'women's' sexual desire as possible. Each creates, as Henstra (1999) says of Carter, women characters 'whose eroticism does not undermine their strength' (p. 110). In *O, The Sadeian Woman* and *The Passion of New Eve*, the emphasis is on 'performativity', which, to use Henstra's language, is also 'contrapuntal', in that audiences and readers are encouraged to think of more than one side of the story, the predator and the prey, within this framework (p. 109).

In *The Passion of New Eve*, there is a more sustained engagement with issues that surface in *The Sadeian Woman* than in Carter's previous novels, and especially with what she identifies more explicitly in *The Sadeian Woman* as the 'gaps' in pornography (p. 16). These gaps occur because pornography, Carter argues in *The Sadeian Woman*, derives 'directly from myth' (p. 6). As such, much of it is essentially 'reactionary' and amounts to no more than 'tableaux of falsification [which] remove our sexual life from the world, from the tactile experience itself' (p. 8). Analysing the kinds of experience which pornography offers the reader, Carter concludes that it fails in two key respects which become important to her two major novels written in the 1980s: *Nights at the Circus* (1984) and *Wise Children* (1991). First, it fails because, unlike in these novels and *The Passion of New Eve*, 'there is no room [...] for tension and the unexpected' (p. 13). This is missing from pornography because it refuses to engage with 'the free expression of desire' (ibid.) that would provide the 'tension' and 'the unexpected' which Carter argues it needs. Second, the perceived 'reader or consumer of pornography is usually a man who subscribes to a particular social fiction of manliness' (p. 14). However, Nicola Pitchford (2002) points out that equally a myth is the notion of what she calls 'the pornographic-cum-automaton reader' because 'each pornographic text, and each new reading occasion, produces it slightly differently' (p. 168).

The frequent twists and turns in *The Passion of New Eve* signify the 'unexpected' which Carter fails to find in much 'conventional' pornography and, as far as a number of the protagonists are concerned, mimic the way in which each new reading of a text, as Pitchford says, produces it slightly differently. The names of two of the key protagonists in *The Passion of New Eve* seem to have arisen from the earlier novel, *Heroes and Villains*. Eve and Lilith are the two possible identities which Jewel and Donally discuss as appropriate for Marianne:

'... Embrace your destiny with style, that's the important thing. Pretend you're Eve at the end of the world.'

'Lilith', said Donally, pedantically. 'Call her Lilith.'

'That's a bad heredity. Besides, I always thought of Lilith as kind of mature.' (p. 124)

One of the first twists is that Eve, at the beginning of the novel, is a misogynistic man, Evelyn, and a second is that Leilah, a naked model and dancer whom he ties and beats, re-emerges as Lilith, a guerrilla fighter.

At one level, Evelyn represents what Carter perceives in *The Sadeian Woman* as the stereotypical male reader of pornography. But he is also a man who beats women, to employ Carter's words from *The Sadeian Woman*, out of 'a Psychic fiction as deeply at the heart of Western culture as the myth of Oedipus', a response, Carter maintains, 'to the bleeding scar left by her castration' (p. 23). This is all too evident when Evelyn parts Leilah's legs in order to examine 'more closely the exquisite negative' of her sex (p. 27), reducing her, like O, to an orifice. Evelyn, here, is a vicious parody of the male, objectifying gaze. In peering at Leilah as if he were a doctor conducting a medical examination, Evelyn reveals his indifference and lack of empathy, with no appreciation of how humiliating such an examination is for women. Indeed, as a narrator, Evelyn is most obviously defective in describing the quality of his feelings in relation to other persons. When he finishes with Leilah, he characteristically writes: 'But soon I grew bored with her. I had enough of her, then more than enough ... the sickness ran its course' (p. 31). Eventually, he admits: 'So I abandoned Leilah to the dying city and took to the freeway.' (p. 37)

Leilah is the opposite archetype to that represented by Evelyn from pornography, the woman whose function is to invite 'fucking'. But there is also something of the BDSM Mistress about her: she flaunts purple painted nipples that match her lips; wears black leather shoes with ankle straps and six-inch heels; and favours mesh stockings that accentuate her legs. Given the way in which she recalls the Domina, it is one of the twists in *The Passion of New Eve* that Leilah can be 'submissive'. She consents to sadomasochistic sex, tied to a bed frame in a cycle of punishment, defecation and beatings which, as in the Sadeian brothel, 'grew more vicious by almost imperceptible degrees' (p. 28). Sarah Gamble (2006b) draws attention to the passage in *Love* in which Annabel 'comes to use sex and masochism as weapons in a relationship in which only voluntary subjugation gains her a warped sense of dominance' (p. 59). In a game of chess, she hits Lee to engineer a response which in turn results in her being forced to kneel, her wrists tied with his belt, and take a beating. But her concluding remark that this will teach *him* to take her queen, subverts the whole dominant–submissive scenario.

In *The Sadeian Woman*, Sade is not represented as depicting sadomasochism as it might be practised by men and women in 'real' life. This, to follow Carter's thesis, is partly because of his negative representation of all things sexual: 'Sade has a curious ability to render every aspect of sexuality suspect, so that we see how the chaste kiss of the sentimental lover differs only in degree from the vampirish love-bite...' (p. 25). At one level, it is possible to argue, as Carter does, that Sade freed female sexuality from its inevitable association with reproduction. But he presents sadomasochism in accord with cultural misogynistic archetypes or stereotypes that reflect wider socially determined anxieties about sadomasochistic sex.

Sarah Gamble (2006b) maintains that, at one level, in Carter's work, pornography is a 'red herring': 'The real locus of her interest...is the attempt to depict reality accurately and unflinchingly through whatever means necessary, no matter how unconventional or controversial' (p. 60). Leilah is a more complex character than might appear in the kind of pornography Carter writes about in *The Sadeian Woman*. Her readiness to be tied to the bed and beaten is redolent of Justine in *The Sadeian Woman*, but her six-inch shoe heels are more a signifier of Juliette than of Justine. Pitchford (2002) argues that desire 'must be artificially produced, or induced, by means of representation' (p. 173). From the outset, Leilah is perceived through the signs and tropes associated with her – the unbuttoned blouse, the painted nipples, the stockings, high heels and fur coat – which are also associated with pornography and, furthermore, appear to signal her availability for sex. Evelyn perceives her as a woman excited by his following her because she sensed the possibility of rape and really wanted to be 'taken'. But, as Leilah also represents the dangerous woman, one of the stereotypes of sadomasochistic fantasy, as mentioned above, Evelyn's attraction to her is a combination of passion and fear: 'from one hand swung her shoes, that would have made a painful weapon'; her garters are a fetish object but also a means by which Evelyn fears she could strangle him; and her finger nails are 'enamelled blades' (pp. 24–25). Leilah, in this sadomasochistic context, anticipates what post-feminists, like Sarah Projanksy (2001), see as women engaging in sexual, bodily behaviour that 'plays' with the male gaze:

> This celebration of women's play with the heterosexual male gaze – their invitation of the gaze and their own fascination with and attention to the object of that gaze (their own bodies) – not only intensifies heterosexuality within the postfeminism depicted in the popular press, but it also ensures a place for femininity in postfeminism. (p. 80)

Consensual sadomasochistic sex or 'play' offers a wider variety of options than the stereotypes. It is also about 'deconstructing' the subject through new, challenging situations, acknowledging how identity, as Pitchford (2002) says, 'can change because each identity participates in multiple discourses' (p. 178). Always at the shoulder of Carter's critique of Sadeian pornography, and the 'pornographic writing' to which the critique gives rise, is a vista of multiple identities played out in multiple contexts but all based in the same body.

Henstra's (1999) argument, mentioned earlier, that, in *The Sadeian Woman*, Carter explores both the dominant and the submissive roles within sadomasochism with equal sympathy for each, highlights how Carter's writing on sexuality often defies singular readings. Merja Makinen takes Patricia Duncker to task, for example, for simplistically reading *The Bloody Chamber and Other Stories* (1979) as 'all men are beasts to women' and for seeing 'the female protagonists as inevitably enacting the roles of victims of male violence' (p. 12). Makinen finds in Carter's work what she calls 'the decolonization of feminine sexuality' in which Carter suggests the need to break away from the 'sadist or masochist, fuck or be fucked, victim or aggressor binarism' and, as Makinen says, argues 'for a wider incorporation of female sexuality ... that it too contains a whole gamut of "perversions" alongside "normal" sex' (ibid.).

THE 'PLAY' AND THE 'PASSION'

The Passion of New Eve shares with the films of Federico Fellini, which Carter much admired, an interest in how 'role-playing, vision, projection, and make-believe' are among the ways in which women can escape beyond themselves (Burke, 1987, p. 72). *The Passion of*

New Eve takes us into a world which is closer to Hoffman's than the Minister's. As the Czech who lives in the apartment above Evelyn observes, 'The age of reason is over' (p. 13). This is a world where, as in Hoffman's, the mass media controls desire; which aspires, as Evelyn hints at the outset, to establish celluloid in a more perfect 'complicity with the phenomenon of persistence of vision' (p. 5). In this respect, *The Passion of New Eve* pursues and develops an important area of enquiry suggested in the previous novel, in which Desiderio complained: 'The motion picture is usually regarded as only a kind of shadow play and few bother to probe the ontological paradoxes it represents' (p. 102). *The Passion of New Eve* explores the paradoxes inherent in American Hollywood culture and especially the 'absent presence' of what the images deny. In particular, it gives priority to what the peep show proprietor in *The Infernal Desire Machines of Doctor Hoffman* describes as 'persistence of vision' (p. 109). If pornography, as defined in *The Sadeian Woman*, fails to provide readers with 'tension' and 'the unexpected', as mentioned earlier, *The Passion of New Eve* refuses to provide the reader with a 'persistence of vision'. This lack of persistence of vision is one of the textual strategies by which Carter, as I have argued, disrupts the dominant submissive binarism and develops what Henstra (1999) has a called a performative, contrapuntal reading of sadomasochism.

In key respects, Tristessa recalls Lazzari in Federico Fellini's *The Nights of Cabiria*, not least through the way in which the latter lives, as Burke (1987) says, 'in a highly visualised world' evident in 'the multimirrored, glassed, and imaged world of his villa' (72). Like Cabiria, 'transported by Lazzari's appearance', Evelyn/Eve projects onto Tristessa, as Burke says of Cabiria, 'her dreams of romantic fulfilment' (73). Although they are surrounded by visual objects, Tristessa and Lazzari are 'ruled by things unseen, whose presence is wholly mental' (ibid.). In Fellini's film *The Nights of Cabiria*, as Burke (1987) says, 'Lazzari appears at a point when Cabiria has taken to play-acting' (ibid.). In Carter's novel, Tristessa appears when Evelyn is learning the relationship between femininity and role play. Cabiria, in Burke's words, 'adapts admirably, becoming a suitable and refreshing companion for Lazzari' (p. 72). For a while, this is true also of Evelyn and Tristessa.

Initially, long before Evelyn becomes Eve and before Evelyn's discovery that Tristessa is a transvestite, Tristessa is the archetypal object of heterosexual male desire. In this regard, the novel disrupts the complicity between 'viewer' and 'viewed' in several ways. First, whilst watching Tristessa on the screen, Evelyn is 'pleasured' by a young woman, 'Catherine Earnshaw', whom he takes with him to see the film. Her willingness to be submissive in 'sucking him off' makes him think of his sadistic Nanny, from whom he believes he has inherited 'his ambivalent attitude towards women' (p. 9). In other words, the kind of pleasure which the movie is supposed to offer the viewer is interrupted, for Evelyn, by pleasure from what is happening to him in the cinema itself. However, there are further layers of interruption. The pleasure derived from Catherine is a blurring of the pleasure of 'real' sex with a celluloid fetishistic image of Woman. Moreover, the young woman's name is not 'Catherine Earnshaw'. Drawing on Emily Bronte's *Wuthering Heights*, Evelyn only calls her that because he cannot remember her true name. But one of the most important complications in this episode is that Tristessa is a man who enjoys dressing as a woman. One of the salient tropes in *The Passion of New Eve* is that there is no event which has, as in pornography, a singular interpretation, for characters within the text or for the reader. Not only gender identities but identities in general are invariably deceptions.

Throughout *The Passion of New Eve*, symbols are inevitably inadequate and often paradoxical. The disruption of the spectacle of Evelyn viewing Tristessa mirrors the gap, discussed above, between 'real' sadomasochism, which is purely about inflicting pain on others, and the fantasy of sadomasochism that becomes embroiled with the infliction of real pain and which developed, according to *The Sadeian Woman*, out of Sade's work. Therefore, at times, *The Passion of New Eve* suggests that sadomasochistic 'fantasy' and 'real' torture are connected, even implying that one leads to the other. Evelyn fantasises about meeting Tristessa tied stark naked to a tree. But then the narrative questions the boundary between this and what the Gestapo did to Baroslav and his wife. The Gestapo raped his wife and cut her into pieces while Baroslav, tied to a tree, was forced to watch. The latter is redolent of the kind of spectacle sketched by de Sade into which he believed sexual fantasy inevitably develops. But in this novel, where 'persistence of vision' is regularly disrupted, the issue raised is whether Sade's 'assumption' is a statement rooted in 'reality' or another of the mythologies by which even consensual, sadomasochistic sexual play itself is rendered disturbing and frightening. The Gestapo violence hovers at the edges of Evelyn's fantasy of Tristessa tied to a tree. It parallels the way in which his fears of being strangled by Leilah's garters or killed by one of her shoe's six-inch spikes, suggesting some kind of female revenge for symbolic castration, hovered at the margins of their first sex together.

The Sadeian Woman is not 'outside' Carter's fiction; her fiction and this essay are integral parts of the same 'project', which interweaves *The Infernal Desire Machines of Doctor Hoffman*, *The Passion of the New Eve* and *The Sadeian Woman* in an exploration of intense sexual passion where the boundaries between sexuality and violence become blurred. Recalling the scene in the tenement doorway in *The Passion of New Eve*, when he forces himself upon Leilah, Evelyn's explanation for his behaviour is that his passion was so intense as to be uncontrollable. Here, Evelyn thinks of his own sexual drive as a kind of demonic possession, which is how *The Sadeian Woman* depicts the libertines in Sade's final extravaganza, the 'hell-game'. However, unlike in her earlier novels, Carter is not interested simply in 'interrupting' conventional thinking about how violence and sexuality are linked, but in the interruption of desire itself.

What most interrupts desire in *The Passion of New Eve* is the complex and somewhat elusive link between the 'body' and identity as a 'performance', which is explored through Leilah's 'performance' on the street and in the clubs, Tristessa's transvestism and Evelyn's enforced sex change. Thus, the way in which Leilah 'seemed to come and go in her body, fretful, wilful, she a visitor in her own flesh' and the 'duplicity [that] gleamed in her eyes' 'disrupt' Evelyn's sex with her (p. 27). But, most complex of all, and most disruptive of the binarisms and archetypes of 'traditional' pornography, is the sex that Evelyn, the involuntary transsexual, has with Tristessa, the voluntary transvestite: 'Masculine and feminine are correlatives which involve one another. I am sure of that – the quality and its negation are locked in necessity' (p. 149). This is the kind of episode, if we follow Carter's critique of pornography in *The Sadeian Woman* to its logical, or rather fantasy, conclusion, that would not be found in pornography.

POST-FEMINISM, FREUD AND IRONY

Although, at the beginning of *The Passion of New Eve*, Evelyn enjoys watching Leilah dress in the mirror, he does not seem to notice the grotesquely erotic nature of her make-up and what she chooses to wear. As a dancer and as the stereotypical predatory, female 'sexual vampire', she subverts the traditional opposition between male spectator and predator and female spectacle and victim. As discussed above, Leilah, as model and naked, erotic dancer, is literally a performer. As such, she assumes a degree of agency over her own subject position as 'colonised' woman. This is evidenced in the extent to which her masquerade is an engagement with the elision of eroticism and exoticism:

> The finicking care she used to give to the creation of this edifice! Applying the rouge to her nether lips and the purple or peony or scarlet grease to her mouth and nipples; powders and unguents all the colours of the rainbow went on to the skin in the sockets of her eyes; with the manual dexterity of an assembler of precision instruments, she glued on the fringe of false eyelashes. The topiary of her hair she would sometimes thread with beads or dust with glinting bronze powder she also applied to her pubic mound. Then she sprayed herself with dark perfumes that enhanced rather than concealed the lingering odour of sexuality that was her own perfume. (p. 29)

For the reader, positioned outside the frame of Evelyn's narrative, which takes for granted the objectification, eroticisation and exoticisation of women, the artificial nature of what Leilah has constructed is difficult to miss. Indeed, some of the language – 'grease', 'glued', 'sprayed', 'sockets' – is as applicable to a factory body-shop as to a human body. Moreover, Leilah is seen as 'an assembler of precision instruments' and the selection of words which cross the boundary between the human and the inhuman is particularly pertinent. Leilah's make-up gives her a metallic quality, evidenced in the words 'sprayed' and 'glinting bronze'. The feminine within the masculine imaginary is exposed here as grotesque. Unlike the reader, alert to the artificiality of what is being presented here, Evelyn elides the constructed Woman with women. Mendoza claimed in *The Infernal Desire Machines of Doctor Hoffman*: 'If a thing were sufficiently artificial, it became absolutely equivalent to the genuine' (p. 102). The account of Leilah as a dancer sets up a dynamic between Leilah as signifier, in control of her own narrative as it were, and Woman as signified, the object in others' narratives. In male-centred culture, women are signified as, for example, wife, mother, whore, 'bird', slapper, more than they are allowed to be 'signifiers'.

Both *The Infernal Desire Machines of Doctor Hoffman* and *The Passion of New Eve* emphasise the mutability of identity. Desiderio and Evelyn/Eve are brought to knowledge through intense, sadistic pain. Both Albertina, an androgynous, shadowy and vague presence throughout *The Infernal Desire Machines of Doctor Hoffman* and Leilah, reborn as Lilith, Adam's first and unacknowledged wife, undergo metamorphosis into guerrilla leaders. Whereas Desiderio is disturbed by this projection of Albertina, Eve recognises the importance of Leilah's transformation from what (s)he perceived as whore/victim.

When Tristessa is captured by Zero, the harem women try to make him aware of the 'maleness' which he has never been able to accept as part of himself. They perform obscene naked dances, 'contemptuously flourishing their fringed holes at him', a parodic inversion of Evelyn's inspection of Leilah's vagina at the beginning of the novel, and 'brandishing mocking buttocks' (p. 128). They show Tristessa a false, carnivalesque version of the masculinity from which he has tried to separate himself. It is a version forged, as the phrase 'their fringed holes' suggests, in peep shows and pornography.

Although *The Passion of New Eve* may be a rewriting of the biblical story of Genesis, its emphasis is upon the consequences of the Garden of Eden story rather upon the original narrative as such. Some of the narratives of twentieth-century psychoanalysis are imbricated in the gender myths and stereotypes that have their origins in the biblical narrative where woman, as inferior to man, is created out of a bone from the man's ribcage and becomes a sexual temptress. Evelyn's accounts of his relationship with Leilah in the early part of the novel clearly depict Leilah in Freudian terms. According to Freud, the child is fused with the mother in what he calls the pre-Oedipal stage, but it is in the Oedipal stage, in which the child identifies or fails to identify anatomically with the father, that the child acquires gender identity. This is the process by which, according to Freud, the female accepts her 'castration' and a sense of 'lack' because she is unable to identify fully with the father and by which the male child, identifying with the father, fears castration. So the female in Freudian psychoanalysis is defined, as Evelyn initially defines Leilah, by an absence or sense of lack.

The initial relationship between Evelyn and Leilah may also be alluding to the ideas of the French psychoanalytic philosopher, Jacques Lacan, who drew on Freud's theories. For Lacan, and mid-twentieth-century French psychoanalytic theory more generally, what is important is the child's entry into language, the 'symbolic'. In the 'Symbolic Order', as the symbolic structure of language and meaning is referred to in European linguistics, the male child sees himself reflected in its 'phallocentricity', or male centricity, while the female finds herself rendered invisible or oppressed. The latter may well be suggested by the way in which Leilah, the female, is tied down by Evelyn, the male. So the episode in which Leilah is tied to the bed and beaten might be read as a description of sado-masochistic sex or as the way in which the Symbolic Order represses female experience. Significantly, Leilah's feet are free so that she can still kick. Within this allegorical reading, the fact that Leilah can still kick suggests that, in any language system in which the female is repressed by male discourse, she has the potential to subvert or overthrow it. This reading would, of course, align itself with the undisguised symbolic civil war which opens the text, in which the Symbolic Order that has dressed women in white boots and mini-skirts as fetish objects is overthrown by what it fetishises. Moreover, Leilah's continued potential to kick out is evident in the way in which her make-up and appearance – high-heeled shoes with ankle straps, mesh stockings – appears to conform to male fetish but, in fact, mimics and mocks it.

As Evelyn watches Leilah dress in front of the mirror in order to dance in theatres and restaurants, he witnesses the emergence of a self from 'the not world' of the mirror. It emerges from behind the world in which Evelyn as a man is used to seeing his desires, preconceptions and sexual views reflected. Watching Leilah dress in order to go to work where she strips for men, Evelyn is cast in a role which is the opposite of the one which is assumed by the men who watch her striptease. The reversal begs the question: is Evelyn interested in and stimulated by Leilah or by the idea of Leilah as erotic, fetish object? In the later novel, *Nights at the Circus*, discussed in Chapter 7, the men who visit Madame Schrek's brothel do not hire the use of the women's bodies, but 'the use of the idea' of them (p. 70).

We normally regard our fantasies as private and unique to our-selves. But are they, as Carter suggests in *Shadow Dance*, socially constructed? Or can they be traced to experiences which have been buried in our subconscious? *The Passion of New Eve* frequently hints at different explanations of the way characters behave, but without necessarily giving them credence. The text teasingly sug-gests, for example, psychoanalytical reasons for Zero's behaviour: that he wishes to humiliate the women by rubbing excrement into their breasts because he may have been humiliated as a child during toilet training. However, Zero's excessively macho behaviour appears to hide homophobia; that his ultimate fear is homosexuality becomes clear when Tristessa is revealed as a man. Indeed, it drives his hatred of Tristessa, whom he believes to be a lesbian who has emasculated him. Ironically, Eve's principal fear, that Zero may suspect that she herself was once a man, leads her to exaggerate her femininity, which, in turn, makes him suspect that she, too, is a lesbian.

One of the key issues for Carter is that the biological differences between men and women are not as important in the construction of gender identities as their elaboration in complex cultural codes which lay down what is appropriate or inappropriate behaviour and physical appearance for each gender. Evelyn's unquestioned assumptions about women's 'lack' are parodied in Beulah, a poetic name for the state of Israel in its future restored condition.

The operation which Mother performs on Evelyn is an elision of a number of male fantasies and anxieties, including a parody of the male fear of castration. Mother behaves in contradictory ways, sadistically ensuring that Evelyn is conscious during the operation, comforting him in a cruelly deep baritone voice, and running her finger up and down the equally cruel phallic knife. There are echoes here of Victorian sadomasochistic pornography in which a male is whipped by a surrogate for his mother. Normally, she would be armed with a rod, which, like Mother's knife, is a symbolic phallus. Within this context, Mother's baritone voice is significant, for in Victorian sadomasochistic pornography, as Steven Marcus (1964) says, references to masculine attributes such as muscular biceps and hairy arms suggested that behind the violent, phallic mother was the father (p. 258). Mother, in *The Passion of New Eve*, is in some respects a development of Mamie Buckskin, who runs the fairground rifle range in *The Infernal Desire Machines of Doctor Hoffman*. She is described as 'a paradox – a fully phallic female with the bosom of a nursing mother and a gun, death-dealing erectile tissue, perpetually at her thigh' (p. 108). In the sadomasochistic sequence in *The Passion of New Eve* between Evelyn and Leilah, the cultural significance assigned to the phallus is debunked in the references to Evelyn's limp cock, his exhaustion and Leilah's greater energy. It is reinforced here by the way in which his genitalia, useless in themselves, are tossed to Sophia. The surgical operation performed by Mother mirrors the linguistic severance performed by the author in the separation of 'lyn' from 'Eve'. In a witty reversal of his earlier patronising regard for Leilah's 'exquisite negative', Eve finds that 'where I remembered my cock was nothing. Only a void, an insistent absence, like a noisy silence' (p. 75). Here, Carter is parodying what she regards in *The Sadeian Woman*, as we have seen, as 'an imaginary fact that pervades the whole of men's attitude towards women' and which 'transforms women from human beings into wounded creatures who were born to bleed' (p. 23). The possibility of a relationship between Evelyn's fetishising of Leilah's clitoris and his violence towards her is an exploration of the argument which surfaces in *The Sadeian Woman*, that the myth of the bleeding wound stimulates the male desire to exercise domination.

The confusion which Evelyn/Eve experiences after the operation is also redolent of Victorian sadomasochistic pornography, in which, as Marcus (1964) says, 'the sexual identity of the figure being beaten is remarkably labile' (p. 259). Indeed, he goes on to point out that the ambiguity of sexual identity seems 'to be part of the pleasure which this fantasy yields' (ibid.). The ambiguity of Evelyn's name is also itself redolent of Victorian sadomasochistic pornography in which naming was often ambiguous.

Ironically, when Mother asks Eve after the operation how he finds himself, he replies: 'I don't find myself at all' (p. 75). At one level, this is because his identity has been so bound up with his physical anatomy. He now finds that he has become his own fantasy! At another level, his problem is that he has seen gender identity in strictly essentialist and binary terms, whereas the novel itself suggests that identities are imaginary and provisional rather than fixed and closed. This is evidenced in the two main characters, as I suggested earlier: Eve, a man trapped as the result of surgery in a female body, and Tristessa, a woman trapped in a man's body masquerading as Woman. Their wedding, in which they are required to assume a conventional subject position as bride and groom, emphasises the 'shadow' or gap, to employ terms from *The Infernal Desire Machines of Doctor Hoffman*, between socially determined subject positions and the more complex lived experiences of the individual. The marriage takes place before a congregation which includes reassembled wax figures such as Jean Harlow and Marilyn Monroe.

Robinson (1991) points out: 'The overall effect of Carter's novels is to drive a wedge between Woman and women, between male-centred metaphysical representations of Woman and the feminine, and women's multiplicitous and heterogeneous self-representations'

(p. 77). *The Passion of New Eve* is typical of Carter's work in that it resists any conventional view of the mother figure. As Ward Jouve (1994) says, in this novel, 'Carter hunted the archetype down to extinction' (p. 157). Jouve, of course, is referring to the end of the novel, in which Eve, initially accompanied by Lilith, engages in a journey back to the source, a parody of mythical journeys to the Underworld. There, Eve finds that 'Mother is a figure of speech, and has retired to a cave beyond consciousness' (p. 184). Carter may have had in mind here Fiedler's (1960) assertion that, in the Age of Reason, 'Satan has become a figure of speech' (p. 128). He argues that the Evil One is evoked by those who no longer believe in him.

The rediscovery of the 'mother' was the linchpin of a great deal of twentieth-century feminist psychoanalytic writing since the 1970s, which focused upon the mother–daughter relationship as an alternative to the emphasis upon the father–son, or even mother–son, relationship in Freudian psychoanalysis. As noted in the discussion of *The Magic Toyshop* in Chapter 4, a line of communication from mother to daughter has been posited as an alternative to male, symbolic communication, which has tended to repress or exclude the female. For many women writers, the presence of the mother figure has served as a muse. However, as Carter's fiction makes clear, the daughter needs both to identify with and to achieve independence from her mother. Against the grain, Carter, as Ward Jouve says, 'never writes from the vantage point of the mother. Always that of the daughter' (p. 160). In her work, she regularly rebuts the mother. That the mother at the end of *The Passion of New Eve* has now become a figure of speech is ambiguous and might suggest Carter's scepticism about the reclamation of the mother, implying also that it is an argument which might trap women in 'motherhood' as distinct from 'mothering'. On the other hand, Carter's daughters always behave in unconventional ways and take on non-stereotypical roles. After managing to escape from Mother's programme before becoming a Virgin Mother produced out of her/himself, Eve is forced to experience a condensed and fantastic version of a woman's life in Zero's harem. In this respect, Eve's observation that '[Zero] was the first man I met when I became a woman' (p. 86) seems an appropriate retribution for the humiliation which, as Evelyn, he heaped on Leilah. Although Mother performs an operation that transforms Evelyn biologically, it is the subsequent experiences which transform Evelyn into Eve. Significantly, Eve is not the agent in what happens to her, which, of course, is the position in which many women find themselves, as Evelyn, as Eve, discovers.

Zero, a one-eyed, one-legged monomaniac, seems to be an exaggerated version of what some women have to endure and may probably be an understatement of what others have to put up with from men. He is physically repulsive and Eve loses her virginity in a parody of the way many men have taken women. But the irony is that Zero is a version of the young Evelyn. He treats the women in his harem in an exaggerated version of the way in which Evelyn treated Leilah. As Eve realises: he 'forced me to know myself as a former violator at the moment of my own violation' (p. 102). I suggested earlier that Zero's fear of lesbianism and the humiliations which he heaps onto his harem may be projections of his fear of an aspect of himself to which he will not admit. In this respect, too, he may be an older version of, and a commentary upon, Evelyn. In tying up Leilah and beating her, Evelyn suggests that he, too, may be afraid of the feminine. Significantly, as we have discussed, when he fantasises about meeting the real Tristessa, he imagines her tied to a tree.

One of the most important distinctions between *The Passion of New Eve* and the novels discussed in the previous chapter is the greater degree of irony with which the focalisation in the novel is presented. Carter's interests in the social processes and the cultural mythologising which determine gender identity, and which turn women into Woman, are pursued in much bolder and more theatrical ways. Whereas realist fiction is written from a perspective through which different issues and widely disparate experiences cohere, *The Passion of New Eve* is overtly concerned with the difficulty of assuming a vantage point from which to write. At the same time, it engages with psychological issues of the 1970s, such as the extent to which gender identity is based on biological difference, the masculinist bias in Freudian psychoanalysis, the dominant submissive binarism in sadomasochistic sexuality and the concept of 'moral pornography', as well as diverse subjects such as separatist feminist movements, actuality as the product of media-generated images, and the ability of Western nations to survive as stable entities.

7

Spectacle, Circus and the Films of Federico Fellini: *Nights at the Circus* (1984)

Nights at the Circus is centred on a Cockney artiste, Fevvers, who, having claimed to have grown wings, has become a famous trapeze artist, a friend of Toulouse-Lautrec and the toast of Europe. At one level, the novel is a ribald, picaresque narrative of her life as a performer in England and Russia at the end of the nineteenth century. Fevvers tells her story to an initially sceptical American reporter, Jack Walser, a wanderer whom Carter, recalling her interest in the work of Herman Melville, describes as a latter-day Ishmael, the narrator of Melville's *Moby Dick*. In the first chapter of Melville's novel, the reader discovers that Ishmael 'is tormented with an everlasting itch for things remote' and that whenever he finds himself 'growing grim about the mouth' he accounts it 'high time to get to sea as soon as possible'. In *Nights at the Circus*, we learn that Walser, too, 'subjected his life to a series of cataclysmic shocks because he loved to hear his bones rattle. That was how he knew he was alive' (p. 10).

Like all of Carter's novels, *Nights at the Circus* is packed with literary and cultural allusions and is indebted to a diverse range of sources. One of the key tropes which scholars have emphasised in relation to this novel is the carnivalesque. But the real subject, as Helen Stoddart (2007) stresses, is the 'overlap between the circus and the carnival/carnivalesque'. She points out that the circus owner Colonel Kearney's name is actually pronounced 'Carny' (p. 115), while Anne Fernihough (1997) argues that the circus 'functions as a debased version of carnival, using all the carnivalesque tropes but showing how, in practice, they can often serve very different ends from the radical utopian ones emphasized by Bakhtin' (cit. Stoddart, ibid.).

THE CARNIVALESQUE

Although Mikhail Bakhtin is only one source for Carter's thinking about the carnivalesque, it is this that has received most attention in Carter scholarship. Carter's interest in carnivalesque demonstrates the concept of 'double allegiance' mentioned in Chapter 1, for, while Carter is clearly indebted to some aspects of Bakhtin's work, she is critical of others as we shall see. Bakhtin's *Rabelais and his World* (1965), placing Rabelais in the cultural context of his milieu, provides an introduction to the carnivalesque in Carter's work. In effect, it is, as Carter appears to recognise in her work, a particular way of looking at European cultural history, or more specifically the transition to modernity in Europe. The book, based on a thesis completed in 1940, applies the term carnivalesque to the varied popular–festive life of the Middle Ages and the Renaissance. Somewhat idealistically, he sees, as Simon Dentith (1995) says, 'the flowering of a gay, affirmative, and militantly anti-authoritarian attitude to life, founded upon a joyful acceptance of the materiality of the body' (p. 66). In this respect, Bakhtin's theory of the carnivalesque bears out Fredric Jameson's thesis, referred to in Chapter 1, that the appearance of the body is a potentially disruptive element of narrative, especially when the larger cultural narratives such as 'Order', 'Civilisation', 'Progress' and 'Destiny' begin to lose their authority. The appeal of the carnivalesque for Bakhtin and Angela Carter is that it valorises the subordinate, the anti-authoritarian and the marginal. Dentith (1995) maintains that carnivalesque writing takes 'the carnival spirit into itself and thus reproduces, within its own structures and by its own practice, the characteristic inversions, parodies and discrownings of carnival proper' (p. 65).

A more important source for the carnival elements in *Nights at the Circus* than Bakhtin, especially when we recognise, as mentioned earlier, that the novel is really concerned with the overlap between carnival and circus, are the films of the Italian director Federico Fellini. Until recently, what has been overlooked in Carter scholarship is the association between twentieth-century interest in the 'carnival' and the political context in which it has developed. Helen Stoddart points out that Mikhail Bakhtin pursued his interest in the carnivalesque in Russia in the 1930s under Stalin. One can see how this context would be of interest to Carter, whose fiction, as we have seen, explores oppressive regimes and social structures. In this regard, there is a parallel to be drawn between Bakhtin's interest in the carnivalesque and Federico Fellini. Fellini pursued his interest in carnival and the circus under 'the humourless and rigid tyranny of Italian fascism' (Fellini, 1976, p. 154).

Carter's use of her source material often involves lifting images and ideas out of their original contexts, as she appears to recognise in them what is unsaid or understated. This is certainly the case in her allegiance to Federico Fellini, whose films, like Carter's later novels, combine spectacle, illusion, carnival, fairy tale and fable. His work includes *La Strada* (1954), in which a young girl from an impoverished family is sold as an assistant to a travelling circus strongman; *Le Notti di Cabiri* (1957), whose chief protagonist is a prostitute, Cabiria Cecarelli; *La Dolce Vita* (1960), mentioned earlier, featuring a journalist attracted to modern society's decadent hedonism; *Satyricon* (1968), a bawdy, erotic fantasy of the last days of Nero's Rome which is also a critique of mid–late-twentieth-century European society; *Roma* (1972), a series of vignettes depicting Fellini's version of the history of the Eternal City; *Amarcord (I Remember)*, concerned with growing up in an Italian village in the 1930s; and a semi–documentary, *I Clowns* (1970). Fellini's films are an important, and largely unrecognised, influence on Carter's middle to late work. Charlotte Crofts (2003) points out that 'Carter's early fiction is saturated with allusion to cinema' (p. 91), but 'in her later work Carter became more interested in mainstream cinema' and her journalism shows 'a scholarly interest in European and world cinema' that includes the films of Richard Round Bertolucci, Peter Greenaway, Jean-Luc Godard and Oshima Nagiska (p. 96). Carter also shared Fellini's interest in sadomasochism, which he linked, as Carter often does in *Nights at the Circus*, with aspects of carnival.

Carter never wrote a novelistic equivalent of, or even a concerted response to, a Fellini film. But in *Nights at the Circus* and *Passion of New Eve*, as we have seen, there are examples of characters, images and ideas that have been borrowed and 'retextualised'. Fellini (1976) himself provides insights into the process: 'Sometimes, at a distance of years, fragments from scenes loom up from nowhere, views of streets, expressions on faces, things said in silence, an indecipherable glance from some character...' (p. 138). What informs Carter's magpie borrowing of material from Fellini, as from many of her other sources, is an engagement with an image, an insight, and frequently the ideology(ies) embedded in or suggested by the original source.

In many respects, *Nights at the Circus* has absorbed the 'carnival spirit'. The novel is packed with inversions, parodies and 'discrownings'. At one level, the circus in the novel *is* a symbol of the hierarchical and patriarchal society which carnival mocks and mimics with its hierarchy of male performers, pursuit of profit and oppression of subordinates.

The male protagonists impose on Fevvers, as Palmer (1987) says, stereotypical interpretations of femininity invented by a patriarchal culture, such as 'Angel of death', 'queen of ambiguities', 'spectacle' and 'freak' (p. 199). However, the circus is also the focus for an alternative carnivalesque, which, like the popular fairs to which Bakhtin refers, demystifies and debunks the established social hierarchy, including its own.

Lorna Sage (1994b) has suggested that *Nights at the Circus* develops the carnival aspect of Carter's earlier novel, *Several Perceptions* (p. 17). Indeed, several specific details in the later novel recall the earlier work. Madame Schreck's manservant Toussaint is lifted from *Several Perceptions*, in which he is the friend of the prostitute, Mrs Boulder (p. 132). Mrs Boulder herself is the source for some of the motifs developed in *Nights at the Circus*, for she is the daughter of a fairground fortune-teller who called herself Madame Sophia. However, the experience of creating Mamie Buckskin, the fairground rifle-range proprietor in *The Infernal Desire Machines of Doctor Hoffman*, with 'death-dealing erectile tissue' always at her thigh, may also have helped her towards the creation of Fevvers in *Nights at the Circus*.

While the carnival of the circus debunks social hierarchy, it is never completely overthrown. Indeed, several critics, and Carter herself, have expressed reservations about Bakhtin's notion of the carnivalesque. Gąsiorek (1995) points out that critics of carnival have maintained:

> that it is often conceived in an essentialising way, as innately oppositional and subversive; that it relies on a nostalgic notion of 'real community'; that it often reinforces existing power structures because it is a licensed form of release from social restraint; and that its transformations take place within certain kinds of discourse but are unable to challenge the hierarchy of discourses, which comfortably contains their apparent subversiveness. (p. 134)

Judith Mayne (1987) also argues:

> [the] assumption that the mode of carnival is by very definition radical, posited from outside the dominant order rather than from within it. ... obscures the extent to which the carnival may exist as

a safety valve, as a controlled eruption that guarantees the maintenance of the existing order. (p. 40)

The reservations which Carter herself expresses, in an interview with Lorna Sage in 1992, are similar to those voiced by Mayne:

> It's interesting that Bakhtin became very fashionable in the 1980s, during the demise of the particular kind of theory that would have put all kinds of questions around the whole idea of the carnivalesque. ... The carnival has to stop. The whole point of the feast of fools is that things went on as they did before, after it stopped. (Sage, 1992, p. 188)

Carter's reservations are evident in the way in which *Nights at the Circus*, through a woman-centred perspective, challenges some of the key features of the carnivalesque itself. As Palmer (1987) points out, 'the beatings and thrashings associated with carnivalistic mirth' are used to 'represent the violence which is rife in a male-dominated culture' (p. 198). This is evident in the circus, at one level a debased carnival, in the clowns' brutal slapstick and the ape-man's beating of his woman friend, in a phrase which recalls Jewel's whipping of his brother in *Heroes and Villains*, 'as though she were a carpet' (p. 115) – that is to say, she is literally reduced to, and treated as, an object.

THE CIRCUS AESTHETIC

Stoddart and Fernihough suggest that *Nights at the Circus* is not simply an exploration of the carnivalesque; it is concerned with the relationship between 'circus' and 'carnival'. This is a dimension of the novel that has received less attention in Carter scholarship than one would expect. Stoddart (2007) has pointed out that the tripartite structure of *Nights at the Circus* 'mimics the classic three-act play' (p. 1). But, additionally, it mirrors the Victorian spectacular, which, like 'The Storming and Capture of Delhi!', mounted by Astley's circus in 1857, often consisted of three parts. Other spectaculars, such as Astley's 'The Bombardment and Capture of Canton' (1858), consisted of a mixture of scenes which transformed exotic places into 'knowable and tangible' locations (Assael, 2005, pp. 75–76). In Carter's novel the alien and alienating world of the circus is transformed into scenes which for the reader are 'knowable and tangible'.

The overlap between carnival and the circus, and not simply carnival *per se*, is at the heart of *Nights at the Circus*, as we have said. Indeed, it is not simply a celebration of the carnivalesque but a more sombre, even darker, piece of investigation. Fellini is an important influence upon this aspect of the novel, particularly in his semi documentary *I Clowns* (1970), in which he describes the circus aesthetic in contradictory terms: 'the smell of sawdust, and of wild animals, the mysterious gloom up there under the dome of the big top, the heart-rendering music, the sense of play and at the same time of an execution, of holiday and butchery, of grace and madness, all of which makes up the circus' (Fellini, 1976, p. 139). Since Carter argued that 'the carnival has to stop. The whole point of the feast of fools is that things went on as they did before, after it stopped', she was unlikely to sustain a celebration of carnival. Not surprisingly, *Nights at the Circus* is much closer to Fellini than to Bakhtin, in that it is concerned with circus as a matrix of paradoxical cultural symbols which mirror the contradiction at the heart of carnival, but offers the author much more in terms of tropes and issues.

The chapter in Carter's novel devoted to clowns in the Petersburg section of the book, to which I shall turn later in this chapter, betrays the influence of a number of Fellini films. In addition to *I Clowns*, it is indebted to '*Le Notti di Cabiria*' ['*Nights of Cabiria*'] (1957). *Nights of Cabiria*, which may well have inspired the title of the novel, is about a prostitute, Cabiria Cecarelli, whose combination of feistiness and naivety anticipates Carter's central protagonist Fevvers, who, like Cabiria, but in a different way and for longer, manages to escape prostitution. Fellini, who shared Carter's lifelong interest in the circus as a cultural phenomenon, undoubtedly influenced the way in which the clowns in the novel signify the combination of the spectacle, illusion and deception of the circus itself. The influence of this film can also be felt in the way both texts interweave past glory with present decay and degradation.

Given Carter's interest in Fellini, one of the sources for Carter's Fevvers as the Winged Victory is likely to have been Fellini's *Amarcord* ['I Remember'], a work which, like *Nights at the Circus*, interleaves popular, carnivalesque and serious culture and recalls, as many of his films of this period do, features of the circus: the busty woman who runs a tobacconist's displays remarkable strength like the circus Strongman; the motorcyclists are the circus acrobatics; the men trying to climb ladders to rescue the mad uncle who, on a day out from the asylum, escapes up a tree indulge in slapstick comedy reminiscent of circus clowns; and the circus clown is recalled by the uncle himself, who produces odd objects like stones and eggs from his pocket. The strongest links between the film and *Nights at the Circus* are those that recall Fevvers. The uncle's musing about the perfection of an egg anticipates the role that the image of the egg has in Carter's novel, in which Fevvers is supposedly hatched from an egg. But the strongest connection between Fellini's film and Carter's novel is the image of the Winged Victory. In Fellini's film, the villagers gather every evening at the statue of the Winged Victory, which commemorates the war heroes, and near the end of the film a snowball fight is interrupted by a large peacock which lands on the statue. Spreading its feathers in a great display of colour, it recalls Fevvers in the early part of *Nights at the Circus*:

> Look at me! With a grand, proud, ironic grace, she exhibited herself before the eyes of the audience as if it were a marvellous present too good to be played with. Look, not touch.
>
> She was twice as large as life and as succinctly finite as any object that is intended to be seen, not handled. Look! Hands off!
>
> LOOK AT ME!
>
> She rose up on tiptoe and slowly twirled round, giving the spectators a comprehensive view of her back: seeing is believing. Then she spread out her superb, heavy arms in a backwards gesture of benediction and, as she did so, her wings spread, too, a polychromatic unfolding fully six feet across. (p. 15)

Prostitution enters into both *Nights at the Circus* and *The Nights of Cabiria*. In both works, prostitution does not simply represent the commodification of the female but is an example of how the female body is a signifier of male, bourgeois illusions. In this respect, the female body is more 'signified' than 'signifier', and it is with this awareness that the awakening of self-consciousness begins. Both Carter's Fevvers and Fellini's Cabiria, as Burke (1987) says of the latter, express their self-consciousness 'in largely physical terms, as she uses her body to create poses and strike attitudes to impress the world. Seeing herself as a body, she sees herself as separate from everyone else' (pp. 71–72). In Carter's novel, Fevvers, a former prostitute, is billed as the 'Cockney Venus', a point to which I will return later; in Fellini's *Amarcord*, a recurring figure is a young woman, Venus, advertising her apparent availability to men on the street and next to a building site. In her study of the Victorian circus, Brenda Assael (2005) points out: 'the performances of female acrobats were controversial not only because of the danger involved but also because of their perceived lewdness', arising in part from tight-fitting bodices, scanty truck hoses, arms cased in fleshings and legs as good as bare to the hip (p. 115).

Stoddart (2000) points out that the circus 'promotes the idea of itself in the popular imagination as embodying a lifestyle unfettered by conventionality or by social restraint', but 'behind this image lie levels of physical discipline, bodily regulation and hardship which are unrivalled by any other western performance art' (p. 175). The acrobat and the clown are a reflection of what Stoddart describes as the paradoxical circus self-image (ibid.). Assael (2005) maintains: 'the acrobat's success depended upon the performer's negotiating various aesthetic codes that were sometimes in conflict'. The tension is the product of 'the public's approval of her "ladylike" athletic exhibitions, on the one hand, and the controversy surrounding her sexually provocative poses and costumes, on the other' (p. 126). This problematic Victorian and early-twentieth-century connection between female acrobats and provocative sexuality was confirmed by the scandal in their own life stories, in which the media and the public took considerable interest. Rennert (1975) reminds us: 'Millions of circus fans the world over followed the torrid romance between the leading woman aerialist of the time, petite Lillian Leitzel, and the leading trapeze artist Alfreda Codona' (p. 11).

Thus, the emphasis upon carnival *per se* in Carter scholarship has resulted in the novel's relation to circus history being overlooked. Of the many subjects and issues that had pride of place in Victorian thinking and debates about the 'circus', none was more important than the way in which the controversy surrounding the female circus acrobat 'made her task of aesthetic negotiation inherently problematic and complex' (p. 126). Whilst Fevvers has been associated with carnival, she is revealed as a much more complex figure when aligned with 'real life' circus acrobats from the Victorian period and the early twentieth century. Influenced by the Winged Victory in Fellini's *Amarcord*, as suggested earlier, Fevvers has a strong symbolic presence. Like Fellini's pheasant, which settles on and becomes part of the Winged Victory war memorial, circus trapeze artists, in Stoddart's words, 'demonstrate human transcendence in the natural world (over animals) and the natural elements (defying gravity and fire), over machinery (wires, bicycles and cannons) and over the possibility of death' (p. 166). But Fevvers becomes more aesthetically and culturally complex when placed in the occluded history of the female circus performer. Stoddart (2000) points out that the first woman flying trapeze artist is usually perceived as Mlle Azella, who performed her act in Holborn in 1868 (p. 171). But Fevvers, who began her trapeze act in the Cirque d'Hiver in Paris and then signed up to travel with the 'Imperial Circus', has affinities with those who followed her, such as the celebrated Lillian Leitzel and Princess Victoria. Leitzel, 'much below medium height, with shoulders abnormally developed by years of gruelling exercise', had an act during which she clung 'by one wrist to a loop on a rope and threw her short body end-over-end for fifty, seventy, a hundred times' (Rennert, 1975, p. 11). Princess Victoria in 1920 was billed as 'the most beautiful and sensational high wire act ever presented' and as 'La belle Victoria on the High Wire' (Rennert, 1975, p. 12). Stoddart (2000) maintains: 'By mid nineteenth century metaphors of flight became attached more exclusively to equilibrists and trapeze artists than equestrians as the former replaced the latter as the sensational focus of the circus' (p. 169). It is against the background of Victorian and early-twentieth-century circus history that Fevvers stands as a complex manifestation of a complicated novel. Indeed, it is within this context that Carter's interest in Fevvers becomes clear. Stoddart (2000) points out that 'the gender and sexuality of the aerialist have frequently been conceived in ambiguous and at times quite contradictory terms', which links Fevvers to Carter's recurring blurring of gender distinctions. She argues: 'So not only were these performers sexually transgressive in terms of the nineteenth-century public stage since they construct a spectacle out of the semi-naked female body, but also because aerial acts provided a stage on which, far from any concessions being made to women's lesser strength, they performed the same moves in the same way as men.' (p. 175)

The clown, more so than even the female acrobat, embodies the paradox at the centre of the circus. Ostensibly, the clown would appear to be a carnivalesque figure. Fellini (1976) admits that:

The clown is the incarnation of a fantastic creature who expresses the irrational aspect of man; he stands for the instinct, for whatever is rebellious in each one of us and whatever stands up to the established order of things. He is the caricature of man's childish and animal aspects, the mocker and the mocked. The clown is a mirror in which man sees himself in a grotesque, deformed, ridiculous image. He is man's shadow. (p. 123)

On the basis of this passage, it would be possible to argue that for Fellini the clown is the circus equivalent of the carnival fool. However, it is important to notice that the clown in Fellini's eyes is not the 'embodiment' of 'man's childish and animal aspects' but the 'caricature' of them. Not surprisingly, given this point, this passage is not Fellini's only word on the subject. For Fellini (1976) there is not only ribaldry and mockery in the circus but, as embodied by the trapeze artist, 'technique, precision and improvisation' (p. 98). In identifying different types of clowns, as I shall discuss later, Fellini complicates the whole question of the clown as carnival, as indeed does Carter. They approach the clown in terms of the dilemma, originating in Victorian thinking about the circus. Assael (2005) explains that the clown, like the acrobat, was 'engaged in a symbolic play arising from the opposing aesthetic impulses on the part of the public that stemmed from community standards, on the one hand, and human interest and desire, on the other' (p. 126). What Carter focuses upon, even more than Fellini, is the circus in relation to 'human interest and desire'. In some respects, *Nights at the Circus* develops Carter's interest in 'pornographic reading' in *The Sadeian Woman*. Her interest and scholarship in the circus would have inspired this approach for, as Assael says, 'taken together, beauty, flirtation, the thrill, and the strong female body produced complex responses on the part of the viewer' (p. 109). At the heart of the novel is not simply Fevvers but different readings of Fevvers, as of the circus itself. Among these different readings is the Victorian pornographic reading of the circus as sexual Other, which, as Assael maintains, stressed 'flirtation' and 'perceived lewdness' and was thought to be evident also in what were regarded as 'indecent posters' advertising various circuses (p. 122). What interests Carter, though, more than Fellini is, to employ Assael's language, the 'problematic and complex' aesthetic negotiation at the heart of the circus. This interest overlaps with her interest, shown in *The Sadeian Woman* and *The Passion of New Eve*, in the complex aesthetic negotiation involved, from the reader's point of view, in different types of pornography.

Thus, *Nights at the Circus* stands more fully revealed in relation to the circus than to the carnival *per se*. In this regard, it is important to remember that the circus, as Stoddart (2000) has pointed out, has a particular aesthetic as a 'site of physical danger, sexual excitement and comedy' and as 'a site of myth, fantasy, symbol'. It is associated with a danger which is 'spectacular and inspiring rather than vital in itself' (p. 188). Of course, the circus, and Fellini's view of the circus, excites Carter much more than does 'pornography' in *The Sadeian Woman*. It has the 'unexpected', which Carter argues was lacking in what she conceived as traditional pornography. Fellini (1976) in his essay 'Why Clowns?' declares that circus 'has its own dimensions, its own authentic atmosphere which cannot be put away in mothballs...has gathered together within itself, in an exemplary way, certain lasting myths: adventure, travel, risk, danger, speed, stepping into the lime- light' (pp. 121–122). In their shared interest in this aspect of the circus, both Carter and Fellini return, sometimes quite subtly, to what circus and pornography may be said to have in common. Fellini suggests 'there is the more mortifying aspect of [circus] which keeps recurring, the fact that people come to see you and you must exhibit yourself...' (p. 122). The use of the word 'exhibit' is very significant here.

Carter's interest in the circus, as a devotee and a scholar, is evident also in the fact that Colonel Kearney is manager of the 'Imperial Circus'. Whilst scholarship has tended to stress the carnivalesque, it has overlooked an important dimension of the circus in terms of colonial discourse. Assael (2005) points out: 'When the circus shifted from the fair to the tent or the amphitheatre, the acts became more elaborate and ornamental, a change that coincided with Britain's transition from colonial authority to imperial power in the second half of the century' (p. 75). In its animal taming acts, the circus became a site of 'the tensions evident in colonial discourse between the ideas of combating barbarism and teaching civility' (p. 69). Cooke's circus in Glasgow, Assael says, 'went so far as to boast that the tamer worked "miracles", drawing important parallels with missionary work' (p. 68). The imperial and colonial aspects of the Victorian circus, as Carter suggests in the novel, were inseparable from the Victorian pornographic reading of the circus as sexual Other. Together, they reflect how the British empire was not only an economic but a sexual project and how within that project sex was embroiled with control, domination and violence.

SPECTACLE AND DESUBJECTIVISATION

Nights at the Circus is set in 'the fag-end, the smouldering cigar-butt, of a nineteenth century which is just about to be ground out in the ashtray of history' (p. 11). It is concerned with cusps. Not only is the novel located at the peak of the nineteenth century but Fevvers is at the peak of her career. But 'cusp' is also the point where two lines of the curve meet. Fevvers, apparently a winged lady, is at the cusp of two physical existences – woman and bird – as well as of reality and illusion, the genuine and the fake.

When we first meet her, Fevvers is signed up with a circus run by Colonel Kearney, a cigar-chewing, bourbon-swilling cliché from Kentucky. The circus provides Carter with a vehicle to explore the interrelationship between fact, fantasy and fiction that Fevvers represents. Although the circus has a history, it is a history which is itself outside 'History', and the same is true of Fevvers herself as a circus aerialist:

> 'Lor' love you, sir!' Fevvers sang out in a voice that clanged like dustbin lids. 'As to my place of birth, why, I first saw the light of day right here in smoky old London, didn't I! Not billed the "Cockney Venus", for nothing sir, though they could just as well 'ave called me "Helen of the Hire Wire", due to the unusual circumstances in which I come ashore – for I never docked via what you might call the *normal channels*, sir, oh, dear me, no; but, just like Helen of Troy, was *hatched*. (p. 7)

Fevvers, like the circus itself, is a combination of 'real' circumstance (smoky old London), self-invention and fantasy (the "Cockney Venus") and spectacle ("Helen of the Hire Wire"). At one level, the circus has not changed since its distant Roman origins when the people came to see the spectacle of chariot racing and exotic wild animals. Nineteenth-century audiences came to see what was risky and dangerous but also what, like Fevvers as the 'bird woman', challenged their understanding of the laws of Nature, the boundaries between the human and non-human and their sense of limits. Stoddart (2000) reminds us that 'the capacity of the human body to perform beyond its normal or even imagined limitations in forms which are entertaining, astonishing and beautiful has always constituted the very core of the circus' (p. 166).

The circus audience temporarily enter a world of spectacle and, when the show is over, they return to a more humdrum reality. But, during the circus, they become caught up in a sequence of spectacles, orchestrated by a 'ringmaster', as paradoxically participant and outsider. For the audience, the return to 'normality' is essential because, although the circus is an exciting experience, it is designed to 'undo' the subject. The audiences attend the circus, to adapt Walser's view of himself, because they want to experience a 'series of cataclysmic shocks' and because they want to hear their bones rattle.

Nights at the Circus is a novel that, like the circus itself, is very much about rattling bones. In effect, Carter keeps the reader 'at the circus' throughout the whole span of the novel, which reproduces the experience of circus spectacle. In fantasy, Laplanche and Pontalis (1986) point out, 'the subject, although always present in the fantasy, may be so in a desubjectivised form, that is to say, in the very syntax of the sequence in question' (p. 26). At its heart, *Nights at the Circus* provides the reader with a 'desubjectivising' experience. Its picaresque, serial narrative, composed of even more events than in Carter's previous novels, includes a great clown's lapse into madness; the defection of Monsieur Lamarck's Educated Apes; and the derailment of the train in a wilderness by a whirlwind. The inventiveness of these events are supplemented by further equally bizarre stories, such as the girl who imitated the dead brought from the grave by the tears of loved ones; the House of Correction set up by a murderess; and the Grand Duke who planned to shrink Fevvers to a miniature and imprison her in a Faberge egg.

Indeed, Fevvers's own narrative 'desubjectivises' the listener, and nowhere is this more apparent than in the novel's opening paragraph, where we experience how Fevvers, who for much of the text is presented through the journalist Walser's eyes, wishes to present herself. Walser's physical discomforture while listening to her is evident: 'The young reporter wanted to keep his wits about him so he juggled with glass, notebook and pencil, surreptitiously looking for a place to stow the glass where she could not keep filling it...' (p. 9). It mirrors his and possibly the reader's sense of being in a new position, caught up in an undecipherable matrix of fictions, fantasies and truth. Immediately unsettling are the contradictions within Fevvers's own self-image as the 'Cockney Venus', underscored by the clash between the classical images of unworldly beauty in Venus and Helen, her 'real' origins in 'smoky old London' and her voice that 'clanged like dustbin lids'. Like the nineteenth-century circus freak show as we have said, she defies the normal limits of nature in being not only a woman but a bird and in being 'hatched' rather than 'born'. However, her references to Venus and Helen are also disturbing because they remind us of the extent to which classical worldviews that underpin Western civilisation are dependent upon spectacles. The story of Helen of Troy, based on the rape of Leda by Zeus in the form of a swan, not only mythologises women but turns classical history into a spectacle, or rather a series of spectacles, which, like the sequence of events in the circus and Fevvers's biography itself, 'desubjectivises' the listener. Just how discomforting the myth of Leda and the swan can be is apparent if we recall W. B. Yeats's poem on the subject, which not only renders the rape vividly but implicitly draws parallels between Helen and the Virgin Mary and between the swan intent upon rape and the Holy Spirit.

To what extent Fevvers in the novel is aware of the misogynistic discourses informing some of her self-referencing is a moot point. She calls herself 'bird woman', ironically invoking the term by which twentieth-century men in private and in music and the media referred to women. Twentieth-century women writers, such as the modernist poet H D, have demythologised Helen from a feminist perspective. But Carter, thinking perhaps of the origins of the unusual physical features which constituted the circus 'freak' show, imagines a 'Helen' who inherits some of both Leda's and the swan's characteristics, in this case the feathers across Fevvers's shoulder. This imagining of a woman who is both bird and human is made especially uncomfortable through the allusion to the rape of Leda. It reminds us of rape victims who are made pregnant by their attackers and, especially in the Victorian period, if they gave birth, would have faced a permanent reminder of what had happened in the genes carried for life by the child from both the mother and her rapist.

In *Nights at the Circus*, Carter uses the figure of Fevvers to further explore cultural discourses informed by patriarchal values and viewpoints. Merja Makinen (1992) has drawn a distinction between 'the disquietingly savage analyses of patriarchy' in the novels of the 1960s and 1970s – *The Magic Toyshop, Heroes and Villains* and *The Passion of New Eve* – and the 'exuberant' last two novels, *Nights at the Circus* and *Wise Children*:

> This is not to argue that the latter novels are not also feminist, but their strategy is different. The violence in the events depicted in the earlier novels (the rapes, the physical and mental abuse of women) and the aggression implicit in the representations, are no longer foregrounded. While similar events may occur in these last two texts, the focus is on mocking and exploding the constrictive

cultural stereotypes and in celebrating the sheer ability of the female protagonists to survive, unscathed by the sexist ideologies. (p. 3)

'Exuberant' is certainly an appropriate adjective to describe the last two novels, but, as I suggested in Chapter 1, it can suggest that these texts are less thoughtful and rigorously written than they are. Their narrative voices appear to be a development, as several critics have noticed, of Puss in 'Puss-in-Boots' from the fourth story of *The Bloody Chamber and Other Stories* (1979). There love, sex and desire are demythologised, as Makinen says, 'in a lighthearted *commedia dell' arte* rendition' (p. 11). For Margaret Atwood (1994), too, the 'humour and gusto' of the earlier story anticipates that of the last novel:

['Puss-in-Boots'] is above all a hymn to here-and-now common sensual pleasure, to ordinary human love, to slap-and-tickle delight – not as an object to be won, achieved or stolen, nor to be reserved by the rich and privileged for themselves, as in de Sade, but available to all, tabby cats as well as young lads and lasses. In spirit it anticipates *Wise Children*, with its rollicking cockney narrative voice; it's *The Marriage of Figaro* rather than *Don Giovanni*: it's no accident that the clever valet Puss is himself named Figaro. It is, in a word, Carter thumbing her nose at de Sade. (pp. 126–127)

(AUTO)BIOGRAPHY AND SELF-DEFINITION

The controlling consciousness of *Nights at the Circus*, as in her subsequent novel *Wise Children*, which is discussed in Chapter 6, is female. In both these texts, the female narrator assumes a position of authority, taking control of her own story–history and asserting herself as the author of her own words and actions. This is evident in Fevvers's personal biography and the way she recounts how she was brought up in a London brothel run by a one-eyed madame known as Nelson, how she escaped from a spell put on her at the dreaded Madame Schreck's museum of women monsters and fled a wealthy necromancer who was intent on having her as a human sacrifice. Magali Michael (1994) points out that in *Nights at the Circus* 'the customary association of authorship and activeness with the male is here reversed' (p. 500).

Even though Fevvers's story in *Nights at the Circus* is written by a male, the male voice is emasculated. Fevvers carefully evades all attempts by Walser to try to fix her identity and, in doing so, she challenges not only male definitions of women but, as Michael (1994) argues, notions of truth and reality (p. 497). Indeed, Walser loses the ability to write because his writing is dependent, like Desiderio's in *The Infernal Desires of Dr Hoffman*, upon his masculinised view of the world.

Notwithstanding Fevvers's apparent lack of understanding of some of her references, such as the misogynism in the story of Helen, the amount of control that she has over the narrative is important because autobiography is one of the strategies by which women can take responsibility for their own sense of self in a restricted and restrictive environment or milieu, challenging the traditional appropriation of women's lives and histories by men. Self-making is an essential element in women's autobiography and the notion of the self as 'a subject in process' is important to both *Nights at the Circus* and *Wise Children*. *Nights at the Circus* is centred on the ambivalence of the 'bird woman' because what is important is how the spectacle is 'read'. The twentieth-century male colloquial term for a woman, 'bird', grounds her as a subject in a particular cultural narrative, but 'bird woman' stresses the possibilities of 'flight'. In keeping with the ribaldry of this novel, but also the controversy created by the Victorian female acrobat's provocative sexuality, when Fevvers first describes her realisation of having grown full wings, 'I spread' (p. 24), she does so in language which conflates the spreading of her wings with the parting of her legs for sex. Her account of herself standing before Lizzie, 'her ripped chemise around her ankles' (p. 24), is indeed redolent of a young woman who has had violent sex in which her clothes have been ripped, cryptically developing the allusion to rape in the Helen story. As a character of working-class, Cockney origins, Fevvers has an uncompromising discourse, which, like the body of the female aerialist, openly engages with what 'polite' society might wish to see treated in a more reserved fashion. Thus, there is an obvious parallel drawn between the development of Fevvers's wings and her breasts and a less predictable confession that she dyed her wings, 'more the colour of that on my private ahem parts' (p. 25). This is an act that elides her spectacle as winged woman with her physical presence as sexual(ised) spectacle.

However, through Fevvers as the Winged Victory come to life, *Nights at the Circus* may be seen literally and metaphorically as a flight of fancy. Morris (1993) argues that Fevvers 'fully embodies the vertiginous freedom of self-making' (p. 157). As a winged lady, she spreads her wings and defies both the law of gravity and, as I suggested above, female 'decorum'. As the embodiment of freedom, the winged Fevvers stands in contrast to the young reporter Walser, whom the clowns of the circus transform into 'a human chicken'; a chicken being significantly a bird without flight:

> Walser had some more fun jumping on the rolling eggs and smashing them, but not as much fun as all that. Bored, he flapped his arms, again.
>
> 'Cock-a-doodle-do! Cock-a-doodle-dooski!'
>
> When he realised the kind ladies were all gone, tears ran unhindered from his eyes. Crowing like a cock, flapping his arms up and down, he sprinted off among the trees. (p. 224)

This episode appears to be a development of a scene from Fellini's *la Dolce Vita* in which a reporter turns a young woman at a party into a chicken by sprinkling her with feathers. *Nights at the Circus* differs from Carter's previous novels in shifting the emphasis of its critique from misogynistic discourse to the personal, social and cultural need for spectacle. Not gainsaying the misogynistic prejudices underpinning much of the spectacle in the novel, Carter appears to be particularly interested in 'fictionality' as much as fantasy. When Fevvers confesses to Walser that she dyes her wings, she stresses that this is 'the only deception which I practice on the public!' (p. 25), which is, like the circus itself, untrue. But the issue that is a recurring concern throughout the text is why there is a need on the part of circus audiences and readers of fictional narrative to suspend disbelief and partake in an experience which extends their understanding of the limits of nature. In this respect, Carter's circus recalls Fellini's Lux theatre in *The Nights of Cabiria*, where the conjuror turns woman into ape and a male head into a female.

It is this confusion of practising deception whilst meeting a need for spectacle that enables Carter, through Fevvers's biography, to link the circus, the brothel and the freak show. Carter, employing the Justine and Juliette binarism discussed in the previous chapter, argues in *The Sadeian Woman*:

> The brothel is also a place of lies, of false appearances. Juliette's virginity is sold successively to fifty buyers and, for each customer, she must act out a part – that she is starving and forced to

sell herself; that it was her mother sold her to the brothel. And so on, a series of flattering charades designed to persuade the customers they are not dealing with a simple business-woman, that the weeping creatures who reluctantly bend themselves to their superior will are, in fact, so many innocent Justines. (p. 84)

SPECTACLE, GENDER AND DISCOMFORT

For the most part, Colonel Kearney notwithstanding, it is women who provide the spectacle in *Nights at the Circus*, such as Mother Nelson the brothel keeper and Madame Schreck who runs the museum, and men who desire it. One of the premises which the novel explores is whether men need the experience of 'desubjectivisation' which spectacle offers and whether, as in the case of Madame Schreck's punters who exchange their regular 'topcoat and topper' for a 'cassock or a ballet-dancer's frock' (p. 61), they need to fulfil fantasies which they keep secret even from those with whom they are most intimate. According to Laplanche and Pontalis (1986), as we noted earlier, at the heart of fantasy is the experience of a 'sequence of images' (p. 26). This is central to the spectacle which Madame Schreck provides her paying clients, including the judge who wears an executioner's hood and pays to stand while a weeping girl spits at him, and others who pay to view a series of tableaux that include the Sleeping Beauty. The conflation of theatre, spectacle and deception is designed to challenge the clients' normal disposition, perspective and bearings: 'There'd be a lot of clanking of chains, there being several doors to open, and it was all dark but for her lantern, which was a penny candle in a skull' (p. 62). At the heart of the experiences of the judge and of the clients who view the Sleeping Beauty is an 'undoing' of women as victims of patriarchy; the weeping girl signifies women who have been orphaned, abused and/or cast out under the law and the sleeping beauty, the quiet unassuming female, parodies the Victorian, male ideal of womanhood.

For the judge, the experience of 'desubjectivisation' is erotic; wearing his black cap and having a noose placed around his neck makes him ejaculate. But for Walser, the loss of his normal equilibrium is essential to his self-development:

Two things, so far, have conspired together to throw Walser off his equilibrium. One: his right arm is injured and, although healing well he cannot write or type until it is better, so he is deprived of his profession. Therefore, for the moment, his disguise disguises – nothing. He is no longer a journalist masquerading as a clown; willy-nilly, force of circumstance has turned him into a *real* clown ... (p. 145)

Walser epitomises the whole process of 'desubjectivisation' with which spectacle, and especially the spectacle of the circus, provides the audience and which the novel seems to have been designed to provide for the reader. The temporary 'escape' which the circus offers the audience is more than that, as what happens to Walser suggests. Applying the make-up of a clown, he finds a 'stranger peering interrogatively back at him out of the glass' (p. 103), as the circus audience finds so much that is 'strange' peering at them. The circus ring is, after all, shaped like an eyeball. The key word here is 'interrogatively', and Carter uses what happens to Walser as a vehicle to explore the ambivalence that audiences frequently feel towards the circus experience. This is an important trope also in Fellini's *I Clown,* which is encapsulated in the description of the 'bug-eyed children teetering between tears and laughter' (p. 118). Wearing his mask, Walser feels uncomfortable, like the circus audience, because he feels 'interrogated', but he is also, like the circus audience, inspired: 'he felt the beginnings of a vertiginous sense of freedom' (p. 103). In thinking that his 'very self, as he had known it, [had] departed from him', Walser experiences what in the novel is one of the key elements of 'circus'. At the Imperial Circus in St Petersburg, the paying customers are required to deposit their furs in the cloakroom so that they leave behind 'the skin of one's own beastliness' (p. 105). However, this is again ironic because what the nineteenth-century audience encountered in the circus was other forms of beastliness, evident, for example, in the behaviour of certain types of clowns. At its heart, the circus, as Walser says of himself, is 'the freedom to juggle with being' (p. 103). Whilst this can be a positive experience, this is not always the case. Walser's experience is not an easy one. Forced to become part of the ape show, he is stripped naked and made to wear a dunce's cap, and is left with a 'dizzy uncertainty about what was human and what was not' (p. 110). It is the proximity of the ape to the human that especially unsettles Walser. This is brought home to him when one of the apes stares into his face, an 'exchange with the speaking eyes of the dumb' (p. 108), which also brings to mind Countess P's panopticon, to which I shall turn in a moment. The clown Buffo the Great parodies the way the circus 'juggle[s] with being'; he 'wears his insides on his outside, and a portion of his most obscene and intimate insides' while 'he stores his brains in the organ which, conventionally stores his piss' (p. 116).

A prerequisite of 'desubjectivisation' through the experience of fantasy and spectacle is that narrative and 'normal' time must be interrupted and that meaning and status, as in Walser's case, must change. These are the conditions that inform the spectacles with which the novel presents the reader and that are mirrored in the experience of spectacle, as in Olga Alexandrova's and Vera Andreyevna's witnessing of the travelling procession by characters within the novel. One of the central spectacles with which the novel presents the reader is Countess P's asylum, based on the French historian Michel Foucault's version of Bentham's panopticon. Like the other spectacles in *Nights at the Circus*, it is based upon a fusion of deception and fantasy. The asylum is intended to rehabilitate women who have murdered their husbands, but what is not known, even to the authorities who permit the construction of the building, is that Countess P successfully murdered her husband when she was eighteen years of age. The spectacle interrupts the narrative of the novel at the same time as it is part of the sequence of images with which it presents the reader. Without signposts and with no discernible tracks leading there, the asylum is outside geography, time and history:

> It was a panopticon she forced them to build, a hollow circle of cells shaped like a doughnut, the inward-facing wall of which was composed of grids of steel and, in the middle of the roofed, central courtyard, there was a round room surrounded by windows. (p. 210)

The circular nature of the artifice brings to mind the circus ring and the circle with which women are identified through images of the womb and the moon. Indeed, it is through a symbol written in blood from her menstrual cycle that Olga is able to communicate her desire for her 'turnkey'. The panopticon 'desubjectivises' the inmates by locking them in bare cells, 'in which was neither privacy nor distraction' (p. 212), and turning them by night into spectres: 'During the hours of darkness, the cells were lit up like so many small theatres in which each actor sat by herself in the trap of her visibility...' (p. 211). But the spectacle of Countess P's panopticon, in which she revolves in her chair at varying speeds around the tier of cells in which her inmates are imprisoned, suggests that much in society can be seen in terms of satisfying not only practical needs but, like the circus, the desire for spectacle.

Although not in the same intense way, the acts in Colonel Kearney's circus are under his gaze from his swivel chair as Countess P's prisoners are under her gaze from her rotating chair. But, like Countess P, and also without realising it, Kearney of Kentucky is trapped in the spectacle he has created: 'Even in the relative privacy of his hotel suite, the Colonel sported his 'trademark' costume – a pair of tightly tailored trousers striped in red and white with a blue waistcoat ornamented with stars' (p. 99). Suggesting Colonel Sanders's Kentucky Fried Chicken and Uncle Sam from American army recruiting posters, he signifies the extent to which the overarching identity of America as a nation is dependent upon a narrative constructed around spectacle: 'the Old Glory itself, topped with a gilt eagle, unfurled with grandiose negligence from a pole propped in the corner – born in Kentucky he might have been, but no Dixie patriot he!' (ibid.). He actually sees in the spectacle of the circus a manifestation of what is at the heart of the American constitution: 'All nations united in the great Ludic Game under the banner of Liberty itself' (p. 102). Fevvers and the Colonel, who has a pig as his closest friend, are very different types of 'spectacle', but in their different ways share a capacity to unsettle those with whom they come into contact.

The importance of spectacle to Western culture is suggested in the novel by the images of martyrdom, of St Catherine, St Lawrence and St Sebastian, and by the spectacle created by the great cities: St Petersburg, Tokyo, Seattle, San Francisco, Chicago and New York. Yet, like the circus itself, the spectacle of the city has a dirty and negative side. After seeing the procession of poor women following a cart laden with coal through the streets of London, Fevvers proclaims: 'The Shining City! The new Jerusalem!' (p. 88). It is impossible to know whether or not she is being ironic. In *Nights of Cabiria* the seedy district of Rome in which Cabiria works is close to the Passeggiata Archeologica, a reminder of Rome's glorious past. Out of costume, Fevvers, walking through the less than spectacular, nineteenth-century London streets, looks 'like any street girl making her way home' (p. 88). The paradox of the circus is encapsulated by Walser, who 'thrilled,

as always, to the shop-soiled yet polyvalent romance of the image'
of the circus ring:

> What a cheap, convenient, expressionist device, this sawdust ring,
> this little O! Round like an eye, with a small vortex in the centre;
> but give it a little rub as if it were Aladdin's wishing lamp and,
> instantly, the circus ring turns into that durably metaphoric, uro-
> bic snake with its tail in its mouth. (p. 107)

Through, for example, Fevvers's description of her experiences in a
Victorian brothel, *Nights at the Circus* explores how the development
of a sophisticated life of the emotions which is perceived as our cultural heritage has relegated certain aspects of sexuality to the social
underground. Carter, as we shall discuss in a moment, follows Fellini
(1976) as seeing in the clown a reflection of how 'the completely
enlightened man has made his grotesque, deformed aspects disappear' (p. 123). In this respect, the location of the narrative at the end
of the nineteenth century is especially significant, for it was during
this period, as Steven Marcus (1964) points out, 'that pornography
and especially pornographic writing became an industry' (p. 2). The
efflorescence of pornography during this period indicates not only a
general disturbance of sexuality, but, as Marcus says, 'dysfunction'
(p. 262). Pornography in general amounted to a reversal of Victorian
moral ideals, and some of it, such as the pornography of sadism,
was a reversal of Victorian ideal moral standards for men (p. 263).
Prostitution itself is seen in the novel as challenging traditional
demarcations of reality and illusion. After all, the women assume a
role and the men pay not for sex but for the simulacra of sex. Hence,
Nights at the Circus takes us through many positions of debasement,
evidenced in worlds assembled and contained for the pleasure of
men, and often betraying the influence of the Marquis de Sade.

Nights at the Circus also reflects the way in which prostitutes during the Victorian period were beginning to be seen in more humane
ways. Reformers such as William Acton sought to educate or persuade the public 'to regard her not as some alien and monstrous
creature but as a fellow human being' (Marcus, 1964, p. 5). Secondly,
they sought to explode the popular myth of 'the harlot's progress'.
The majority of prostitutes did not succumb to death or venereal disease as was popularly thought, but returned to a regular course of
life – through finding work of some other kind, opening small shops
or lodging houses, emigration or marriage (p. 6). In other words, the

revised conception of prostitutes as 'fellow human beings' and of prostitution as a transitory state recommended acceptance of the interrelationship of the legitimate and the illegitimate, whereas previously the latter had been denied or banished to the underground of 'civilisation'. The consequences of the latter are evident in the way in which Madame Schreck's subterranean museum is the darker side of Ma Nelson's. However, more importantly, the emergence of a more liberal and sympathetic view of prostitutes challenged the conventional opposition of subject and object in which prostitutes were an example of the way women were objectified by men. This is clearly alluded to, for example, in the episode in which a wealthy gentleman purchases Fevvers from the museum of women monsters and tries to kill her with his sword, a symbol of his phallic power, in a ritual which does not hide the hair-fine boundary between sacrifice and intercourse. Fevvers challenges him with her blade, defying, as Michael (1994) says, 'accepted notions of women as naturally and inevitably passive objects' (p. 502).

Moreover, *Nights at the Circus* pursues the implications of the revised ways in which prostitutes were being seen in late Victorian England in two further respects. Prostitution in the novel is seen as the product of economic need, dispelling the myth that the women involved take pleasure in sex, and is employed so as to confound the distinction between 'good' and 'bad' women. Walser suggests as much when he admits that he has known many whores fine enough to have been his wife. Here, of course, Carter is blurring the distinction between what were often the only two options available to women in the nineteenth century: prostitution or marriage. Indeed, the economic and ideological oppression of women is kept to the fore throughout the novel by Lizzie, a strong Marxist and a former prostitute herself. Carter argues in *The Sadeian Woman*: 'The marriage bed is a particularly delusive refuge from the world because all wives of necessity fuck by contract. Prostitutes are at least decently paid on the nail' (p. 9). In other words, wife and prostitute are both entrapped within an economic system that exploits women, but the prostitute is sometimes more aware of her position than is the wife.

THE CLOWN

Earlier in this chapter, I drew attention to Carter's and Fellini's interest in the overlap between the circus and pornography and how the circus was read 'pornographically' in the Victorian period. In *Nights at the Circus*, Buffo most conspicuously conflates whores and clowns, demonstrating an understanding of how both are centred on exhibition. In both cases, punters pay for a fantasy, unable to separate the 'reality' from the deception of the spectacle:

> We are the whores of mirth, for, like a whore, we know what we are; we know we are mere hirelings hard at work and yet those who hire us see us as beings perpetually at play. Our work is their pleasure and so they think our work must be our pleasure, too, so there is always an abyss between their notion of our work as play, and ours, of their leisure as our labour. (p. 119)

In the clown chapter, Carter, like Fellini, looks behind the mask of the clown and, like Fellini, finds a drunk. Fellini's *Amarcord*, as I noted earlier, interweaves episodes reminiscent of the circus with carnivalesque and toilet humour. Anna Hunt (2006) draws attention to how in *Nights at the Circus*, in 'the lugubrious liminality of Clown's Alley', the masks 'allow incognito indulgence in a ridiculous and perverse display of toilet humour' (p. 147). It is not simply the toilet humour but the 'ridiculous and perverse display' that links Carter's fiction and Fellini's films. The lodgings of the clowns could not be more different from the spectacle of the circus, having 'the lugubrious atmosphere of a prison or a mad-house' (p. 116), a feature which seems to be a direct borrowing from Fellini (1976), who felt there was 'something of the madhouse in the circus' (pp. 120–121).

Stoddart (2007) points out that *Nights at the Circus* 'appears to have been inspired by a whole series of European clowns of the late nineteenth and early twentieth centuries, several of whom...are mentioned by the chief clown, "Great Buffo"'. His act recalls their acts in the way it makes use of props which 'either do not do what they are supposed to or completely fall apart' (p. 115). Moreover, Carter's musical clowns, Grick and Grock, mirror the 'real life' double act 'Grock and Brick' (p. 116). Carter, like Fellini in 'Why Clowns?', focuses on the paradox of the clown, but she does so from a different perspective. Fellini distinguishes between the 'white clown', who frightens children because he stands for duty and 'repression', and the Auguste, with whom children identify because 'like the gosling or the puppy, [he] is always ill-treated' (p. 126). Like Kearney, Countess P and Madame Schreck, Buffo is an unsettling figure. When children shy away from the clown, it may be because he represents, like the grotesque in the fairy story, the end of innocence and timelessness, which they can glimpse but not fully understand. At one level, the clowns in *Nights at the Circus* are roguish, trickster figures whose cocked, conical caps mirror carnival's Lord of Misrule. Certainly, in their bow ties, they seem to mock respectable society. But there is more to them than that. Their white, grotesquely made-up faces parody the preserved, made-up faces of the dead and the mimicry of the made-up transvestite.

Like Fellini's *I Clown*, Carter's chapter ends in an extravagant clown funeral. A coffin is brought into the ring draped in a Union Jack. There are several ways of reading Carter's 'tumultuous resurrection of the clown'. At one level, it may be seen as a parody of resurrection itself and of the point that Melville makes at the end of *Moby Dick* when Ishmael rises to the surface in a coffin from the wreck of the Pequod, that if there is an afterlife then it has to be through the coffin itself. But, in breaking out of the coffin, Buffo has to break through the Union Jack, which in its association with Empire can be seen as a flag of oppression. As 'mockery of mockeries', the clown also parodies the way that the oppressed, including slaves signified by the circus elephants who endlessly rattle their chains, survive by mimicking the language and behaviour of their oppressors. Buffo observes that beneath the clown's mask are 'the features of those who were once proud to be visible' (p. 119). Carter explores how, in Assael's (2005) words, 'the clown's pathos emerged from his combination of contradictory roles – as jolly performer and struggling artist' (p. 100). The source here may again be the essay by Fellini, for whom the Auguste clown was 'an image of the subproletariat: the hungry, the lame, the rejected, those capable of revolt perhaps but not of revolution' (p. 125). In this regard, *Nights at the Circus* once again reflects Carter's circus scholarship, for, as Assael points out: 'Although the clown occupied an essential role in the circus, his world outside the ring was paradoxically marked by social isolation and abject poverty, sickness, and melancholy' (p. 100).

Fevvers's laughter links her with the circus clown, even though she is an aerialist, a feature which reinforces the novel's roots in the 'real' circus, and in the overlap between circus and carnival. Fellini's essay may again have been a key influence here. He points out that Gelsomnia and Cabiria in his films are both Augustes: 'They are not women, they are asexual; they are the Happy Hooligan from the strip cartoon' (p. 129). Fellini (1976) argues that 'the white clown stands for elegance, grace, harmony, intelligence, lucidity, which are posited in a moral way as ideal, unique, indisputable divinities.' But to the 'Cockney Venus', who is more Auguste than white, these might all be attractive attributes if, to employ Fellini's words, 'they were not so priggishly displayed' (p. 124). Carter's novel takes 'priggishness' much further than does Fellini, seeing it as integral to a sexist and colonialist hierarchy.

The female circus performer has a different significance for Carter than for Fellini. Gelsomnia, Fellini's female clown in *La Strada* (1954), sold by her impoverished mother to a circus strongman, journeys into silence and servitude. The movement of the novel, as the description of the escape from the asylum illustrates, is beyond language into song – women's songs are a celebration and break the enforced silence – and through carnivalesque into a conjurer's world; in Siberia, Fevvers and her companions take a train which ceases to exist as soon as they turn their backs on it. In *Revolution in Poetic Language* (1984), and in subsequent works, Julia Kristeva argues for greater recognition of the joy and physical sensation to be found in the music of language, which are not normally experienced in public utterance. This 'joy' has its origins literally in 'baby language', enunciated with the appearance of delight, and associated with the 'mother tongue' as the parent croons 'baby sound' back to the babbling infant. The women, escaping from the panopticon, reclaim their 'mother tongues'. Within this context, the fact that one of the prisoners in the asylum writes her notes to a warder who befriends her in menstrual blood – conventionally seen as 'dirty' and a demarcation between men and women – proves significant. Her 'love words' to another woman are outside of the male tradition of 'love words' because they are written to another woman and because they are written, literally and metaphorically, in the womb's blood.

As half-woman and half-swan orphan, and as someone who claims to have been hatched, Fevvers, of course, was born outside the classic Oedipal triangle in which, according to Freudian psychoanalysis, the girl child acquires a secondary sense of identity, inferior to the male child. Moreover, as 'Virgin Whore', Fevvers is at the cusp of the two polarised categories – 'virgin' and 'whore' – in which women have been categorised in Western culture.

Throughout *Nights at the Circus*, gender identity is part of display and spectacle. A woman may masochistically identify with a spectacle that is oppressive, or, as in Fevvers's case, construct 'femininity' as a masquerade which ultimately deconstructs it in terms of the tyranny of the male Look. Mary Doane (1982) explains:

> The masquerade, in flaunting femininity, holds it at a distance... [its] resistance to patriarchal positioning would therefore lie in its denial of the production of femininity as closeness, as presence-to-itself, as, precisely imagistic.... The masquerade doubles representation; it is constituted by a hyperbolisation of the accoutrements of femininity. (pp. 81–82)

Indeed, Fevvers lives through entertainment, masquerade and spectacle by making a living from 'a hyperbolisation of the accoutrements of femininity':

> [Fevvers] cocked her head to relish the shine of the lamps, like footlights, like stage-lights; it was as good as a stiff brandy, to see those footlights, and beyond them, the eyes fixed upon her with astonishment, with awe, the eyes that told her who she was.
>
> She would be the blonde of blondes, again, just as soon as she found peroxide; it was as easy as that, and, meanwhile, who cared! (p. 290)

The contrast with her in the novel is most obviously Mignon, initially a Marilyn Monroe figure, who is the opposite of masquerade. She assumes the image but, unlike Fevvers, she does not realise that that is all it is. In fact, Fevvers is closer to Mae West than to Marilyn Monroe. In *The Sadeian Woman*, the two – West and Monroe – are contrasted:

> Mae West's joke upon her audience was, however, a superior kind of double bluff. She was in reality a sexually free woman, economically independent, who wrote her own starring vehicles in her early days in the theatre.... (pp. 60–61)

Carter herself said that Fevvers 'is basically Mae West with wings' (Haffenden, 1985, p. 88). Rendered silent as a female spectacle, Mignon is a version of 'the entranced maiden' who, as Judie Newman (1990) says, 'stands as emblematic of the patriarchal view of woman' (p. 116). The point is sharply made through the contrast between Mignon and the clowns; although both wear make-up, the

clowns are still in charge of their personae. In fact, they actually
achieve liberation through their masks. Women in the novel are seen
in terms of binarisms – either as goddesses and angels or as sub-
human. Mignon becomes a battered wife who is beaten by the Ape
Man and abandoned to a hungry tiger by her lover, the Strong Man.
The subordinate position of the women performers in the circus is
portrayed as comparable to that of the troupe of performing apes –
although both troupes eventually rebel. There are cruel parodies of
a woman as an 'entranced maiden', totally under male control, in the
women on display in the museum of death: the sleeping beauty who
never wakes up and the miniature woman who never grows up.
Eventually, through the intervention of Fevvers and Lizzie, Mignon
rejects the role of victim and creates herself anew in a lesbian relationship with the Princess in the dancing tigers act.

Walser, blinkered through focusing on whether Fevvers is true
or false, does not realise that masquerade engages with a phallic
construction of femininity: 'She would be the blonde of blondes,
again, just as soon as she found peroxide; it was as easy as that, and,
meanwhile who cared!' (p. 290). Through her masquerade, Fevvers
reverses the conventional masculine and female positions until, as I
explained earlier, she turns her gaze on him: 'And she fixed Walser
with a piercing, judging regard, as if to ascertain just how far she
could go with him...It flickered through his mind: Is she really a
man?' (p. 35).

As Desiderio's life changes when he falls in love with Albertina,
Walser's life changes when he falls in love with Fevvers. In the
course of the novel, he becomes insane but recovers to return to
Fevvers's arms. For a while, Carter's narrative has the potential to
develop along conventional lines: an ostensibly radical woman falls
in love with a man and is transformed into Woman and marries him.
Even though Carter reverses the gender roles, the potential ending is
now the same as in the fairy tales where a prince rescues a maiden
who falls in love with him. In fact, Fevvers begins to lose the control
she has won over her own life and begins to look like 'only a poor
freak down on her luck' (p. 290). In a parody of ageing, her wings
now become troublesome appendages – 'she could not spread two
wings, she spread one – lopsided angel, partial and shabby splen-
dour!' (ibid.). Failing against male images of female goddesses – 'No
Venus, or Helen' – when Fevvers feels whole again it is in Walser's
gaze. However, Lizzie warns Fevvers of the tyranny of the happy
ending, observing candidly: 'You're fading away' (p. 280). It is also

possible, though, to read the novel at this point with a focus on the transformation which Walser has undergone. Carter once explained that he had 'to be broken down' before he could become 'not a fit mate for Fevvers at all, but a serious person' (Haffenden, 1985, p. 89). Running after the others, Walser soon forgets his quest 'in his enchantment at the sight of dappled starlight on the snow' (p. 224). Significantly, this echoes the flight from the House of Correction, when 'the white world around them looked newly made' (p. 218). In order to become a reconstructed male, Walser has to become a 'blank sheet' upon which he can inscribe a new beginning. Turned upside down, literally and metaphorically, in a fireman's lift by the Shaman, Walser sees his past life in 'concrete but discrete fragments' (p. 238). Earlier, I suggested that the women's songs represent a reclamation of the 'joy' in language experienced by the babbling infant and by 'the mother tongue' which croons back those sounds to the child. In symbolic language which tends to privilege the male point of view, this 'joy' is often lost. Significantly, when turned upside down, Walser begins to 'babble helplessly in a language unknown to the Shaman' (ibid.).

In the asylum, which is structured as Bentham's panopticon so that each prisoner is held under permanent observation, the countess and the warders are also imprisoned and watched. The panopticon serves as an image of the way in which in society at large all are imprisoned. In many ways, *Nights at the Circus* takes up where *The Passion of New Eve* leaves off. It is located in a post-modern, post-cultural space that is as much beyond America as it is beyond postwar Europe, 'the unfortunate bedraggled orphan' (Haffenden, 1985, p. 87). Indeed, all the principal premises upon which twentieth-century America and the Americanised future for late capitalist society are founded collapse in the course of the novel. Walser, who represents post-Enlightenment, rational enquiry, is transformed through his experiences as a clown and through his love for Fevvers, while Colonel Kearney's entrepreneurialism is left in ruins after the circus is seized by outlaws. Fevvers's laughter at the end of the book, as Michael Wood (1984) says, indicates that she has not only 'understood the joke of life' but also 'the freedom that lives in jokes' (p. 16). At one level, the circus in the novel, as in Dickens's *Hard Times*, represents an alternative to what in *The Passion of New Eve* is 'the phenomena of the persistence of vision'. Fevvers's boast at the end of the narrative – 'I fooled you then' – is partly a confidence trick as well as a description of her sense of being. When she says in the last line of the novel 'It just goes to show there's nothing like confidence' (p. 295), the word 'confidence' is double-edged. As Carter commented: 'She's had the confidence to pull it all off, after all' (Haffenden, 1985, p. 90). But the word 'confidence' conflates Fevvers's confidence in herself with her skill as a trickster. The conclusion invites the reader to enter once again the fictionality of the circus as narrative and the narrative as circus.

8

Illegitimate Power and Theatre: *Wise Children* (1991)

In *Wise Children*, Dora Chance, an ex-musical hall and variety theatre star, is writing her autobiography on her seventy-fifth birthday. The narrative has the impact of her speaking voice and, as Kate Webb (1994) says, appears to transcend the word processor on which she is writing (pp. 294–295). It positions us as if we were in the audience of a theatre listening to a stand-up comedian: it draws attention to itself, frequently postpones the subject and prods us into attention.

The shift in focus from the circus in the previous novel, *Nights at the Circus*, to the music hall in *Wise Children* is understandable in the context of the way in which the two were juxtaposed in European cinema, which, as we have seen, had a profound influence on Carter's fiction. In European, especially French, cinema there was a great deal of interest in the relationship between the music hall, the circus and the cinema. This is probably most evident in French cinema of the 1930s, in the work of Jean Renoir, where the focus on music hall, as in *Wise Children*, is on the way in which it made use of circus acts. But in Carter's novel, as in Renoir's films, there is a particular interest in the way in which music hall, as Dudley Andrew (1992) says, threw 'in its lot with more modern practices the cinema knew best how to exploit' (p. 25). Thus, *Wise Children* is a text that is written at the boundary between music hall and cinema, anchored in an awareness of how the former made increasingly better use of 'hidden technology, on continual novelty, on illusionism, on the female body, on scale and increasingly on narrative' (ibid.). But, through the focus on Dora and Nora, who lived through the transition from music hall to cinema, Carter, like the film directors Jean Renoir and Christian Jacque, examines how the music hall 'could only fabricate the intimacy of the circus as one of its illusions' (ibid.).

151

The music halls in which Dora and Nora built their careers developed from the entertainment of saloon bars in the first part of the nineteenth century. In these bars, there was an auditorium, in which the audience sat, drank and smoked at tables as they might in a public house. The music hall, perceived as illegitimate theatre because of its origins and often ribald content, posed a threat to 'serious' theatres, especially in London, where for much of the nineteenth century it attracted larger audiences. Music hall programmes consisted of speciality acts, which were also taken on by circuses, comedy and popular song. It was not long before the music halls in London and in some of the larger northern cities gave way to what became known as 'variety theatres'. Having their origins in the music hall, they too might be perceived as having an ironic, dialectic relationship with serious theatre. But, because their ambience more closely resembled 'legitimate' theatre, this dialectic is even more pronounced. Instead of tables in a large hall, the auditorium of the variety theatre consisted of stalls, circles and boxes, and there was a separate bar.

The grand Parisian entertainment halls left behind the café concert and the street entertainment in which the music hall had its roots. But still, as Dudley Andrew maintains, the music hall 'dared to pretend to thrive on intimacy and audience contact' (ibid.). Through Dora's memoirs, the music hall which we encounter in *Wise Children* is a music hall that is on the cusp of the café concert and the large entertainment halls.

The circus's circular auditorium extends outwards from the centre in ever-increasing circles, like the circles created when a stone is dropped into still water; a metaphor for how the travelling circus sent out ripples of excitement and mystery through the communities which they visited. As the trapeze swung out over the 'auditorium' in the Victorian Big Top, wild animals passed close to the spectators and clowns leapt over the circus ring into the auditorium, audiences were made to feel as if they were part of the spectacle. The variety theatre, however, offered a different kind of experience from the circus. There was more distance between the performers and the audience, and this had to be negotiated in the act itself. What the circus created, as Carter explores in *Nights at the Circus*, was a dual sense of exhibition and participation which was embedded in its structures. The variety theatre and the music hall, through participation and, as Dora and Nora suggest, often lewdness, did not so much remove as mock the structural gap between audience and performer.

Victorian social hierarchy was created and sustained not by contact but by non-contact. Variety theatre and music hall purported to break down the spatial barriers upon which social hierarchies depended. They did this through the ways in which their performers used and subverted the spatial symbolism and codified practices of 'legitimate' theatre. In this regard, in the variety theatre and the music hall act, like the circus act discussed in Chapter 7, there is a complex relationship between the discipline of the performer and the performance as carnival. In both *Wise Children* and *Nights at the Circus*, Carter is interested in how even the exuberance and carnival in the variety and circus acts are products of rehearsal and hard work. In each text, she examines this paradox within the wider circus/variety theatre and music hall aesthetic. 'Serious' theatre provides a potentially subversive cultural space which is further developed, prioritised and promoted in 'illegitimate' theatre and circus. But this subversive space is sustained through the expertise and discipline of the artist–performer, who, in turn, reflects the values and perseverance of conventional society. The paradox of the circus-cum-variety theatre carnival is embedded in the body of the performer. When Dora declares 'What a joy it is to dance and sing', she invokes the corporeal liberation of 'theatre' and, especially, variety theatre. The concept of joy unfetters the body and permits participation in what lies beyond its normal limits. Yet the joy is created by 'song and dance', which in her case is the product of learned skills and discipline.

Theatricality, as an important part of the narrative content as well as the style of each of the last two novels, produces a sense of expansiveness which belies the carefulness with which it is woven throughout the texts. This is evident in the way it is reflected in the geography of the novels. *Nights at the Circus* and *Wise Children* begin in London. After her 'conquests on the continent', Fevvers in *Nights at the Circus* has returned home to London, where, in a description that links the worlds of the two novels, 'the principal industries are the music hall and the confidence trick' (p. 8). Here Fevvers and her adopted mother, Lizzie, tell her story to Walser. Dora begins her narrative with a sociological sketch of how London has changed, observing that, while once you could think of the city divided by the river, now 'there's been a diaspora of the affluent' (p. 1). Then through the plot devices of a touring circus and touring theatre, respectively, each narrative takes us to other parts of the globe. *Nights at the Circus* is divided into three parts, as we have seen, each

Angela Carter

labelled in terms of a geographical location. Michael (1994) points out that the movement toward increasingly remote places 'is accompanied by a movement away from the stable ground of reality and toward the ever more fantastic' (p. 495). In *Wise Children*, Ranulph's zeal to spread Shakespearean theatre to the farthest reaches of the globe takes him to Canada, America, the Far East and Tasmania. But this 'movement' in the text, like the representation of the fantastic, is carefully planned and executed.

The way in which the music hall can be seen as being at a cusp in entertainment history parallels the way in which the text is also located at an important cusp in British history. In *Nights at the Circus*, Mignon, according to Carter herself, is 'supposed to be Europe, the unfortunate, bedraggled orphan – Europe after the war – which is why she carries such a weight of literary and musical references on her frail shoulders' (Haffenden, 1985, p. 87). *Wise Children* begins with Britain, to use Carter's own words, as 'an advanced, industrialised, post-imperialist country in decline' (Wandor, 1983, p. 73). As Dora Chance observes: 'these days, there is no such thing as a penny any more and it is as if this foggy old three-cornered island were dangling from a cloud' (p. 112).

Wise Children associates Britain's imperial decline with that of the British theatre and, through the trope of the degenerating family line which Carter no doubt borrowed from Edgar Allan Poe, with the demise of the Hazards as a theatrical family. The first wife of Melchior, who is called 'Mr British Theatre', is now in a wheelchair, while Tristram has become the 'weak but charming' host of a sadomasochistic television game show, 'Lashings of Lolly', which appears to draw on music hall. Hazard himself appears in the show and is humiliated: the 'last gasp of the imperial Hazard dynasty that bestrode the British theatre like a colossus for a century and a half' (p. 10). The interweaving of the decline of the theatre with the demise of the British empire is parodied in the English colony of actors who travel to America, playing Disraeli, Queen Victoria and Florence Nightingale.

According to Dora, there are a number of indications of Britain's decline. One of them is the disappearance of the Lyons teashops. The nostalgia with which she describes them betrays that sense of cultural loss which, as discussed in Chapter 1, Carter observed in Britain:

Do you remember the Lyons teashops? Thick, curly white plaster on the shopfronts, like walking into a wedding cake, and the name in gold: J. Lyons.

Poached eggs on toast keeping snug in little tin pigeon holes as you shuffled down the counter. The moist and fruity Bath buns with crumbs of rock candy glistening on the top, and a little pat of butter lined up alongside. The girl would pour hot water, whoosh! in a steaming column into a fat white pot and there you were, your good, hot cup of tea, with leaves left in the bottom of the cup, afterwards, to tell your fortune with. (p. 111)

The demise of the Lyons teashops is seen as part of a larger socio-cultural change, in which the 'Americanisation' of Britain played a large part, reflected in the London railway stations. At Waterloo and Victoria stations, there is 'nowhere you can get a decent cup of tea, all they give you is Harvey Wallbangers, filthy cappuccino' (p. 3). Intriguingly, they are compared with the railway station in David Lean's film *Brief Encounter* (1946), where two middle-aged people, a suburban housewife and a local doctor, meet in the buffet. It is an especially pertinent allusion in a novel in which extramarital affairs are a strong trope. Like Carter's novel, the film is a retrospective narrative; Laura sits at home with her husband, listening to a recording of Rachmaninov's Second Piano Concerto, enacting the reveries of her affair. It is not clear in the film how much is based on memory and how much on fantasy.

The most obvious symbol of post-war Britain and imperial decline in the novel is the music hall comedian Gorgeous George, a parody of the English patron saint. He has the map of the world tattooed on his body. As Dora notes, he is 'not a comic at all but an enormous statement' (p. 66). Some of the irony is of his own design; he flexes his muscles to 'God Save the King' and 'Rule Britannia'; the Cape of Good Hope is at his navel and 'the Falkland Islands disappear down the crack of his bum' (p. 67). Some of it is the product of circumstance. The tattooed map is pink, but in limelight – suggesting the way hindsight has changed the way we see the British Empire – it is turned into 'a morbid raspberry colour that looked bad for his health', perhaps suggesting how the Empire has eventually proved bad for the psychological and economic health of Britain. When Dora last sees George, he is a pathetic street beggar who approaches her for a cup of tea. The irony here is that George returns to the street, where music hall began, but as a beggar, not an entertainer.

But there is a further irony which comes unwittingly from George himself. In his heyday, his catch phrase was: 'Nothing queer about our George.' It suggests an anxiety about homosexuality which may be his own, but may also be part of English culture. The music hall, as in Sarah Waters's *Tipping the Velvet* (1999), influenced by Carter, provided a cultural space in which the rigid boundaries between genders and sexualities could be challenged. Carter, through the narrator Dora, may be having fun with traditional concepts of English masculinity, with anal fixation – George plays Bottom in *Midsummer Night's Dream* – and with sexual violence; George carries a golf club, an object with phallic as well as chauvinistic connotations.

The exploration of the boundary between genders and sexualities is a further element which links the music hall with the circus. As mentioned earlier, music halls and the circus frequently engaged the same speciality acts, including acrobats and trapeze artists. Indeed, Fevvers in *Nights at the Circus* is first launched at a variety theatre in Holborn, London. Like the circus performance, discussed in Chapter 7, the variety and music hall act negotiated and renegotiated public discourses around taste and decency and sought to satisfy popular enthusiasms and desires. The way in which semi-nude, female, circus acrobats, exhibiting self-conscious physical poses, were subject to 'pornographic reading' in the Victorian period is mirrored in the controversy and scandal with which female variety performers were often associated. Carter suggests in *Wise Children*, through the careers of Dora and Nora, that the scandal associated with female variety theatre performers often arose from what they deliberately sought to suggest or signify by their performances. There were numerous music hall stars of whom this might be said. Marie Lloyd dressed provocatively, sometimes as a naïve schoolgirl, to sing her more lewd songs, which she delivered with winks and gestures, while the 'signifying' nature of the performances by distinguished male impersonators, such as Ella Shields and Vesta Tilley, challenged conventional assumptions about gender and sexuality. But Carter's novel further suggests that these performances were not easily read as passive pornographic texts because of the way in which they actively engaged with, mimicked and mocked dominant cultural ideas. Ironically, as Carter implies in *Wise Children*, the 'scandal' that the performers sought to invoke in their acts sometimes followed them in their offstage lives.

While in one respect *Wise Children*, like *Nights at the Circus* and the music hall itself, is at the cusp of a particular history, in another respect it is paradoxically outside history. Dora, as an illegitimate child, is someone who has been excluded from established society. Chedgzoy (1995) maintains: '*Wise Children* records the pain of cultural exclusion and exile from the legitimate family' (p. 74). Dora's mother is a foundling who had sex with the patriarchal Melchior Hazard. However, although Melchior is their biological father, Dora and her twin sister were brought up by Melchior's twin brother, Peregrine. Ironically, Peregrine is the biological father of Melchior's 'legitimate' twin daughters, Saskia and Imogen. Twins run through the Hazard family; Tristram and Gareth are twins by Melchior's third marriage, mirroring the way in which the novel interweaves legitimacy and illegitimacy. However, even more important than the physical presence of twins in the novel is the concept of 'twinning'.

The twins in the novel mirror the ways in which the circus and the music hall are twinned. In this regard, *Nights at the Circus* and *Wise Children* are twinned as texts. In *Nights at the Circus*, as we have seen, the carnival of the clowns is both thrilling and terrifying. The clown's mask suggests something sinister as well as comic. In *Wise Children*, the spirit of the carnivalesque is embodied, literally, in the ever-expanding, Rabelaisian Perry, whose mask hides a dangerous paedophile. He is the proverbial American sugar daddy, but also the wicked uncle who seduces Dora when she is thirteen. Towards the end of the novel, Dora reflects on her love-making with Perry, when for a moment they were prepared to 'fuck the house down'; in carnivalesque terms, to overturn the social order which is embodied in a house which is itself full of secrets:

> While we were doing it, everything seemed possible, I must say. But that is the illusion of the act. Now I remember how everything seemed possible when I was doing it, but as soon as I stopped, not, as if fucking were the origin of illusion.
>
> 'Life's a carnival', he said. He was an illusionist, remember.
>
> 'The carnival's got to stop, some time, Perry,' I said: 'You listen to the news, that'll take the smile off your face.'
>
> 'News? What news?' (p. 222)

Perry represents the dark side of the clown, which, perhaps, some children sense.

The carnivalesque in Carter's fiction is a theme, and not necessarily simply a position from which she writes, as some critics have presumed. In *Wise Children*, the thematising of the carnivalesque is evident in the tension which Webb (1994) has identified at its heart between the avowed intention of the narrator, Dora Chance, to exorcise the family lies, skeletons and secrets and the obvious interest in the way in which these stories overturn the established social order.

At the outset of the novel, Dora's work on her memoirs is linked to the dustbin being blown over, when 'all the trash spills out' (p. 3). The day on which she starts the narrative is a topsy-turvy combination of wind and sunshine. This binarism reflects the duality at the core of the text. The wind is said to get into the blood and turn a person wild. Later in the novel, it is the wind, like the skeletons in the family cupboards, that whips 'round the wings and the bare backstage corners' (p. 83).

THEATRE, THEATRICALITY AND CARNIVAL

The stories embedded in *Wise Children* generally concern women who are oppressed by men and who are literally and metaphorically excluded from, or marginalised within, male versions of history. Within this context, the priority given to theatre, often associated with subversion, and to women taking control of their own 'story' or 'history' is very significant. Alison Findlay (1999) points out that 'the Renaissance idea of history is male'; it was believed that women should appear at the margins of history because 'all daughters of Eve should be subject to their husbands' and 'history is concerned with matters of state: the lives of governors and national politics rather than the everyday existence of the population' (p. 164). Carter's interest in the theatre came from a number of sources, of which the most important were Shakespeare and Renaissance drama, variety theatre and music hall, and the theatre of Japan and China, for which the work of Bertolt Brecht prepared her.

It is hard to believe that Carter, as a student of English at Bristol University in the 1960s, was not influenced by Brecht's essay 'Alienation Effects in Chinese Acting'. But, even if she were not, Brecht's essay provides a useful theoretical framework within which to read Carter's work in relation to the theatre. Although Brecht compares the alienating effects of Chinese theatre with the realism of mainstream European theatre, the origins of his interest in alienation as a dramatic strategy is located in popular, folk traditions: 'This effort to make the incidents represented appear strange to the public can be seen in a primitive form in the theatrical and pictorial displays at the old popular fairs' (Willett, 1964, p. 91). Carter would certainly have applauded this thesis and, considering

Brecht's next sentence, it probably had a direct influence on *Nights at the Circus* and maybe even her interest in Fellini's *I Clown*, discussed in Chapter 7: 'The way the clowns speak and the way the panoramas are painted both embody an act of alienation' (ibid.).

Theatre, as subject or metaphor, and 'theatricality', embedded in the prose style and in the flamboyance of the text's ideas, have always characterised Carter's fiction. They are more developed and even more pronounced features of her later work. But in the later novels they are also handled with a greater degree of irony. In *Wise Children*, theatre is a theme, as the circus is a theme of *Nights at the Circus*. It is significant that the narrators of both *Wise Children* and *Nights at the Circus* are professional performers. Kate Webb (1994) has drawn attention to the variety of stars who make guest appearances in the novel, including Charlie Chaplin, Judy Garland, Fred Astaire and his wife Adele, Ginger Rogers, Ruby Keeler, Jessie Mathews, Josephine Baker, Jack Warner, W. C. Fields. Gloria Swanson, Paul Robeson, Orson Welles, and Noel Coward (p. 296). Dora's birthday, which she spends on her memoirs, is also Shakespeare's birthday and the novel is written around a mock Shakespearean plot involving disguises, the search for true parentage and false trails. Indeed, at the end of *Wise Children*, we have a list of 'Dramatis Personae (in order of appearance)' (p. 233).

Wise Children is concerned with the tangled history of two theatrical families: the Hazard dynasty, which has dominated English (Shakespearean) theatre for one-and-a-half centuries, and its illegitimate progeny, represented by Dora and Nora Chance, who had a novelty act but also worked as extras and took part in strip shows. Dora and Nora's 'carnivalesque' is a product of theatre, as Buffo and the clowns in *Nights at the Circus* are creations of the circus. Although the two sides of the Hazard family and of the theatre are twinned, as has been argued, they might be seen as confronting each other. The legitimate Hazard theatre dynasty and its twin, the illegitimate theatre, see each reflected in the other. But in each there is also an absent presence. The legitimate and illegitimate in each case are based upon a dialectic with the illegitimate and legitimate, respectively, which each only half-acknowledges; just as with one physical twin there is also the absent presence of the other.

Illegitimacy has always been an important trope in Carter's novels. Desiderio in *The Infernal Desire Machines of Doctor Hoffman* is the illegitimate son of a prostitute's relationship with an Indian, and Buzz in *Love* is the product of the sex his mother had, again while working as a prostitute, with an American serviceman. However, in *Wise Children*, the linking of seventeenth-century theatre and illegitimacy provided Carter with a means of developing illegitimacy in its various guises as a theme. As Alison Findlay (1994) points out, in the seventeenth century, the theatre and bastards were often seen as occupying an equivocal area, spatially and ideologically. Like the bastard, the theatre was perceived as socially disruptive and occupied a similar position to the bastard in the cultural landscape: 'a liminal area outside the law', making its subversive potential visible (p. 214).

The extent to which Carter's last two novels are located in the theatre or circus, as sites of illegitimate power, is evident from the voices of Fevvers and Dora themselves. Dora's voice, as mentioned at the beginning of this chapter, is redolent of that of a music hall performer. However, it also possesses many of the characteristics of bastard speech in seventeenth-century theatre. Like the bastard in the theatre, Dora speaks from what might be described as a 'downstage' position and, like the bastard in the theatre, from this downstage position, she undercuts the authority of the multi-levelled reality represented, literally and metaphorically, on the stage. As she says herself, she and Nora seemed 'destined, from birth, to be the lovely ephemera of the theatre' (p. 58). During their professional life, they have danced the boards in music halls, have taken roles as extras in ill-fated Hollywood musicals and, stripped to G-strings, have taken part in strip shows.

Like the Renaissance stage bastard, Dora can move from one level of reality to another more easily than those who occupy a fixed position. Indeed, *Wise Children*, intertwining the different zigzagging family, professional and social lines between the two families, the legitimate and the illegitimate, is a mirror of the Renaissance stage, which, as Findlay (1994) says, 'was composed of very disparate modes which co-existed and intertwined' (p. 220). In particular, since Melchior and Peregrine, Dora's and Nora's father and uncle, are twins (who is the father and who is the uncle?), the novel reflects the way in which the Renaissance theatre disrupted the fixed nature of classic theatre. Of course, from a Puritan perspective, playhouses were seen as places of erotic exchange which destabilised clear distinctions between the classes and genders. Indeed, Dora's autobiographical narrative begins by bemoaning the loss of clear distinctions in London's social geography generally.

THE SHAKESPEARE PLOT

Thus, in *Wise Children*, Carter appears to write from the theatre conceived as a location of illegitimate power, pursuing the creative possibilities in the way in which in the Renaissance 'illegitimacy' and 'theatre' were often linked. From this vantage point, she is able to explore different sites of the illegitimate power associated with theatre, such as the carnivalesque, the mask, the brothel, and the social margins. Indeed, the source of the carnivalesque in *Wise Children* was undoubtedly Shakespeare, as suggested by an interview Carter gave in 1991. Here, she criticised the way in which Shakespeare's recognition as a canonical writer has led to a misrepresentation of his work:

> intellectuals... are still reluctant to treat him as popular culture. ... You mention folk culture and people immediately assume you're going to talk about porridge and clog dancing, there's this William Morris and Arnold Wesker prospect, truly the bourne from which no traveller returns. Shakespeare, like Picasso, is one of the great hinge-figures that sum up the past – one of the great Janus-figures that sum up the past as well as opening all the doors toward the future. ... I like a *Midsummer Night's Dream* almost beyond reason, because it's beautiful and funny and camp – and glamorous, and cynical. ... English popular culture is very odd, its got some very odd and unreconstructed elements in it. There's no other country in the world where you have pantomime with men dressed as women and women dressed as men. ... It's part of the great tradition of British art, is all that 'smut' and transvestism and so on. (Sage, 1992a, pp. 186–187)

Bakhtin might have regarded the carnivalesque in Shakespeare to be controlled within and by the larger Symbolic Order of the plays. But, while Carter clearly believed that the carnivalesque in Shakespeare has not received the attention it deserves, her primary interest is in the way in which the Shakespearian aesthetic and the carnival overlap. A year after Carter's death, Salman Rushdie (1993) described *Wise Children* as an 'oo-er- guy, brush-up-your-Shakespeare comedy' (p. xi). Certainly, *Wise Children* should encourage us to 'brush-up' Carter's Shakespeare.

An important insight into how Carter thought of Shakespeare is provided by her short prose piece, 'Overture and Incidental Music for *A Midsummer Night's Dream'* from *Black Venus* (1985). Indeed, *Black Venus* as a project is very relevant to a discussion of Carter's interest in the illegitimate and its relationship to the theatre in *Wise Children*. It is a collection of her short fiction written between the late 1970s and early 1980s, supposedly resurrecting episodes and versions of events that have not made it into the official records. Hence 'The Cabinet of Edgar Allan Poe' inserts into the literary biography of Poe an account of the significance of the black muse, his dead mother's legacy. Sage (1994b) points out that 'Overture and Incidental Music for *A Midsummer Night's Dream'* places the reader 'behind the plot, before the curtain rises, eavesdropping on the suppressed subtext' (p. 45). Carter suggests that the Court of Oberon and Titania has been idealised over the centuries and that the original Court was a much less sedate place. Like the wind which Dora observes to whip around backstage, Carter exposes what is hidden behind the scenes: the Golden Herm is a hermaphrodite, lusted after by Oberon, who sees him/her as a boy, through which Carter pursues her interest in the blurring of sexual boundaries. In a carnivalesque spirit, Carter gives us the 'reality' behind the English midsummer fantasy: all the fairies have head colds. Moreover:

> Puck is no more polymorphously perverse than all the rest of these sub-microscopic particles, his peers, yet there is something particularly rancid and offensive about his buggery and his undinism and his frotteurism and his scopophilia and his – indeed, my very paper would *blush*, go pink as an invoice, should I write down upon it some of the things Puck gets up to down in the reeds by the river, as he is distantly related to the great bad god Pan and, when in the mood, behaves in a manner uncommon in an English wood, although familiar in the English public school. (*Burning Your Boats*, p. 70)

It is important to appreciate the full implications of the relationship between the two texts which Carter encourages us to question by calling her story an 'overture and incidental music'. An 'overture' is normally an introduction, which reverses the chronological relationship between the two texts and does not have to have a close relationship in style to the main piece of music. Carter is really saying that *A Midsummer Night's Dream* is predicated on an absence. If Shakespeare's play is situated in a dream-world, the ever-present absence is what the Grimm brothers realised in their 'dark necromantic forest'.

The spirit of the carnivalesque which we find in 'Overture and Incidental Music for *A Midsummer Night's Dream*' pervades the account of the night of the fire which destroys the Hazard Mansion, marking the end of the great tradition of the English theatre, in *Wise Children*:

> The fire had unleashed a kind of madness.... The tenor and me weren't the only ones who'd succumbed to nature, either. Nothing whets the appetite like a disaster. Out of the corner of my eye, I spotted Coriolanus stoutly buggering Banquo's ghost under the pergola in the snowy rose-garden whilst, beside the snow-caked sundial, a gentleman who'd come as Cleopatra was orally pleasuring another dressed as Toby Belch. Not only that. I spied with my little eye an egg-shaped depression in a snow-drift on the parterre surmounted by the lead soubrette who was grinding away for dear life in the woman-on-top position and it turned out the moaning recipient of her favours was who else but my now definitively ex-lover, his cap was gone, but his bells were all tinkling, and he made her a star in her own right in his next production. (p. 103)

As in 'Overture and Incidental Music for *A Midsummer Night's Dream*', Carter presents a fantasy, or an interpretation of a fantasy. There is a confusion of roles here which leaves us wondering whether the people are themselves or the characters whose costumes they are wearing. The night of madness subverts the sense of decorum and sophistication that mediates the public's perception of theatre and the so-called 'serious' arts. This view is suggested by the setting – a traditional English garden – where there is an emphasis on purity: there is a 'snowy rose-garden' and 'snow-caked sundial'. It is also conveyed through the contrast between the words which describe the features of the garden and the Anglo-Saxon description of the activities taking place. Coriolanus 'buggering' Banquo's ghost and Cleopatra having oral sex with Tony Belch seem somehow contrary to the kind of spiritual and moral uplift which 'Theatre' is often thought to provide. However, this behaviour is exactly the kind of thing we might expect of Coriolanus. Cleopatra is actually behaving in character, as is Toby Belch. The carnivalesque spirit of the episode is reinforced by the fact that much of the sex that is taking place – sodomy and oral sex – lies outside what is conventionally represented as the 'norm'. In other words, from the conventional perspective of established society these may be regarded as 'illegitimate' activities:

> So there was an orgiastic aspect to this night of disaster and all around the blazing mansion, lit by the red and flickering flames milled the lamenting revellers in togas, kilts, tights, breeches, hooped skirts, winding sheets, mini-crinolines, like guests at a masquerade who've all gone suddenly to hell. (p. 103)

The theatre in the seventeenth century was a much more carnivalesque institution than it is today. It was much more a place for meeting and drinking and in the performances themselves there was more interaction between the actors and the audiences and within the audience itself than in Victorian and contemporary theatre. As such, theatres were often spaces marked by internal difference, antagonism and cultural tensions. The ambience of the theatre is reflected in Shakespeare's plays themselves which interleave serious subjects and plotlines with riotously vernacular counterpoints. However, as Carter herself was well aware, the more 'serious' subjects have often been stressed at the expense of the crossover between carnival and theatre.

Both *Nights at the Circus* and *Wise Children* pursue the coexistence of these two strands, the 'serious' and the carnivalesque, at a number of levels. In *Wise Children*, as in Shakespeare's plays, the language moves through a number of registers without violating the integrity of the work as a whole. Some of the prose is sharp and original, as in the description of Melchior's eyes as 'warm and dark and sexy as the inside of a London cab in wartime' (p. 72); or the description of scrapbook cuttings 'turned by time to the colour of freckles on the back of an old lady's hand' (p. 78); or the description of how 'Nora threw her heart away as if it were a used bus ticket' (p. 80). However, at other times, Carter incorporates familiar colloquialisms such as the description of 'a face like a month of Sundays' (p. 82) or the description of Nora as 'a martyr to fertility' (p. 81). Nevertheless, the interweaving of the literary with the colloquial is successful.

At the heart of the novel, Dora attempts to maintain a view of the world which, in describing a toy theatre, she summarises in terms of masked drama: 'the comic mask, the tragic mask, one mouth turned up at the ends, the other down, the presiding geniuses – just like life' (p. 58). In *Wise Children*, Dora and Nora dress up as they used to when they were younger, but they realise that even then they knew that it was all a masquerade. Now Dora observes wryly:

> Our fingernails match our toenails match our lipstick match our rouge. Revlon, Fire and Ice. The habit of applying war paint outlasts the battle; haven't had a man for yonks but still we slap it on. (p. 6)

In this regard, once again, there are parallels with *Nights at the Circus*. Of particular relevance to both novels are Brecht's realisations that 'the oppressors do not always appear in the same mask' and that 'masks cannot always be stripped off in the same way' (p. 192). At the heart of the novels is the central paradox which, according to Brecht, masked drama sought to uncover: 'The actors can do without (or with the minimum of) make-up, appearing 'natural', and the whole thing can be a fake; they can wear grotesque masks and can represent the truth' (Willett, 1964, p. 110). In *Nights at the Circus*, there is something grotesque yet 'real' about Fevvers. Dora in her 'warpaint' in *Wise Children* wears a mask in which truth is realised.

9
The Body, Illness, Ageing and Disruption: An Overview

Carter's novels, in which conventional narratives are deconstructed and their oppressive ideologies exposed, would seem to confirm Jameson's (1986) thesis that, when everything else appears to have been stripped away, only 'body manifestations are retained' (p. 321). Jameson argues that the body is potentially one of the most disruptive elements of narrative. This is especially evident in the popular genres upon which Carter drew in her work, such as fairy tales, science fiction, apocalyptic or 'Last days' narratives, gothic narrative and horror fiction. Very often these are texts which, like Carter's works, question the validity of key concepts such as 'civilisation', 'history' and 'progress'. In such contexts, the appearance of the body, according to Jameson, usually produces 'an awakening of fresh sight' which 'diverts a conventional narrative logic of the unfolding story in some *new* vertical direction' (p. 307).

THE BODY AS A SITE OF DISRUPTION

The disruptive function of the body in a work which challenges concepts such as civilisation and history is apparent even from a cursory reflection upon some of Carter's most recalcitrant 'bodies' discussed in the course of this book, such as the somewhat parodic gothic figure, Honeybuzzard; the spectral victim, Ghislaine; the man-inside-a-woman's-body, Eve; the transsexual, Tristessa; and the woman as bird, Fevvers; or upon the whole host of minor 'grotesques' that populate her fiction. But there are other characters, too, who, while they cannot be described as a grotesque, are positioned as 'Other' and associated with 'disruption'. This is evident, for example, in *The Magic Toyshop* (1967) – a novel especially sceptical

166

of grand narratives – which begins with Melanie's discovery that 'she was made of flesh and blood'. From the outset, this realisation disrupts the unfolding story:

> For hours she stared at herself, naked, in the mirror of her ward-robe; she would follow with her finger the elegant structure of her rib-cage, where the heart fluttered under the flesh like a bird under a blanket, and she would draw down the long line from breast-bone to navel (which was a mysterious cavern or grotto), and she would rasp her palms against her bud-wing shoulderblades. (p. 1)

In this passage, the unfolding narrative is checked by the multiple layers of symbolic and cultural meaning attached to the female body. The excitement and sense of self-satisfaction which Melanie experiences in this narcissistic enjoyment of her own physical being fragments, and is threatened by, the social construction of Woman. As Melanie tries on various preconceived images of Woman and female sexuality, the reader becomes more aware than Melanie of the cultural history at her shoulder. Instead of seeing only herself in the mirror, Melanie measures herself against different images of the female body as Woman.

Jameson provides us with a particularly appropriate framework within which to read *The Magic Toyshop* because its deconstructive method strips away the majority of discourses that determine the identity of the female as Woman. Carter adopts a similar approach to her principal protagonists in her subsequent novels, from *Love* to *The Passion of New Eve*, which, of all her work, focuses most starkly upon the manifestation of the body. Through these novels, it is possible to trace the development of one of the key tropes of Carter's 1970s fiction, the simultaneous eroticisation and deconstruction of the cultural construction of the body. In *Love* (1971), Lee's body is rendered sensual and is deconstructed at the same time:

> [Annabel] took a technical pleasure in observing the musculature of his shoulders and the play of snowlight on the golden down which covered them for he was of a furry texture. He was col-ourful to look at and also reminded her of Canova's nude, heroic statue of Napoleon in Wellington House. ... She was especially pleased when she caught a glimpse of his leonine left profile. She found him continuously interesting to look at but it hardly

occurred to her the young man was more than a collection of coloured surfaces. (p. 30)

While it was still a little unusual for a text at this time to eroticise the male nude, despite the influence of authors such as D. H. Lawrence, this attempt to do so is especially contentious. Lee is mediated through the eyes of Annabel and the eroticisation says more about her than about Lee's body. The description of Melanie's body at the beginning of *The Magic Toyshop* employs words which associate it with the larger world of nature: 'fluttered', 'like a bird', 'bud-wing' and 'cavern'. There is an element of mystery and, through the references to birds, of spirituality. But the description of Lee's body is undercut by some of the words which are used; 'musculature', 'play', 'texture', 'profile' and 'surfaces' are words which belong to the language of art criticism. The focus shifts from the body, which is placed and yet not placed within a particular heroic tradition of the male nude, to the observer. The representation of the body here is the product of a worrying detachment.

Thus, the human body and our perception of it are acknowledged in Carter's work as being a product of our individual psyches as much as particular cultural histories. All Carter's novels demonstrate an interest, albeit a characteristically sceptical one, in psychoanalysis and the ways in which it has influenced our thinking about our selves, our identities, our sexuality and our relationships with others. Elaine Jordan (1990) points out: 'playing the psychoanalytically questionable distinction between the real world of sense and the fantasy world of dreams, she collapses the one into the other' (p. 91).

One psychoanalytic trope dominates Carter's fiction more than others. While there is an absence of mothers in Carter's fiction, there are often characters who experience the loss of their mothers. For example, Morris's mother in *Shadow Dance* is killed in an air raid during the war; Melanie in *The Magic Toyshop* loses both her parents in a plane crash; Lee's mother in *Love* is lost to him when she suffers a nervous breakdown; and Marianne's mother in *Heroes and Villains* dies broken-hearted two years after her son's death. During the war years, of course, a generation of children suffered enforced separation from their mothers. As noted earlier, Carter herself experienced this, having been taken from London in the year in which she was born to live with her grandmother in the coal-mining village of Wath-upon-Dearne in South Yorkshire. Her experiences of evacuation coloured her view of industrial Britain. She came to see it as 'matriarchal', 'a community where women ruled the roost', and through a lens which she admitted was 'romantic' (p. 8). Carter's account of her upbringing during these years in 'The Mother Lode' provides us with a clear indication of how, for Carter, loss is replaced by something tangible and apprehensive. Although Carter grew fond of her grandmother, the initial account of her suggests that Carter's mother has been replaced by a disturbing presence:

> My maternal grandmother seemed to my infant self a woman of such physical and spiritual heaviness she might have been born with a greater degree of gravity than most people...she effort-lessly imparted a sense of my sex's ascendancy in the scheme of things, every word and gesture of hers displayed a natural dom-inance, a native savagery, and I am very grateful for all that, now, although the core of steel was a bit inconvenient when I was look-ing for boyfriends in the South in the late fifties, when girls were supposed to be as soft and as pink as a nursuree. (pp. 8–9)

In *The Magic Toyshop*, the mother is replaced by an aunt who has been rendered dumb and the father by a frightening patriarchal figure, Uncle Philip, whose entry into the novel is delayed, so that his 'presence', described in terms which evoke primal fears and anxieties, precedes him.

The disruptive body in Carter's fiction is often associated with a grotesque trait, as in the case of Honeybuzzard, Uncle Philip or Zero, or with a sense of loss, as in the case of Melanie, Annabel, Marianne, Fevvers and Dora. The latter is often imbricated in a loss of the mother. Thus, while there is an acknowledgement in Carter's fiction that identity is bound up with the way in which the body changes over time, for example through illness and ageing, illness and ageing are not approached simply as biological fact, existing outside cultural discourse and metaphor. Her approach, then, appears to be a very different one from that taken by cultural theorists, such as Susan Sontag, who have argued for taking illness out of metaphorical contexts. However, even though Carter employs illness as metaphor, she, too, is concerned with the deconstruction of illness. In Carter's fiction, illness and ageing are often conditions through which to explore the relationship between women, espe-cially between younger and older women, and between men and women within the context of patriarchy.

ILLNESS AND METAPHOR IN CARTER'S EARLY FICTION

Carter's interest in contexts and situations in which her characters are located at a boundary between 'reality' and 'fantasy' leads, almost inevitably, to an exploration of 'mental illness' in her work. In her early fiction, Carter seems interested in melancholic figures for whom, in the words of the French psychoanalyst, Julia Kristeva (1987), 'sadness is in reality the only object' (p. 22). Kristeva quarrels with Freud's interpretation of the melancholic/depressive as simply displacing hatred of an 'Other' into his or her own ego. For Kristeva, the melancholic is unable to displace the loss of the mother into language. Whereas others are able to deal with the loss of the mother by, for example, eroticising the lost object, the melancholic in Kristeva's view dies in her place:

> Signs are arbitrary because language begins with a *denegation* (*Verneinung*) of loss, at the same time as a depression occasioned by mourning. 'I have lost an indispensable object which happens to be, in the last instance, my mother', the speaking being seems to say. But no, I have found her again in signs, or rather because I accept to lose her, I have not lost her (here is the *denegation*), I can get her back in language. (p. 55)

Without suggesting that the melancholic figure in Carter's work can only be understood in terms of the failure of the *denegation* to which Kristeva refers, there is a connection to be drawn between the absence of mother figures in Carter's novels, the preponderance of characters who have lost their mothers and an abiding interest, in the early novels, in melancholy.

The concern with illness in Carter's work is focused on mental, rather than physical, illness. In *Love*, Lee's mother's illness comes between him and his mother in two respects, each of which suggests the difficulty which he has, in Kristeva's terms, in achieving *denegation* through language. The most graphic event in the relationship between Lee and his mother occurs when she interrupts his school's Empire Day festival: 'his mother, naked and painted all over with cabbalistic signs, burst into the crowded playground and fell writhing and weeping on the asphalt before him' (p. 10). This incident is linked to what he perceives as his mother's mental illness but, as in novels of the 1960s and 1970s, such as Ken Kesey's *One Flew Over the Cuckoo's Nest*, mental illness is not approached as an illness but is invoked to serve as a metaphor. In her novels, unlike the majority of fiction which employs mental illness as a textual trope, Carter frequently metaphorises illness to deconstruct cultural myths. In this case, the shadow which Lee's mother casts across his participation in Empire Day is an inverse mirror image of how the male, according to Freudian psychology, supposedly comes between the child and the mother, or in post-Freudian psychology the way in which the symbolic, personified in the father, disrupts the semiotic of the mother–child relationship. There are further possible readings of this incident, of course. At one level, his mother represents the return of the colonised. At another level, she is a return of the repressed mother shunned in Freudian psychology by the boy child, who sees her as castrated.

As a child, Lee is also persistently exposed to what is seen as his mother's 'persistent delusion that her sallow, dark baby, child of a dark stranger, was touched with the diabolic' (p. 11). This association with the devil is described in terms which bring to mind the nineteenth-century association of the African man with Satan, reminding the reader of one of the connotations of the letter 'S', which Lee carried as a child in the Empire Day tableau. But this connection between Lee and his mother determines the way in which his future, and his close connection with Buzz and ultimately Annabel, prove to be both 'feminine' and, in a sense, diabolic.

In the early novels, mental illness associated with the female is often associated with acts of 'difference' and sometimes violence. In *Heroes and Villains*, mental illness and ageing are linked in the analysis of the event by which Marianne's elderly nurse kills her father. She is described as acting in a 'fit of senile frenzy' (p. 15) and, by her uncle, as 'seriously maladjusted' (ibid.). The association of women with mental illness in Carter's early fiction through exaggerated acts of behaviour mocks the way in which women in the late nineteenth and early twentieth centuries were linked with highly emotional, unpredictable and hysterical behaviour. But it is also part of a larger trope in Carter's early novels, the fragility of identity perceived as both a cultural and a corporeal phenomenon. Again, this is evident in Lee's Empire Day festival.

The children in Lee's Empire Day tableau carry in turn the individual letters of the school's motto around their necks: 'Do right because it is right' (p. 10). The school's motto is not simply a motto but an induction into a particular way of perceiving one's life and behaviour which, on this particular day, is imbricated in Empire and colonisation. The motto begs the questions: 'What do we mean by right?' and 'Whose right do we mean when we speak of right?' Unknown to Lee, but possibly recognised by the reader, carried in this way, the school's motto reminds us of the way in which children in Kenya and Wales were shamed for not speaking the language of their coloniser by being forced to wear a sign around their neck in their indigenous language. It is significant that the word 'right' is singular. Lee's mother's interruption of Empire Day is not an act of mental illness, as Lee initially perceives it, but an event of mental and bodily difference which exposes the Empire Day pageant as an act designed to celebrate imperialism, to induct the children into the imperialist project and to homogenise identity. His mother epitomises, in her mind and body, the plurality of identities and rights which is Other to the school motto.

Thus, women in Carter's early novels are associated with mental illness which is often a trope for identity. This, as in the case of the children on Empire Day, is a mental and corporeal identity that is fragile in the sense that it can be disrupted. In pursuing this aspect of identity, Carter overturns the conventional binarism of an unstable, irrational female identity, epitomised in popular culture in the representation of emotionally unstable women who commit acts of violence, and stable, rational male identity. The binarism of mental and physical illness which Carter seeks to complicate in her early fiction is introduced at the outset of *Heroes and Villains*. Marianne, captured by the Barbarians, asks Jewel: 'What sicknesses do Barbarians get?' After he has listed the physical diseases from which they suffer, she asks, thinking about the behaviour of her nurse: 'Do Barbarians go mad?' (p. 27). The sicknesses which Jewel lists are: 'fevers from bad water. Cancers, when you grow old, if not before, or if you grow old, that is. Tetanus if you cut yourself. And that withering of the blood...' (ibid.). Jewel's brother, we learn, is dying from gangrene, which, in the way Marianne thinks of gangrene in the body of another barbarian she has seen, is described as one might describe a sexually transmitted disease such as syphilis: 'gangrene would have crept over him like ivy' (p. 26).

In the early fiction, male protagonists are not initially associated with mental illness, nor usually life-denying illnesses such as those from which the Barbarians in *Heroes and Villains* suffer, but ostensibly minor illnesses that are disruptive, such as cold and fevers. In *Shadow Dance*, Morris, who, as discussed in Chapter 2, is implicated in his friend Honeybuzzard's mutilation of Ghislaine's face, is said to have 'caught streaming colds in the summer when his eyes and nose ran like rivers' (p. 108). In *The Magic Toyshop*, when Finn enters Melanie's bed, 'his whole body was shaking' and his 'forehead burned with fever' (p. 170). Although Finn has a fever and is burning, he demonstrates the symptoms of being cold, such as shivering and teeth chattering.

Males catching colds or being overtaken by fevers are linked in the early texts with being excessively cold. Even in summer, Morris in *Shadow Dance* is described as 'still mortifying his flesh in dark, heavy, miserable, winter-weight corduroy' (p. 108). In *The Magic Toyshop*, Jonathon's attic is very cold: 'He was gnawed and pinched with cold; the scabs on his knees showed up a bright purple because of the cold and his nose was red and raw-looking' (p. 81). Finn comes to Melanie's bed, wet and muddy from having been outdoors. The language in both these later incidents suggests some kind of penance through physical suffering. The text overturns the traditional association of the male in Freudian psychology with being intact while the female is associated with a sense of lack. It is as if Carter's fiction is implying that the male is associated with a fundamental sense of guilt which requires the mortification of the flesh. But there is also a suggestion that males have a deep sense of loss that needs to be assuaged. When Finn asks to come into Melanie's bed, she is reminded of when she was a child and she would go to her mother's room for comfort and security. The sick male, in the case of Morris, Finn and even Jonathon, is a figure who is estranged and needs the comfort of the female: Morris has a handkerchief which Edna has ironed and which he is afraid to 'desecrate' (p. 108) by blowing his nose into it, an act which here signifies sexual violation; Finn needs to enter Melanie's bed and share her body warmth and Melanie brings Jonathon a hot drink. However, whereas Melanie used to go to her mother's room for comfort because she believed she could see ghosts, the male protagonists seek comfort from physical symptoms, not admitting, as Melanie did when she thought that she saw ghosts, their emotional needs. The obvious exception is the episode in which Honeybuzzard, having drugged Morris with sleeping pills, crawls into Emily's bed, seeking comfort from her because he is so 'tired'. They are interrupted by Morris's groaning. In keeping with the trope in Carter's early and 1970s fiction that men seek to ease a deep sense of loss, Morris bemoans the belief that he has killed his mother. Held by Emily, who is naked, he takes solace in resting on

her breasts while she thinks of herself comforting him as she might
a younger sister or brother.

WOMEN AND AGE IN CARTER'S FICTION

Wise Children is the novel that has the most sustained focus upon
how ageing is not only a biological but a sociocultural phenomenon.
It conflates ageing with the way in which the history of ordinary
women has been occluded by histories centred upon men. Through
a narrator who is both elderly and a woman, Carter conflates feminist appreciation of the importance of autobiography to women and
the changing values ascribed to oral histories of the elderly after
the 1970s. Pam Morris (1993) points out that autobiography helped
women discover that their emotions, circumstances, frustrations,
and desires were shared by other women (p. 60). In the 1970s, 'life
story review' was seen as increasingly important as one of the ways
in which elderly people could fulfil the need to make sense of their
lives while providing posterity with histories that had been previously marginalised or silenced. In *Wise Children*, Dora is energised
by her past. In depicting those aspects of women's lives which, in
Morris's words, 'have been erased, ignored, demeaned, mystified
and even idealised' (ibid.), Dora's autobiography challenges the
notion of history as a narrative written by men, by the young and,
as I shall discuss later, by the legitimate.

Central to Dora's narrative is the importance of retaining context.
In recounting her sister Nora's first sexual experience with her first
boyfriend, Pantomime Goose, by whom she became pregnant, Dora
cautions:

> Don't be sad for her. Don't run away with the idea that it was a
> squalid, furtive miserable thing, to make love for the first time on
> a cold night in a back alley with a married man with strong drink
> on his breath. He was the one she wanted, warts and all, she *would*
> have him, by hook or by crook. (p. 81)

Dora's narrative seeks to remember and preserve how Nora and
she herself felt at particular moments in their lives. For her this is
preferable to adopting the kind of retrospective which primarily
seeks to understand people's lives and especially the mistakes that
they made. Similarly, she recreates the enthusiasm and passion of

her grandma for keeping a scrapbook of Dora and Nora's achievements as artistes. When they teased her about this, their own old age seemed a long way off:

> We felt bad when we saw those scrapbooks, we remembered how we'd teased her, we'd brought home sausage rolls, and crocodile handbags, but she's kept on snipping out the cuttings, pasting them in. Piles of scrapbooks, the cuttings turned by time to the colour of the freckles on the back of an old lady's hands. Her hand, my hand as it is now. When you touch the old newsprint, it turns into brown dust, like the dust of bones. (p. 78)

Carter scholarship has always had much to say about the relationship between gender and the body, femaleness and femininity, and pansexuality in her fiction. However, it has ignored the presence of the older female, especially that of the postmenopausal woman, such as Aunt Margaret in *The Magic Toyshop* and Mrs Green in *Heroes and Villains*. As suggested earlier, the representation of age in Carter's early novels is both 'real' and 'one-dimensional', no doubt because of the way in which her work emerged from a long-standing interest in premodern narratives such as fairy tales. Even her young characters sacrifice at least some of their verisimilitude to the parodic and transformative narratives in which they are often presented as, unwittingly, the object. But the fairy-tale element in Carter's depiction of age is especially apparent in the case of older females, who are often complicit in the oppression of their sex, such as Madame Schreck in *Nights at the Circus*, or, reminiscent of Rider Haggard's *She*, hide behind a masque of youth, as in the case of Princess Abyssinia in that novel. In the circus ring, Abyssinia looks like a child but 'close to, her face, though neither lined nor wrinkled, was ancient as granite, with the blunt, introspective features of Gauguin's women' (p. 106).

Madame Schreck is a particularly negative representation of postmenopausal woman in Carter's work: 'Madame Schreck is up and dressed and stood there before me in her black dress and a thick veil such as a Spanish widow wears that comes down to her knees, and her mittens on, all complete' (p. 58). She is inseparable from her museum, whose sense of macabre theatre she seems to have internalised. Ironically, her widow's clothes give her a Gothic vitality which appears to be denied to the body within: 'What a shock I got when I felt the rasp of her finger-tips on my palm, for they were indeed hard, as if there were no flesh on 'em' (p. 59). Instead of the wolf in the old grandmother's clothes in 'Red Riding Hood', Carter's narrator, recalling the puppet master Uncle Philip in *The Magic Toyshop*, believes that 'under those lugubrious garments of hers you might find nothing but some kind of wicked puppet that pulled its own strings' (p. 58).

The portrayal of Madame Schreck in her large safe, hugging its riches, stands in sharp contradistinction to more positive representations of postmenopausal women. If Carter's negative representations of postmenopausal women seem to have been influenced by older women in fairy stories and fables, these positive images are probably the product of the years Carter spent as a child with her grandmother in Yorkshire during the Second World War. The physical and emotional solidity of Aunt Margaret in *The Magic Toyshop* and Mrs Green in *Heroes and Villains* echoes Carter's own description of her grandmother in her autobiographical essay, 'The Mother Lode', in *Shaking A Leg* (1997).

In *Heroes and Villains*, Mrs Green has 'a room to herself because she was old and dignified' (p. 36) and she is 'a solid and unmistakeable figure' (p. 37). In her essay, 'The Mother Lode', Carter recalls her grandmother as she appeared to her as an infant. Although not that young, Mrs Green, like Aunt Margaret in *The Magic Toyshop*, is seen too through a young pair of eyes. When Marianne first sees Mrs Green, she is regaining consciousness from a snake bite, symbolically reminding us of Eve, who, metaphorically 'bitten' in the Garden of Eden, enters time and a cycle of prepuberty, menstruation and the postmenopause. Mrs Green, like Carter's grandmother, has been through and is now 'beyond' the cycle and thereby has a different relationship to time. In the essay 'The Mother Lode', *The Magic Toyshop* and *Heroes and Villains*, standing outside the female body cycle is analogous of having lived through the cycle of 'innocence', 'experience' and 'beyond experience'.

In some respects, it might be tempting to see Mrs Green and Aunt Margaret as surrogate mother figures. Each gets to know her new charge in the kitchen, which is traditionally a 'female space' but one which also associates women with servility and domesticity. Each provides food and kindness to a homeless, young female. Yet they are also 'removed' from Melanie and Marianne and from the role of mother. Mrs Green gazes at the children of the small family groups with 'fear and sadness'. From her space outside 'experience' and female corporeality, she is able to bring an understanding of the passive–assertive struggle within the young mother:

> This woman was perhaps a year or so younger than she, certainly very young. She had snakes tattooed around her wrists; the tail of each snake disappeared succinctly into its own mouth. She wore no stockings or shoes. Her dress was made of a stolen blanket patterned with large dark blue and black checks, a dress as rectangular in design as a box, cut deep at the breast for nursing. Her right knee showed through a tear. She wore a dead wrist watch on her arm... (p. 44)

The description of the mother is associated with two consciousnesses: Mrs Green's and Marianne's. At one level, the symbolism, like Melanie's snakebite, which suggests a temporal connection between the two young women, connotes Eve in the Garden of Eden and her induction into time and the female cycle. The snakes around her wrists suggest that she is shackled by them and by the female cycle. The tear at her knee suggests the 'tear' in the vagina which takes a woman into a particular female version of time. Swallowing their own tails, the snakes suggest a circle which signifies the life cycle, the female cycle and a place outside the circle which both young women have yet to understand and in which Mrs Green is located. Wearing a wristwatch that has stopped, the young mother is 'frozen' in time in so far as she repeats an endlessly recurring cycle of female experience, but, unlike Mrs Green, she is too young to understand fully the nature of the cycle.

In 'The Mother Lode', Carter describes a visit to her grandmother which is centred on a retrospective understanding of how she and her grandmother occupied a different relationship to time. Like many of the young women in her novels, Carter, perceives herself as caught up in an ongoing identity struggle marked by the intensity with which she uses her own body as a signifier of unpredictable possibilities:

> When I was eighteen, I went to visit her rigged out in all the atrocious sartorial splendour of the underground high-style of the late fifties, black-mesh stockings, spike-heeled shoes, bum-hugging skirt, jacket with a black fox collar. She laughed so much she wet herself. 'You wait a few years and you'll be old and ugly, just like me,' she cackled. She herself dressed in dark dresses of heavy

rayon crêpe, with grey Lisle stockings bound under the knee with two loops of knotted elastic. (p. 8)

In how she is dressed, Carter is redolent of the young, black, female erotic dancer Leilah in *The Passion of New Eve*, discussed in Chapter 6.

Carter metaphorically wears a wristwatch that has stopped. To an eighteen-year-old, there is no real awareness of anything other than the present moment. With her usual candidness, Carter's grandmother, who is as outside fashion as outside body cycles, begins her granddaughter's induction into time. Eventually, she will be able to see what she once celebrated as 'atrocious'. In their polarisation, granddaughter and grandmother represent the innocence of youth and the experience of age. But, within this scenario, there are subtle indications of a more complex dialectic. The word 'cackled' might well describe an old woman's voice, but it is also a word which is used in fairy tales to describe the voice of an old witch. The elision of 'witch' and 'old age' in fairy stories establishes a way in which elderly women in Western cultural discourse can be seen as menacing. In fairy stories, they often prey on the young, preparing, as in Hansel and Gretel, to literally consume their youth. What Carter does here, though she only realises it later, is to literally present her innocence to her grandmother.

Like Leilah in *The Passion of New Eve*, the young Carter with her grandmother seems to be what she saw in *The Sadeian Woman* as one of the archetypes of pornography interested in inviting sex. At the beginning of the female cycle, unlike the young mother in *Heroes and Villains*, the eighteen-year-old Carter, who sheds menstrual blood, stands in contradistinction to the grandmother who wets herself, a reminder that she is postmenopausal. The young Carter is dressed in a style which has sadomasochistic overtones, as discussed in relation to Leilah in *The Passion of New Eve* in Chapter 6. Unlike Leilah, who is very aware of the way she dresses and of how she is dressing fetishistically to satisfy the voyeurism of her paying audience, the young Carter seems innocent of the way she fetishises herself. Her outfit includes spike-heels and black mesh stockings, signifying perhaps a domina from sadomasochistic fantasy, but the black fur around her collar and the short skirt might unwittingly signal her sexual availability. The way she dresses epitomises the way in which she may be negotiating different sexual polarities while suggesting that all gender and sexual play involves such a negotiation of opposites.

However, it is not only the eighteen-year-old Carter who is dressed according to cultural stereotypes. Whilst her grandmother, through her age, is freed from intense engagement with the body as performance, she is dressed in a way that confirms the way in which postmenopausal women are seen, unaware of how her dark sober garb conflates menopausal identity with widowhood. Much the same point is made in the representation of Aunt Margaret in *The Magic Toyshop*:

> Like Mrs Rundle, she wore black – a shapeless sweater and drag-gled skirt, black stockings (one with a big potato in the heel), trodden down black shoes that slapped the floor sharply as she moved. She smiled a nervous, hungry sort of smile, opening her arms to welcome them as Finn had done. (p. 40)

The Magic Toyshop explores the way in which elderly women like Aunt Margaret are denied a voice; Aunt Margaret is dumb and has to communicate by means of a slate and chalk.

The letter which Melanie writes to Mrs Rundle, with whom Aunt Margaret is compared here, is a vehicle by which Carter introduces another dimension of her representation of the relationship between young women and postmenopausal women. The letter is structured around expectations and conflicts. Melanie's letter writing is frequently revised as she considers and reconsiders what it would be appropriate for someone of her age to say to someone of Mrs Rundle's age. The letter becomes an exercise in communication and non-communication: 'We had a good journey but it was tiring. We hope you had a good journey' (p. 78). The difficulty in finding not only something to say but how to say it is reflected in the repetitive, over-formal, balanced sentences: 'Victoria and I share a room. Aunt Margaret seems very fond of Victoria, already' (p. 79). What emerges is Melanie's and the reader's growing awareness of the extent to which each must be a stranger to the other: 'What could she tell Mrs Rundle, who was now if she had ever been much more than a stranger, living at a distance, forgetting them, putting them into her past, memories packed with other memories in her bulging handbag?' (p. 78).

Mrs Green cares for Marianne, despite being complicit in the ritual which is intended to bind Marianne and Jewel together. She makes astute observations in clipped statements that reflect acumen and knowledge that have come from experience and age. They bring her closer to those to whom she offers empathy, constructive advice and support but they also draw attention to the boundary around her that her age and status create. To the young mother, Mrs Green says: 'I should keep them warm, if I were you' (p. 44); and to Marianne, she remarks: 'It's all very different from what you've been accustomed to, dear' (p. 45) and 'Bread's a bit of a luxury' (p. 42). Commenting on the young males, she almost dismisses them: 'Wild boys, all' (p. 40). Marianne watches transfixed as Mrs Green prepares her first breakfast. At one level, the surprisingly detailed description of the process highlights Mrs Green's culinary skills, acquired in the course of her lifetime, but, at another level, it defamiliarises them as well as Mrs Green herself.

There are no characters in Carter's novels who actually age over the course of the narrative. Although happening suddenly, there is the case of Finn in *The Magic Toyshop* who, after his fall in the puppet theatre, is said to have 'stumped like an old man', 'transformed into this lump of unbaked dough' (p. 134). Indeed, there are many characters who, as discussed in the course of this book, undergo transformation and, in some cases, for example Evelyn in *The Passion of New Eve*, it is as sudden as this. However, Carter's novels do provide us with a sense of characters having aged in a specific socio-historical context before the narrative begins, as it were. *Nights at the Circus* gives us a glimpse into the kind of past in which Madame Schreck has grown up and aged: 'Esmeralda's old man, the Human Eel, told me how this Madame Schreck, as she called herself, had indeed started out in life as a Living Skeleton, touring the sideshows, and always was a bony woman' (p. 59). There is a similar insight into Mrs Green, who seems to have, as Melanie thinks of Mrs Rundle, a few principal memories to which age in Carter's novels seem to 'reduce' a particular life: she keeps a framed, faded photograph of the Professor of Economics' wife for whom she once worked on a wooden box which holds her personal belongings, such as a few dresses, several aprons, her hair pins and a book, *Great Expectations*, which she has forgotten how to read. The fact that she has forgotten how to read implies, like the description in *The Magic Toyshop* of how Finn 'stumped like an old man', the wasting aspect of ageing. There are similar suggestions of the negative aspects of ageing in many of Carter's novels, including *Wise Children*, the only novel which unravels in detail how its central protagonists have aged through a particular milieu, but, on the whole, that novel presents ageing in a positive, carnivalesque spirit.

The representation of identity in Carter's fiction eschews the mind–body dualism and conceives of the body as a fusion of the mental and the corporeal. The early fiction betrays the influence of post-feminist and Euro-American Gothic, discussed in Chapter 2, particularly in its emphasis upon melancholy, solipsistic behaviours and evidence of 'difference'. Across the depiction of what some protagonists label forms of mental illness but which, in the novels, are often a manifestation of difference, there is a sense of need, associated with a deep sense of loss and of lack, which challenges the explanation of male and female identities in Freudian psychology. Through the portrayal of ostensibly bizarre events and sometimes quite minor examples of illness, Carter challenges, and in some cases mocks, the conventional association of females with emotional needs and male protagonists with physical illness. While the actual process of ageing over the course of a narrative is not a feature of Carter's fiction, there is an interest, which can be traced back to her relationship with her grandmother, in women who have aged. This is a subject which in her later work is treated in a more spirited and carnivalesque way than in her earlier writings. Illness and ageing, however briefly presented, are employed as metaphors and tropes in Carter's fiction, but are, simultaneously, demythologising textual strategies.

Afterword

In the course of this book, we have discussed Carter's work in the light of new criticism and new critical ideas that have emerged since her death, some of which her fiction might be seen as anticipating. Another way of approaching Carter's work in the twenty-first century is to consider its influence on other writers. In this regard, this Afterword is really a note toward a project to which a number of critical works published in the second decade after Carter's death have already contributed but which has yet to be fully undertaken: what was Carter's legacy to the novel, especially to the British novel, at the end of the late twentieth and twenty-first centuries?

When Carter first started publishing, her novels appeared original and, as she continued to write, each work seemed more radical than the previous one. As suggested in Chapter 1, they seemed not to belong to an English tradition of the novel but to invoke a European, prenovelistic form. However, in the second decade after her death, it is clear that she has proved an important influence on the late twentieth and early twenty-first century British novel. Rubinson (2005) points out: 'Carter's experiments with genres like science fiction, gothic fiction, pornography and fairy tales helped pave the way for a wider critique of gender and genre...' (p. 3).

Carter's translations and alternative versions of fairy tales had a major impact upon the work of women writers who sought to make revisions of traditional fairy stories the basis of their own feminist work. The most notable works, written for adults or children, which, under the influence of Carter's writings, pushed back the boundaries of the fairy tale, include: Margaret Atwood's *Bluebeard's Egg* (1983), Babette Coles's *Princess Smarty Pants* (1986), Judy Corbalis's *The Wrestling Princess and Other Stories* (1986), Lynne Tillman's *The Trouble with Beauty* (1990), and Emma Donoghue's *Kissing the Witch* (1997). Her influence can clearly be seen on Joy Williams's contentious novel *The Changeling* (1978) and her recurrent concern with gender boundaries has influenced Wesley Stace's more recent novel *Misfortune* (2005), which concerns a boy brought up as a girl.

At the centre of the matrix of irony, parody and fantasy in Carter's fairy stories and, as discussed in Chapter 3, in *The Magic Toyshop* is a critique of how myths, fables and a variety of cultural fictions construct female identity. The overlap between these works and those which they influenced lies in how, as Onega (2006) maintains, apparently realistic episodes 'have a distinctive fairy tale flavour' (p. 20). This is evident from a comparison of *The Magic Toyshop* with one of the most important late twentieth-century novels which it influenced, Jeanette Winterson's *Oranges Are Not the Only Fruit*. Narrated retrospectively by an adult protagonist, Winterson's novel begins with her childhood recollections and traces her gradual sexual awakening into adolescence. Both texts share the harshness and cruelty of fairy-tale step-parents and what Onega (2006) describes in regard to Winterson's *Oranges* as total blindness 'to the child's sense of shame or self-respect' (ibid.). In each text, the young female protagonist, as Onega says of Winterson's novel, 'like a fairy tale heroine... has to console herself [in] the power of her imagination' (ibid.). The linearity of Carter's fiction and Winterson's *Oranges*, as Onega (2006) maintains of the latter, 'is constantly interrupted by the interpolation of fairytales and fragments of myth which recur with a difference and/or elaborate on key motifs...' (p. 22).

However, Carter's Gothic writing, referred to in the course of this book as post-Gothic, has also had a profound effect on the development of modern fiction. Tanith Lee's fiction, which includes *Birthgrave* (1975) and *The Blood of Roses* (1999), is especially indebted to Carter's fiction, which her work resembles in its playfulness with language and the way in which it fuses the genres of the fairy tale, Gothic and science fiction. In both Carter's and Winterson's fiction, too, there is a strong interest in the Gothic, but, in utilising Gothic motifs and plot devices, both authors present a critique of Gothic in a form which is not so much feminist Gothic as, to use a term introduced in Chapter 1, post-feminist Gothic. One of the recurring Gothic tropes that are rewritten from a feminist or post-feminist perspective in the wake of Carter's own revision of them is Mary Shelley's Gothic retelling of the creation myth, *Frankenstein*. Winterson's *Boating for Beginners* (1985) presents a post-feminist revision of Mary Shelley's novel in which God is made by accident out of a piece of gateau and a giant electric toaster. A previously secret manuscript written by Noah suggests, in what Onega (2006) describes as 'a ludicrous pastiche of Mary Shelley's Frankenstein' (p. 39), that Noah/Man created God. Winterson's text is very much like a Carter novel in its carnivalesque parodies and quite outrageous themes. The nameless creature which Noah creates turns the Hebraic notion that God's name should be unpronounceable on its head, as he becomes known as 'Yahweh the Unpronounceable'. What we have here is a radical

Angela Carter

alternative reading of the Bible as Carter's *The Passion of New Eve* is a revision of Genesis. Onega (2006) points out:

> The fact that, in this 'alternative' version of Genesis, it is Noah who creates God, and not the other way round is in keeping with Feuerbach's radical view that the idea of God was created by man to express the divine within himself, and that the beginning, middle and end of Religion is MAN. (p. 39)

Boating for Beginners also recalls *the Passion of New Eve* in its emphasis upon pansexuality: Noah, like Tristessa in Carter's novel, is a transvestite whom the Unpronounceable calls 'mother'. Marlene is a transvestite who, like Eve, wants her penis back (in her case, Noah's daughters-in-law provide her with a penis removed from someone else) and Noah's daughters-in-law run a clinic providing therapy in women's sexuality and change-of-sex operations, reminding us that, while Carter's Evelyn undergoes a change-of-sex operation, s/he, like Marlene, needs help in coping with the psychological transformation.

Fay Weldon's *The Life and Loves of a She-Devil* (1983), which has come to occupy a similar status in her *oeuvre* as *Nights at the Circus* in Carter's fiction, may also be said to share Carter's feminist/post-feminist interest in the Gothic. It overturns the way in which feminist Gothic focused upon the female as victim. The key protagonist, Ruth, is initially a victim of her husband's adultery with a beautiful and wealthy romance novelist, Mary Fisher. Instead of accepting her position, she wreaks revenge on her husband, which includes burning down their house so that their two sons have to live with her husband and Mary, who has remained childless up to this point in her life; arranging for Mary's aged mother to be thrown out of her nursing home so that she has to live with her daughter; destroying her husband's business and, by placing a temporary employee in his office to alter his books, having him jailed for embezzlement.

More widely, *The Life and Loves of a She-Devil* is redolent of Carter's fiction in the way in which it overturns a number of myths and fictions, recognising the importance of cultural discourse in determining social 'reality' for women. First, it is ironic that Mary Fisher is a romance novelist, as romance fiction conventionally suggests that a woman's destiny is to meet and fall in love with a handsome and, preferably, rich man. At the outset of conventional romance fiction, the female protagonist is usually independent and self-supporting, but in need of a man to complete her life, where-upon she invariably 'sacrifices' her independence to share her life with her male lover. Weldon's novel is written from the perspec-tive of the 'other' woman, who, in this text, is 'othered' in several respects; not only is she the 'victim' but, by sociocultural 'norms', she is unattractive. Second, in overturning Gothic conventions, and particularly *Frankenstein*, Ruth decides to have herself 'remade' by cosmetic surgery. As suggested earlier, there are a number of sites of violence in this text, as there are in Carter's *The Passion of New Eve*: Ruth burns down the house, uses Mary's aged mother to bring about her own ends, destroys her husband's career and reputation, and dismantles Mary's life. In her sadomasochistic relationship with her husband's trial judge, her own body becomes a site of pain as it does in the cosmetic surgery she decides to undergo, redolent of the way in which Evelyn's body, but not through his choice, becomes a site of pain. McKinstry (1994) points out that 'the site of violence is narrowed...to the female body itself' and that, at one level, it is a 'violent tale of self-loathing, self-destruction as a means of improvement, where the body itself becomes the site of struggle' (p. 105). In choosing cosmetic surgery, Ruth ironically reflects the way in which many women who decide to go down this path suc-cumb to the dominant, sociocultural ideals of how a female should look. Elisabeth Bronfen (1994) finds that what most 'radically irri-tates' her about Ruth is that she 'gain[s] power by confirming to excess the cultural formations' that turn women 'prematurely into inert and meaningless beings' (p. 73).

The Life and Loves of a She-Devil highlights how Weldon's fiction is indebted to Carter for its ironic exposure of the pain which women suffer, as Evelyn discovers in *The Passion of New Eve*, in becoming female and Woman. In this regard, Ruth's escape to a female, sep-aratist community, as Eve finds in *The Passion of New Eve*, does not provide any easy solace:

> Ruth joined a commune of separatist feminists. These women had no truck with the male world; they accepted her readily as one of themselves. She called herself Millie Mason. Like them, she wore jeans, T-shirt, boots and a duffle jacket: they did not ask her for credentials. She was female and had suffered for it, and that was enough...The Wimmin, as they called themselves, lived just outside the city, in a cluster of caravans around an old farmhouse. They worked a four-acre field, growing pulses, grain, comfrey

and yarrow, which they treated and sold in health food shops throughout the land. (chapter 29)

Fay Weldon also shares Carter's and Winterson's interest in the prescriptive power of fairy tales for women. Walker (1994) sees *The Life and Loves of a She-Devil* as 'a novel saturated with fairy-tale motifs': Mary Fisher is a princess in the tower; Ruth 'is compounded of Cinderella's jealous stepsisters and the evil fairy who contrives to bring Mary Fisher down from her tower'; and the style of the novel is 'incantatory', employing the language of spells (pp. 13–14). In this regard, Walker (1994) stresses: 'Weldon both extends and inverts the Cinderella story to demonstrate the awful power of the ideals of romantic love and physical beauty' (p. 15). To her list of Weldon's allusions to fairy tales, Walker might also have added 'The Ugly Duckling', for *The Life and Loves of a She-Devil* is really a version of the ugly duckling story, in which transformation is obtained by surgery rather than nature.

Carter's influence on late twentieth and twenty-first-century women writers who overturn the expectations of genre to challenge society's expectations of women as Woman is evident also in Emma Tennant's *Faustine* (1992), which Rubinson (2005) argues 'rewrites the Faust legend with a woman as the Faust figure'. In this text, Muriel Twyman, 'reaching the age at which women "become invisible" in a "Centrefold world" ', makes a pact with the devil's representative for 'twenty-four years of youth, beauty, riches and power' (p. 195). Like Carter's fiction, this is a novel about people who are invisible, outside the social mainstream, such as the elderly.

What we might describe as Carter's middle fiction, including *The Passion of New Eve*, has had an important influence on Jeanette Winterson and upon one of her works in particular. In its exploration of the themes mentioned above, gender, sexual and female identity, Winterson's *The Passion* (1987) is clearly a novel dependent upon the type of writing which Carter pioneered. It interweaves the parallel stories of two witnesses to the Napoleonic Wars at a time when Hegelian World History was approaching its impending apocalypse. In this regard, and in its title, it recalls *The Passion of New Eve*, which is similarly concerned with World History reaching a critical moment and interweaves the lives of two participants/witnesses to what is happening. Despite the differences between *The Passion* and *The Passion of New Eve*, they have a number of features in common. In each text, a 'woman' is passed from one enslavement to another.

Winterson's Villanelle, a Venetian boatman's daughter, is sold by her husband as an army prostitute. In Carter's novel, Evelyn, as a result of an operation carried out by 'Mother', becomes a transsexual. As a result of a mistake by her natural mother, Villanelle becomes a bisexual woman with, like Carter's Tristessa, a predilection to transvestism. As Evelyn/Eve must live without his male sexual organs, Villanelle must live without a heart. Both novels develop the play of religious and sexual meanings within the word 'Passion'.

Although both Carter's and Winterson's fiction is interrupted by fragments of myth, fable and fairy tale, as discussed above, Carter went further than Winterson has been prepared to go and, in this regard, Kathy Acker's work is closer to Carter's fiction. Acker finds, like Carter, to quote what Pitchford (2002) says of Acker's work, 'in the discrepancies among various (undeniably oppressive) narratives of identity, subversive pleasure, humour and agency' (p. 60). Moreover, as Pitchford says of Acker, but bringing Carter to the fore as a major influence on her work: 'The plagiaristic, pastiche technique of Kathy Acker's writing ... breaks up the homogeneity of culture, exposing the numerous and varied discourses that at any moment influence and shape each of us' (p. 59). Within this framework, Acker and Carter occupy a space which Acker defines in her novel *In Memoriam to Identity* (1990): 'Porn and exile and fear and violence/ Are part of us' ('The Beginning of the Life of Rimbaud'). At one level, Pitchford (2002) suggests: 'One would be hard pressed to find a style that differed more from Kathy Acker's blunt, street-smart polemics than the purple prose of British writer Angela Carter' (p. 105). But what they have in common, Pitchford finds, is 'a postmodernist view of history as the transmission not so much of facts but of texts' (pp. 105–106).

The part that images from a range of visual and verbal texts play in shaping the present for women writers such as Acker, Weldon and Winterson takes us back to Carter and to what Pitchford calls her 'quotational tactics'. By this, she means the way in which Carter's method, more allusive than Acker's direct approach, is to recognise that 'literary meaning, rather than being autonomous and fixed, changes according to the circumstances under which a reader uses a text' (p. 106). One of Carter's most important pieces of 'retextualisation' was the use which she made of speculative fiction in *Heroes and Villains*, *The Infernal Desire Machines of Doctor Hoffmann*, and, eventually, *The Passion of New Eve*. Rubinson (2005) argues that 'Carter took a genre that was traditionally dominated by male writers and characterized by sexist tropes, and made it work for feminist ends' (p. 175).

Carter's exploration in her dystopian novels of the kind of society that would emerge in a post-apocalyptic world paved the way for a feminist mode of speculative fiction exemplified by Margaret Atwood's *The Handmaid's Tale* (1985). Like *The Passion of New Eve*, it belongs to an American strain of post-apocalyptic fiction, but it has its roots in the religious and political fundamentalism of the 1980s. Although it is a very different novel from *The Passion of New Eve*, aspects of it betray some of the ways in which Carter opened up the possibilities of this kind of writing for women authors. Like *Heroes and Villains*, *The Infernal Desire Machines of Doctor Hoffmann* and *The Passion of New Eve*, Atwood's novel looks both to the future and to present society, of which it presents a critique. Whilst this may be said of most speculative fiction, Atwood and Carter refocus conventional, male-centred writing of this kind upon the body, especially the female body, and the way in which it is defined by language and discourse. Thus, the dystopian tale brings to the fore notions of forbidden desires and practices which invoke a wider history of female sexual discourse. Central to *The Handmaid's Tale*, as to Carter's fiction, is the way in which women are encouraged, expected and/or coerced to pursue specific realisations of female identity.

Carter's later work, especially *Nights at the Circus*, has had an important influence on the careers of a number of key writers working across a range of genres. Pat Barker was actually taught by Carter on an Arvon Foundation Course and her influence can be seen in several aspects of *Regeneration*: its common touch, black humour and music-hall elements. But *Nights at the Circus* and *Wise Children* probably had the most extensive influence on the work of the Welsh-born writer Sarah Waters. Like *Wise Children*, *Tipping the Velvet* is narrated by an ex-music hall 'turn' and depicts events that have long passed. In both novels, the narrative voice is a site where the literary meets the vernacular; the title of Walters's novel is Victorian slang for cunnilingus. *Tipping the Velvet* (1998) shares with Carter's *Wise Children* a concern with the aesthetic of the music hall, and especially with the overlap between 'serious' and 'popular' theatre. Although it is a different novel from *Wise Children*, elements of the central protagonist's biography bring to mind the life histories of Fevvers in *Nights at the Circus* and Dora in *Wise Children*. Waters's Nancy Astley has 'risen' from the Oyster bars and, like Fevvers, from prostitution through a life which includes being a male impersonator and an aristocrat's 'plaything'.

How Carter's fiction opened the portal for works like *Tipping the Velvet* is evident in Waters's Carter-like interest in the ways in which the Victorian music hall 'played' with the codified representations of serious theatre and of gender and sexuality. Waters, like Carter, is especially interested in the dialectic between the music hall and wider society, especially as far as assumptions about gender and sexuality were concerned. The exploration of androgyny, a recurring theme in Carter's work, is to the fore in Waters's novel. Nancy, or Nan King as she is known by her androgynous stage name, is initially associated with oysters, which are hermaphroditic, and later, disguised as a man, she performs sexual acts on gay men. But the real emphasis in the text is upon lesbian relationships that push back the boundaries of gender and sexual identity. Like *Nights at the Circus* and *Wise Children*, Waters's novel exposes how respectable Victorian society and the Victorian sexual underground are interwoven, and both Carter and Waters are indebted to how this is revealed in Victorian pornography. Like *The Passion of New Eve* and *The Sadeian Woman*, *Tipping the Velvet* revises the notion of pornography; a vehicle for 'illegitimate' sexuality which, like the illegitimate theatre described in Chapter 8, exists in a continuous dialectic with the legitimate, and vice versa.

The central relationship in Waters's novel is between two women, one a very experienced male impersonator. Its choice of a performer as a central protagonist anchors, as in Carter's novels, a concern with identity itself as a performance. Moreover, like *Wise Children*, *Tipping the Velvet* reflects how the scandal which impersonators like Kitty generated through their acts recalled the 'real-life' performers, some of whom are discussed Chapter 8, and the scandal of their lives offstage. When Nan learns that her female lover Kitty and Walter have married, she takes to the streets in her theatrical costumes, signifying the integration of the theatre and the world of the performer outside the theatre and undermining any notion of the music hall as a world of spectacle and illusion removed from the 'real' world.

Although the texts discussed here are only a handful of those for which Carter paved the way, they suggest the extent of her influence as a postmodern writer on late twentieth-century and twenty-first-century fiction written by women. The term 'postmodern' is complex. Rubinson (2005) suggests: 'Scholars have viewed postmodern literature as critical, protesting, deconstructing, demythologizing, de-naturalizing, and subversive' (p. 196). He also makes the point: 'Because contemporary or postmodern fiction is so often discussed in terms of what it is *against* it is easy to lose sight of what it stands *for*' (p. 196). This is a question which can probably only be explored by a fuller discussion of the feminist and post-feminist works for which Carter paved the way. They share with Carter's fiction the struggle to make sense of human history through a focus on the gendered nature of cultural discourse, language systems and symbolic orders; the exploration of the social norms of sex and morality; and the exposition of power relations in different societies and contexts. Placing Carter's works, as here, in context with even a few of the authors whom she has influenced underscores how Carter's fiction is situated not just in theoretical debates over representation but in concrete issues around social relations. McKinstry (1994) says of Weldon's *The Life and Loves of a She-Devil*: 'Weldon takes the female body as symbol and turns that symbol back into flesh-and-blood, but flesh-and-blood dismembered by the symbolic demands on it' (p. 105). She might as well have been describing Carter's fiction.

Select Bibliography

MAJOR WORKS BY ANGELA CARTER

Novels

Shadow Dance (London: Heinemann, 1966; repr. as *Honeybuzzard*, New York: Simon & Schuster, 1966; London: Pan, 1968; London, Virago: 1995).

The Magic Toyshop (London: Heinemann, 1967; New York: Simon & Schuster, 1968; London: Virago, 1981).

Several Perceptions (London: Heinemann, 1968; New York: Simon & Schuster, 1968; London: Pan, 1970; London: Virago Press, 1995).

Heroes and Villains (London: Heinemann, 1969; New York: Simon & Schuster, 1969; Harmondsworth, Middx: Penguin, 1981).

Love (London: Rupert Hart-Davis, 1971; rev. London: Chatto and Windus, 1987; New York: Viking Penguin, 1988; London: Picador, 1988).

The Infernal Desire Machines of Doctor Hoffman (London: Rupert Hart-Davis, 1972; repr. as *The War of Dreams*, New York: Bard/Avon Books, 1977; Harmondsworth, Middx: Penguin, 1982).

The Passion of New Eve (London: Gollancz, 1977; New York: Harcourt Brace Jovanovich, 1977; London: Virago, 1982).

Nights at the Circus (London: Chatto and Windus, 1984; New York: Viking, 1985; London: Pan, 1985).

Wise Children (London: Chatto and Windus, 1991; New York: Farrar, Straus, and Giroux, 1992; London: Vintage, 1992).

Short fiction

Fireworks: Nine Profane Pieces (London: Quartet Books, 1974; New York: Harper and Row, 1981; rev. London: Chatto and Windus, 1987; London: Virago, 1988).

The Bloody Chamber and Other Stories (London: Gollancz, 1979; New York: Harper and Row, 1980; Harmondsworth, Middx: Penguin, 1981).

Black Venus's Tale (with woodcuts by Philip Sutton) (London: Next Editions in association with Faber, 1980).

Black Venus (London: Chatto and Windus, 1985; repr. as *Saints and Strangers*, New York: Viking Penguin, 1987; London: Picador in association with Chatto and Windus, 1986).

American Ghosts & Old World Wonders (London: Chatto and Windus, 1993; London: Vintage, 1994).

Burning Your Boats: The Collected Angela Carter: Stories, intr. Salman Rushdie (London: Chatto and Windus, 1995).

Children's fiction

Miss Z. The Dark Young Lady (illustrated by Keith Eros) (London: Heinemann, 1970; New York: Simon & Schuster, 1970).
The Donkey Prince (illustrated by Keith Eros) (New York: Simon & Schuster, 1970).
Martin Leman's Comic and Curious Cats (illustrated by Martin Leman) (London: Gollancz, 1979; London: Gollancz paperback, 1988).
Moonshadow (paintings by Justin Todd) (London: Gollancz, 1982).

OTHER WORKS

Unicorn (Leeds: Location Press, 1966).
Come Unto These Yellow Sands: Four Radio Plays (Newcastle upon Tyne: Bloodaxe Books, 1985; Dufour Editions, 1985).
Jordan, Neil (dir.), *The Company of Wolves* (ITC Entertainment/Palace Production, 1984).
Wheatley, David (dir.), *The Magic Toyshop* (Granada Television, 1987).
'The Kitchen Child', *Short and Curlies* (Channel Four, 1990).
The Holy Family Album (Channel Four, 1991).

Non-fiction

The Sadeian Woman: An Exercise in Cultural History (London: Virago, 1979; repr. as The Sadeian Woman and the Ideology of Pornography, New York: Pantheon, 1979).
The Fairy Tales of Charles Perrault (London: Gollancz, 1977; New York: Bard Books, 1979) (edited; includes a foreword by Carter).
Nothing Sacred: Selected Writings (London: Virago, 1982; rev. 1992).
Shaking a Leg: Collected Writings (ed. Jenny Uglow) (Harmondsworth: Penguin, 1998).
Sleeping Beauty and Other Favourite Fairy Tales (London: Gollancz, 1982; New York: Schoken, 1989; London: Gollancz, 1991) (edited and translated).
Memoirs of a Midget (introduction to Walter de la Mare) (Oxford: Oxford University Press, 1982).
The Puzzleheaded Girl (introduction to Christina Stead) (London: Virago, 1984).
Wayward Girls and Wicked Women (edited) (London: Virago, 1990).
Duck Feet (introduction to Gilbert Hernandez) (London: Titan Books, 1988).
Images of Frida Kahlo (London: Redstone Press, 1989).
The Virago Book of Fairy Tales (edited) (London: Virago, 1990; repr. 1991).
Jane Eyre (introduction to Charlotte Brontë) (London: Virago: 1990).
Expletives Deleted: Selected Writings (London: Chatto and Windus, 1992; repr. London: Vintage, 1993).
The Second Virago Book of Fairy Tales (edited) (London: Virago, 1992; repr. 1993).

CRITICISM OF ANGELA CARTER'S WORK AND
OTHER RELEVANT SECONDARY SOURCES

Albinski, Nan Bowman, *Women's Utopias in British and American Fiction* (London and New York: Routledge, 1988).

Alexander, Flora, *Contemporary Women Novelists* (London: Arnold, 1989).

Alvarez, Antonia, 'On Translating Metaphor', *Meta*, 38, 2 (September 1993): 479–490.

Andrew, Dudley, 'Family Diversions: French Popular Cinema and the Music-hall', in *Popular European Cinema*, eds Richard Dyer and Ginette Vincendeau (London and New York: Routledge, 1992).

Armstrong, Isobel, 'Woolf by the Lake, Woolf at the Circus: Carter and Tradition', *Flesh and the Mirror: Essays on the Art of Angela Carter*, ed. Lorna Sage (London: Virago, 1994).

Assael, Brenda, *Circus and Victorian Society* (Charlottesville and London: University of Virginia Press, 2005).

Atwood, Margaret, 'Magic Token through the Dark Forest', *The Observer*, (23 February 1992), 61.

Bakhtin, Mikhail, *Rabelais and His World*, trans. Helene Iswolsky (Cambridge, Mass.: MIT Press, 1968).

Barker, Paul, 'The Return of The Magic Story-Teller', *Independent on Sunday* (8 January 1995), 14–16.

Barreca, Regina, *Fay Weldon's Wicked Fictions* (Hanover and London: University Press of New England, 1994).

Baudrillard, Jean, *Symbolic Exchange and Death* (1976), trans. Iain Hamilton Grant (London: Sage, 1993).

Bayley, John, 'Fighting for the Crown', *New York Review of Books*, (23 April 1992), 9–11.

Bell, Michael, 'Narrations as Action: Goethe's "Bekenntnisse Einer Schonen Seele" and Angela Carter's *Nights at the Circus*', *German Life and Letters*, 45, 1 (January 1992), 16–32.

Belsey, Catherine, *Critical Practice* (London and New York: Methuen, 1980).

Boston, Richard, 'Logic in a Schizophrenic World', *New York Times Book Review*, (2 March 1969), 42.

Brabon, Benjamin A. and Stéphanie Genz, 'Introduction. Postfeminist Gothic', *Gothic Studies*, 9, 2 (November 2007a), 1–6.

Brabon, Benjamin A. and Stéphanie Genz (eds), *Postfeminist Gothic: Critical Interventions in Contemporary Gothic* (Basingstoke: Palgrave Macmillan, 2007b).

Bristow, Joseph and Trev Lynn Broughton (eds), *The Infernal Desires of Angela Carter: fiction, femininity, feminism* (London: Longman, 1997).

Brockway, James, 'Gothic Pyrotechnics', *Books and Bookmen*, 20, 5 (February 1975), 55–56.

Bronfen, Elisabeth, ' "Say Your Goodbyes and Go" ': Death and Women's Power in Fay Weldon's Fiction', in *Fay Weldon's Wicked Fictions*, ed. Regina Barreca (Hanover and London: University Press of New England, 1994).

Brown, Richard, 'Postmodern Americas in the Fiction of Angela Carter, Martin Amis and Ian McEwan', in *Forked Tongues?: Comparing Twentieth-century British and American Literature*, eds Ann Massa and Alistair Stead. (Harlow and New York: Longman, 1994).

Bryant, Sylvia, 'Re-constructing Oedipus through "Beauty and the Beast"', *Criticism* 31, 4 (Fall 1989), 439–453.

Burke, Frank, *Federico Fellini: Variety Lights to La Dolce Vita* (London: Columbus Books, 1987).

Carr, Helen, *From My Guy To Sci-Fi: Genre and Women's Writing in the Postmodern World* (London: Pandora Press, 1989).

Carroll, Rachel, 'Return of the Century: Time, Modernity, and the End of History in Angela Carter's *Nights at the Circus*', *Yearbook of English Studies*, 30, (2000), 187–201.

Chedgzoy, Kate, *Shakespeare's Queer Children: Sexual Politics and Contemporary Culture* (Manchester: Manchester University Press, 1995).

Clark, Robert, 'Angela Carter's Desire Machine', *Women's Studies*, 14, 2 (1987), 147–161.

Collick, John, 'Wolves through the Window: Writing Dreams/Dreaming Films/Filming Dreams', *Critical Survey*, 3, 3 (1991), 281–289.

Connor, Steven, *The English Novel in History 1950–1995* (London and New York: Routledge, 1996).

Crofts, Charlotte, *'Anagrams of Desire': Angela Carter's Writing for Radio, Film and Television* (Manchester: Manchester University Press, 2003).

Cronan Rose, Ellen, 'Through the Looking Glass: When Women Tell Fairy Tales', in *The Voyage In: Fictions of Female Development*, ed. Elizabeth Abel *et al*. (London: University Press of New England, 1983).

Crow, Thomas, *The Rise of the Sixties: American and European Art in the Era of Dissent* (London: George Weidenfield & Nicolson, 1996).

Day, Aidan, *The Rational Glass* (Manchester: Manchester University Press, 1998).

Dentith, Simon, *Bakhtinian Thought: An Introductory Reader* (London and New York: Routledge, 1995).

Doane, Mary Ann, 'Film and the Masquerade: Theorising the Female Spectator', *Screen*, 23 (September/October 1982), 74–87.

Docherty, Thomas, *On Modern Authority: The Theory and Condition of Writing 1500 to the Present Day* (Brighton: Harvester, 1987).

Duncker, Patricia, 'Re-imagining the Fairy Tales: Angela Carter's Bloody Chambers' *Literature and History* 10, 1 (Spring 1984), 3–14.

Duncker, Patricia, 'Queer Gothic: Angela Carter and the Lost Narratives of Sexual Subversion', *Critical Survey*, 8, 1 (1996), 58–68.

Dworkin, Andrea, *Pornography: Men Possessing Women* (London: The Women's Press, 1981).

Easton, Alison (ed.) *Angela Carter* (Basingstoke: Macmillan, 2000).

Fernihough, Anne, '"Is She Fact or Is She Fiction?" Angela Carter and the Enigma of Woman', *Textual Practice*, 11, 1 (1997), 89–107.

Federico Fellini, *Fellini on Fellini*, eds Anna Keel and Christian Strich, trans. Isabel Quigley (London: Eyre Methuen, 1976).

Fiedler, Leslie A., *Love and Death in the American Novel* (1960; repr. London: Granada-Paladin, 1970).

Findlay, Alison, *Illegitimate Power: Bastards in Renaissance Drama* (Manchester and New York: Manchester University Press, 1994).

Findlay, Alison, *A Feminist Perspective on Renaissance Drama* (Oxford: Blackwell, 1999).

Fitzgerald, Jennifer, 'Selfhood and Community: Psychoanalysis and Discourse in *Beloved*', *Modern Fiction Studies*, 39, 3–4 (1993), 669–687.

Fowl, Melinda G., 'Angela Carter's *The Bloody Chamber* Revisited', *Critical Survey*. 3, 1 (1991), 67–79.

Freud, Sigmund, *The Interpretation of Dreams* (New York: Avon, 1965).

Fruchart, Anna Watz, 'Convulsive Beauty and Compulsive Desire: The Surrealist Pattern of *Shadow Dance*', *Re-Visiting Angela Carter: Texts, Contexts, Intertexts*, ed. Rebecca Munford (Basingstoke: Palgrave Macmillan, 2006).

Gamble, Sarah, *Angela Carter: Writing from the Front Line* (Edinburgh: Edinburgh University Press, 1997).

Gamble, Sarah (ed.), *The Routledge Companion to Feminism and Postfeminism* (1998; repr. London and New York, 2001).

Gamble, Sarah (ed.), *The Fiction of Angela Carter: A Reader's Guide to Essential Criticism* (Basingstoke: Palgrave Macmillan, 2001).

Gamble, Sarah, *Angela Carter: A Literary Life* (Basingstoke: Palgrave Macmillan, 2005).

Gamble, Sarah, ' "There's no place like home": Angela Carter's rewriting of the domestic', *LIT: Literature Interpretation Theory*, 17, 3–4 (July–December 2006a), 277–301.

Gamble, Sarah, 'Something Sacred: Angela Carter, Jean-Luc Godard and the Sixties', *Re-Visiting Angela Carter: Texts, Contexts, Intertexts*, ed. Rebecca Munford (Basingstoke: Palgrave Macmillan, 2006b).

Gąsiorek, Andrzej, *Post-war British Fiction: Realism and After* (London and New York: Arnold, 1995).

Genz, Stéphanie, '(Re)Making the Body Beautiful: Postfeminist Cinderellas and Gothic tales of Transformation', in *Postfeminist Gothic: Critical Interventions in Contemporary Gothic*, eds Benjamin A. Brabon and Stéphanie Genz (Basingstoke: Palgrave Macmillan, 2007).

Gerrard, Nicci, 'Angela Carter is Now More Popular than Virginia Woolf ...', *The Observer, Life*, (9 July 1995), 20–23.

Gustar, Jennifer J., *Living with Disbelief in the Fictions of Angela Carter* (Brighton: Sussex Academic, 2008).

Gustar, Jennifer, 'Re-membering Cassandra, or Oedipus Gets Hysterical: Contestatory Madness and Illuminating Magic in Angela Carter's *Nights at the Circus*', *Tulsa Studies in Women's Literature*, 23, 2 (Fall 2004), 339–369.

Haffenden, John, *Novelists in Interview* (London and New York: Methuen, 1985).

Hanson, Clare, 'Each Other: Images of Otherness in the Short Fiction of Doris Lessing, Jean Rhys and Angela Carter', *Journal of the Short Story in English*, 10 (Spring 1988), 67–82.

Harman, Claire, 'Demon-lovers and Sticking-plaster', *Independent on Sunday* (30 October 1994), 37.

Henstra, Sarah M., 'The Pressure of New Wine: Performative Reading in Angela Carter's *The Sadeian Woman*', *Textual Practice*, 13, 1 (1999), 97–117.

Hogan, David, *Dark Romance: Sexuality in the Horror Film* (Jefferson: McFarland & Co. Inc., 1986).

Hunt, Anna, 'The Margins of the Imaginative Life: The Abject and the Grotesque in Angela Carter and Jonathan Swift', in *Re-Visiting Angela Carter: Texts, Contexts, Intertexts*, ed. Rebecca Munford (Basingstoke: Palgrave Macmillan, 2006).

Hutcheon, Linda, *The Politics of Postmodernism* (London and New York: Routledge, 1989).

Irigaray, Luce, *This Sex Which Is Not One* (Ithaca, NY: Cornell University Press, 1985).

Jackson, Rosemary, *Fantasy: The Literature of Subversion* (London and New York: Methuen, 1981).

Jameson, Fredric, 'On Magic Realism in Film', *Critical Inquiry*, 12, 2 (1986), 301–325.

Jordan, Elaine, 'Enthralment: Angela Carter's Speculative Fictions', *Plotting Change: Contemporary Women's Fiction*, ed. Linda Anderson (London: Edward Arnold, 1990).

Jordan, Elaine, 'The Dangers of Angela Carter', in *New Feminist Discourses: Critical Essays and Theories and Texts*, ed. Isobel Armstrong (London and New York: Routledge, 1992).

Jordan, Elaine, 'The Dangerous Edge,' in *Flesh and the Mirror: Essays on the Art of Angela Carter*, ed. Lorna Sage (London: Virago, 1994).

Jouve, Nicole Ward, 'Mother is a Figure of Speech', *Flesh and the Mirror: Essays on the Art of Angela Carter*, ed. Lorna Sage (London: Virago, 1994).

Kappeller, Suzanne, *The Pornography of Representation* (London: Polity Press, 1986).

Katsavos, Anna, 'An Interview with Angela Carter', *Review of Contemporary Fiction*, 14, 3 (Fall 1994), 11–17.

Kaveney, Roz, 'New New World Dreams: Angela Carter and Science Fiction', *Flesh and the Mirror: Essays on the Art of Angela Carter*, ed. Lorna Sage (London: Virago, 1994).

Klein, Melanie, *The Selected Melanie Klein*, ed. Juliet Mitchell (Harmondsworth, Middx: Penguin Books, 1991).

Kristeva, Julia, *Semiotike, Recherches pour une Semanalyse* (Paris: Seuil, 1969).

Kristeva, Julia, *Powers of Horror: an essay on Abjection*, trans. L. S. Roudiez (New York, Columbia University Press, 1982).

Kristeva, Julia, *Revolution in Poetic Language* (New York: Columbia University Press, 1984).

Kristeva, Julia, *Black Sun: Depression and Melancholia* (1987), trans. Leon S. Roudiez (New York: Columbia University Press, 1989).

Laplanche, Jean and Jean-Bertrand Pontalis, 'Fantasy and the Origins of Sexuality', in *Formations of Fantasy*, ed. Victor Burgin *et al.* (London: Methuen, 1986).

Lechte, John, *Julia Kristeva* (London and New York: Routledge, 1990).

Lee, Alison, *Realism and Power: Postmodern British Fiction* (London and New York: Routledge, 1990).

Lee, Hermione, 'Angela Carter's Profane Pleasures', *The Times Literary Supplement*, 4655 (19 June 1992), 5–6.

Lee, Hermione, ' "A Room of One's Own, or a Bloody Chamber?": Angela Carter and Political Correctness', in *Flesh and the Mirror: Essays on the Art of Angela Carter*, ed. Lorna Sage (London: Virago: 1994).

Lewis, Peter, 'The Making Magic', *Independent*, (3 April 1993), 24–26.

López, Gemma, *Seductions in Narrative: Subjectivity and Desire in the Works of Angela Carter and Jeanette Winterson* (Amherst, New York: Cambria Press, 2007).

MacAndrew, Elizabeth, *The Gothic Tradition in Fiction* (New York: Columbia University Press, 1979).

Mckinstry, Susan, 'Fay Weldon's *Life and Loves of a She-Devil*; The Speaking Body', *Fay Weldon's Wicked Fictions*, ed. Regina Barreca (Hanover and London: University Press of New England, 1994).

McLaughlin, Becky, 'Perverse Pleasure and the Fetishized Text: The Deathly Erotics of Carter's *The Bloody Chamber*', *Style*, 29, 3 (Fall 1995), 404–422.

Makinen, Merja, 'Angela Carter's *The Bloody Chamber* and the Decolonization of Feminine Sexuality', *Feminist Review*, 42 (Autumn 1992), 2–15.

Marcus, Steven, *The Other Victorians: A Study of Sexuality and Pornography in Mid-Nineteenth Century England* (1964; repr. London: Weidenfeld and Nicolson, 1966).

Martin, Sara, 'The Power of Monstrous Women: Fay Weldon's *The Life and Loves of a She-Devil* (1983), Angela Carter's *Nights at the Circus* (1984) and Jeanette Winterson's *Sexing the Cherry* (1989)', *Journal of Gender Studies*, 8, 2 (July 1999), 193–210.

Matus, Jill, 'Blonde, Black and Hottentot Venus: Context and Critique in Angela Carter's *Black Venus*', *Studies in Short Fiction*, 28 (Fall 1991), 467–476.

Mayne, Judith, *Cinema and Spectatorship* (New York: Barnes and Noble, 1987).

Meaney, Gerardine, *(Un)like Subjects: Women, Theory and Fiction* (London and New York: Routledge, 1993).

Michael, Magali Cornier, 'Angela Carter's *Nights at the Circus:* An Engaged Feminism via Subversive Postmodern Strategies', *Contemporary Literature*, 35, 3 (Fall 1994), 492–521.

Morris, Pam, *Literature and Feminism: An Introduction* (Oxford: Blackwell, 1993).

Munford, Rebecca, 'ReVamping the Gothic: Representations of the Gothic Heroine in Angela Carter's *Nights at the Circus*', *Paradoxa: Studies in World Literary Genres*, 17 (2002), 235–256.

Munford, Rebecca (ed.), *Re-Visiting Angela Carter: Texts, Contexts, Intertexts* (Basingstoke: Palgrave Macmillan, 2006).

Munford, Rebecca, ' "The Desecration of the Temple": or, Sexuality as Terrorism? Angela Carter's (Post-) feminist Gothic Heroines', *Gothic Studies*, 9, 2 (November 2007), 58–70.

Nead, Lynda, *The Female Nude: Art, Obscenity and Sexuality* (London and New York: Routledge, 1992).

Newman, Judie, 'The Revenge of the Trance Maiden: Intertextuality and Alison Lurie', in *Plotting Change: Contemporary Women's Fiction*, ed. Linda Anderson (London: Edward Arnold, 1990).

O'Day, Marc, 'Mutability is Having a Field Day', in *Flesh and the Mirror: Essays on the Art of Angela Carter* ed. Lorna Sage (London: Virago, 1994).

Onega, Susana, *Jeanette Winterson* (Manchester and New York: Manchester University Press, 2006).

Palmer, Paulina, 'From "Coded Mannequin" to Bird Woman: Angela Carter's Magic Flight', *Women Reading Women's Writing*, ed. Sue Roe (Brighton: Harvester, 1987).

Palmer, Paulina, *Contemporary Women's Fiction: Narrative Practice and Feminist Theory* (London and New York: Harvester Wheatsheaf, 1989).

Peach, Linden, *British Influence on the Birth of American Literature* (London: Macmillan and New York: St Martin's Press, 1982).

Peach, Linden, 'The Journalist as Philosopher and Cultural Critic. The Case of Angela Carter', in *The Journalistic Imagination: Literary Journalism from Defoe to Capote and Carter*, eds Richard Keeble and Sharon Wheeler (London and New York: Routledge, 2007).

Peach, Linden and Angela Burton, *English as a Creative Art: Literary Concepts Linked to Creative Writing* (London: David Fulton, 1995).

Perez-Gil, Maria Del Mar, 'The Alchemy of the Self in Angela Carter's *The Passion of New Eve*', *Studies in the Novel*, 39, 2 (Summer 2007), 216–235.

Pitchford, Nicola, *Tactical Readings: Feminist Postmodernism in the Novels of Kathy Acker and Angela Carter* (Cranbury, NJ: Bucknell University Press; London: Associated University Presses, 2002).

Projanksy, Sarah, *Watching Rape: Film and Television in a Postfeminist Culture* (New York: New York University Press, 2001).

Punter, David, *The Literature of Terror: A History of Gothic Fictions from 1765 to the Present Day: The Modern Gothic* (London and New York: Longman, 1996).

Punter, David, 'Essential Imaginings: The Novels of Angela Carter and Russell Hoban', in *The British and Irish Novel Since 1960*, ed. James Acheson (London: Macmillan and New York: St Martin's Press, 1991).

Reed, Toni, *Demon-lovers and their Victims in British Fiction* (Lexington, Ky.: The University Press of Kentucky, 1988).

Rennert, Jack, *100 Years of Circus Posters* (London: Michael Dempsey, 1975).

Robinson, Sally, *Engendering the Subject: Gender and Self-representation in Contemporary Women's Fiction* (Albany, NY: State University of New York Press, 1991).

Roe, Sue, 'The Disorder of *Love*: Angela Carter's Surrealist Collage', *Flesh and the Mirror: Essays on the Art of Angela Carter*, ed. Lorna Sage (London: Virago: 1994).

Rose, Jacqueline, *Why War? – Psychoanalysis, Politics and the Return to Melanie Klein* (Oxford and Cambridge, Mass.: Blackwell, 1993).

Rose, Mary Beth, *The Expense of Spirit: Love and Sexuality in English Renaissance Drama* (London and Ithaca, NY: Cornell University Press, 1988).

Rubinson, Gregory J., "On the Beach of Elsewhere': Angela Carter's Moral Pornography and the Critique of Gender Archetypes', *Women's Studies* 29, 6 (Dec 2000), 717–741.

Rubinson, Gregory J., *The Fiction of Rushdie, Barnes, Winterson and Carter: Breaking Cultural and Literary Boundaries in the Work of Four Postmodernists* (Jefferson, North Carolina and London: McFarland & Company, Inc., Publishers, 2005).

Rushdie, Salman, 'Introduction', in Carter, Angela, *Burning Your Boats: The Collected Angela Carter: Stories* (London: Chatto and Windus, 1995).

Russell, Lorena, 'Dog-Women and She-Devils: The Queering Field of Monstrous Women', *International Journal of Sexuality and Gender Studies*, 5, 2 (2000), 177–193.

Sage, Lorna, 'Breaking the Spell of the Past', *The Times Literary Supplement*, 4307 (18 October 1985), 1169.

Sage, Lorna, 'Angela Carter interviewed by Lorna Sage', in *New Writing*, eds Bradbury, Malcolm and Cooke (London: Minerva Press, 1992a).

Sage, Lorna, *Women in the House of Fiction* (Basingstoke: Macmillan, 1992b).

Sage, Lorna, *Angela Carter* (Plymouth: Northcote House in association with the British Council, 1994a).

Sage, Lorna (ed.), *Flesh and the Mirror: Essays on the Art of Angela Carter* (London: Virago, 1994b).

Sanders, Julie, 'Bubblegum and Revolution: Angela Carter's Hybrid Shakespeare', *Re-Visiting Angela Carter: Texts, Contexts and Intertexts*, ed. Rebecca Munford (Basingstoke: Palgrave Macmillan, 2006).

Sceats, Sarah, 'Oral Sex: Vampiric Transgression and the Writing of Angela Carter', *Tulsa Studies in Women's Literature*, 20, 1 (Spring 2001), 107–122.

Schmidt, Ricarda, 'The Journey of the Subject in Angela Carter's Fiction', *Textual Practice*, 3 (1989), 56–75.

Schor, Naomi, 'Fetishism and its Ironies', *Nineteenth-Century French Studies*, 17, 1/2 (Fall/Winter 1988/89), 89–97.

Selmon, Stephen, 'Magic Realism as Post-colonial Discourse', *Canadian Literature*, 116 (1989), 9–24.

Siegel, Carol, 'Postmodern Women Novelists Review Victorian Male Masochism', *Genders*, 11 (1991), 1–16.

Simon, Julia, *Rewriting the Body: Desire, Gender and Power in Selected Novels by Angela Carter* (London: Peter Lang, 2004).

Smith, Patricia Juliana, '"The Queen of the Waste Land": the endgames of modernism in Angela Carter's *Magic Toyshop*', *Modern Languages Quarterly*, 67, 3 (September 2006), 333–362.

Sontag, Susan, *Illness as Metaphor* (New York: Farrar, Straus and Giroux, 1978).

Springer, Kimberly, 'Third Wave Black Feminism?', *Signs: Journal of Women in Culture and Society*, 27, 4 (2002), 1059–1082.

Steinem, Gloria, Foreword, *To be Read: Telling the Truth and Changing Face of Feminism*, ed. Rebecca Walker (New York: Anchor Books, 1995).

Stoddart, Helen, *Rings of Desire: Circus History and Representation* (Manchester: Manchester University Press, 2000).

Stoddart, Helen, *Angela Carter's Nights at the Circus*, Routledge Guides to Literature (London and New York: Routledge, 2007).

Studlar, Gaylyn, 'Visual Pleasures and the Masochistic Aesthetic', *Journal of Film Studies* 37, 2 (Spring 1985), 5–26.

Studlar, Gaylyn, 'Masochism, Masquerade, and the Erotic Metamorphoses of Marleine Dietrich', in *Fabrications: Costume and the Female Body*, eds. Jane Gaines and Charlotte Herzog (London and New York: Routledge, 1990).

Suleiman, Susan Rubin, 'The Fate of the Surrealist Imagination in the Society of the Spectacle', in *Flesh and the Mirror: Essays on the Art of Angela Carter*, ed. Lorna Sage (London: Virago, 1994).

Toye, Margaret E., 'Eating their Way Out of Patriarchy: Consuming the Female Panopticon in Angela Carter's *Nights at the Circus*', *Women's Studies*, 36, 7 (October 2007), 477–506.

Turim, Maureen, *The Films of Oshima Nagisa: Images of a Japanese Iconoclast* (Berkeley: University of California Press, 1998).

Turner, Rory P. B., 'Subjects and Symbols: Transformations of Identity in *Nights at the Circus*', *Folklore Forum*, 20 (1987), 39–60.

Walker, Nancy, 'Witch Weldon: Fay Weldon's Use of the Fairy Tale Tradition', in *Fay Weldon's Wicked Fictions*, ed. Regina Barreca (Hanover and London: University Press of New England, 1994).

Wandor, Michelene (ed.), *On Gender and Writing* (London: Pandora Press, 1983).

Warner, Marina, 'Angela Carter: Bottle Blonde, Double Drag', in *Flesh and the Mirror: Essays on the Art of Angela Carter*, ed. Lorna Sage (London: Virago: 1994).

Webb, Kate, 'Seriously Funny: *Wise Children*', in *Flesh and the Mirror: Essays on the Art of Angela Carter*, ed. Lorna Sage (London: Virago, 1994).

Whelehan, Imelda, *Modern Feminist Thought From Second Wave to Post feminism* (Edinburgh: Edinburgh University Press, 1995).

Williams, Linda Ruth, *Critical Desire: Psychoanalysis and the Literary Subject* (London and New York: Arnold, 1995).

Willett, John (ed. and trans.), *Brecht on Theatre: The Development of an Aesthetic* (London: Methuen, 1964).

Wood, Michael, 'Stories of Black and White', *London Review of Books*, 6, 18 (4 October 1984), 16–17.

Zipes, Jack, *Fairy Tales and the Art of Subversion* (London and New York: Routledge, 1988).

Index